To Joan and Ron
With Love + Best

SCAL

AND

SPANNER

A DOCTOR REMEMBERS

By

Dr H. John Powell.

from H. John Powell

ISBN 1 897 887 40 X

A British Library Cataloguing-in-Publication data. A catalogue record for this book is available from the British Library.

Published by Natula Publications,
5 St Margaret's Avenue, Christchurch, Dorset BH23 1JD
www.natula.co.uk

All illustrations in this book belong to the author.

Front Cover Illustration:
The Operating Theatre at the Wesley Guild Hospital, Ilesha, Nigeria

Back Cover Illustration (from top to bottom):
Dr H. John Powell sailing off the Cornish coast; Off-duty nurses; The Red Pepper Market in Ilesha; Lepers from the leper compound outside their church

This book is for Barbara, remembering her unfailing love and support that enabled me to cope with so many medical and other adventures in and around Ilesha, Nigeria

Also for Florence, whose love and encouragement was of tremendous help to me in recording these recollections of those adventures.

Dr H. John Powell is the son of a Methodist Minister. He was educated at Kingswood School, Bath where he first felt the call to medical service in Africa. He trained for a medical degree in Edinburgh with the Edinburgh Medical Missionary Society, later commencing work in the Livingstone Dispensary, 39 Cowgate, Edinburgh, as resident physician in 1941.

He was sent to Nigeria by the Methodist Missionary Society arriving in September 1942 at The Wesley Guild Hospital in Ilesha, in the southwest of that country.

He spent 10 fascinating years in the medical service there during which time he married Barbara Hogge, S.R.N of the R.I.E. They had 3 children: - Gillian, now a Macmillan nurse, who lives in the Doncaster area; Carol, also a nurse, who lives with her G.P husband Dr P.Wood in Longiddry; and his son, Alan, who deals in property, commercial and private housing in the Doncaster area.

After service in Nigeria, Dr Powell worked as a G.P. in Mexborough, South Yorkshire where he looked after the health of the mining, steel and rail workers for the next 30 years.

He retired to Cornwall, buying a boat and sailing the Cornish seas from South Mawes to Falmouth for 20 years.

Sadly, his wife of 49 happy years died in 1993. He was married, in 1995, to Florence, sister of James Leask of the Bank of Scotland, herself an Edinburgh graduate and a most highly regarded teacher of the young. They have now moved to Highcliffe, Dorset to be a little nearer civilisation (?) and their young folk and remain in good health, despite *Anno Domini.*

His complete autobiography is now taking shape on his new computer toy!

CONTENTS

SCALPEL AND SPANNER

A Doctor Remembers

PREFACE

I quote from my 1947 annual report of a year spent in the 65 bed Mission hospital at Ilesha in the southwest 'bush' country of Nigeria. I wrote that the doctor there 'should be able to pass lightly from the intricate workings of a diesel engine to the comparative simplicity of a gastro-enterostomy'. After all, engine and human body are both pump operated and now that our engineering brothers have been able cleverly to copy the marvels of the human brain into computer science, both engines and humans are thus computer controlled. They have come into close relationship. So the doctor needs to have the 'hands on' ability to palpate his patient's abdomen seeking for signs of serious trouble, and to feel both by touch and sound the telltale vibrations of his hospital's lighting generator, for it is likely that he will be responsible for the diagnosis and treatment of both human and engineering systems in that hospital.

This work consists of a collection of real life incidents personally experienced by me during my ten years service in the Wesley Guild Hospital at Ilesha and recorded by the word-pictures in the pages that follow. Many are medical, some personal with titbits of medical palaver thrown in. Some are a mite technical and certainly rather sanguinary with quantities of blood lost and blood regained. Some sport quite a spot of fun and lots of less serious activities.

It is my hope that such stories will portray the huge and urgent need for medical help in that great country. They reveal how some of those needs are met, sometimes not devoid of a little spicy entertainment! They also try to demonstrate the approach of Christian love and goodwill towards mankind that are the basis of that hospital's work. So here in these pages you will find sorrow and joy, despair and triumph; expectations sometimes sadly unrealised and hopes very often happily fulfilled. There is the scalpel and the spanner. There is fun and frolic. There are new plans, new beginnings and new achievements.

Above all there is advance into a wider and more expert future for this hospital's service in the name of Christ and for His sake.

Can you take it? Try. Read on. Smile. Weep. Laugh. Enjoy it!

Acknowledgements

My wife, Florence, for her patience during my preoccupations, and for her editorial skills in furthering the progress of these medical scribbles into book form.

Sheila Herringshaw for her faithful typing and computer processing of this book with all its strange medical phraseology, and her unstinting help, encouragement and advice.

Peter Armstrong for his willing expertise in assisting my efforts at computer operation, and for much wise advice in all the aspects that have helped to bring this work into print.

Also, posthumously, the help, friendship and cheerful competence of Hezekiah Awodiya of Ilesha, as we journeyed together by night and day in the Operating Theatre of the Wesley Guild Hospital, Ilesha, Nigeria.

CHAPTER 1

Dream to Action

Nitrous oxide is such a delightful anaesthetic. The wretched pain vanished and I drifted gently into a world of whirling nothingness that revolved in circles of black. My mind relaxed and not even dreams of sandy beaches, foaming waves, and great palm tree fronds waving quietly in an onshore breeze disturbed the calmness of unconsciousness.

Violent toothache from a badly decayed lower molar had woken me - a prefect in the Upper House dormitory of Kingswood School, Bath. Action was needed. Pain drove me to seek my housemaster after morning prayers in the chapel. I found him in the masters' common room. "Yes of course, Powell" he said, "off you go to the dentist in the city, and I'll get the secretary to ring him; I'll tell your form master too."

So out with my bicycle and down Lansdown Hill I sped to be kindly received by an efficient white-coated man with a pair of Guy's dental forceps in his right hand and a rubber facemask in his left.

"Make yourself comfortable and open your mouth wide" said he. I did so. "Very wide please, now bite this" and a big rubber-covered gag was thrust between my teeth, so arranged as to leave access for his murderous instrument as it sought the offending molar. Then the 'laughing gas'!

From the depths of painless blackness there spoke a kindly voice. "Come on, old chap, wake up, it's all over." I felt the need to spit some salty stuff as a bowl came under my chin. I gently pushed from my mouth the same salty stuff and behold, it was blood! Mumbling a "Thank you" I accepted a glycerine and thymol mouthwash. Please note that the blood was mine own.

That of others will be found, as this book's title may suggest, in following chapters, being inevitably associated with the word 'scalpel'. (Relax please; it's not all blood and guts - just little bits!)

Being encouraged to return to school I found my bike and often standing on the pedals, depending on the gradient, mounted the hill, found the senior Day Room and sat quietly to recover my breath and composure. I felt reluctant to go into the morning Greek class and stayed, relaxing quietly, probing with my tongue the hole in my gum.

My mind mused peacefully, and thoughts entered... I was studying more advanced Latin and Greek with a rather vague notion of following my dear father into the ministry of the church. Did I really wish to proceed with this idea? Thinking it over I realised that this was not really my true desire.

I mused on. Suddenly my thoughts crystallised. I would abandon this vague intention. Had this seed been sown in my mind seven years previously, when at age eleven I had watched 'Magic Lantern' slides shown by Rev. Deaville Walker? These revealed the desperate condition of the people of Africa, who were in great need of medical help to combat the dangerous and deadly diseases from which they were suffering. I would train as a doctor and offer my services in medical missionary work. It was like a revelation. This was what I really wanted to do. Such was indeed my true desire.

Again thought demanded action. I rose, left the Day Room, and went immediately to make a request to see my headmaster, A.B.Sackett MA. MC. "A medical missionary?" said he, that man who had such a profound understanding of boys. He too acted at once. Consultations followed rapidly, with my father, with the Methodist Missionary Society who were prepared to accept me as a missionary candidate, and offered help with university fees; with the Edinburgh Medical Missionary Society who would accept me as a student, and also offered financial help and residence in their hostel in George Square, Edinburgh.

And the stage was set. Just a curriculum change from Classics to Chemistry, Physics and Biology, and six months to bring these subjects to Oxford and Cambridge credit standards in my brain, quite a slog, but good exercise.

Somehow I managed to retain enough information to pass the exam in those subjects; so at last I stepped onto Waverley platform from the Scottish Express, complete with my bicycle, suitcase and my parental blessing, their good wishes, their prayers, and their wonderful help. And so to George Square…and to student life...

At Edinburgh University the vast anatomy dissection room contained many wooden tables each burdened with a naked cadaver, each surrounded by a small group of four or five students. Each one wielded a scalpel, and each one carefully attacked with it the body part allotted to them for the purpose of discovering the internal secrets of a human being.

What fun it was to dissect with a sharpish scalpel the anatomy of some long forgotten preserved corpse in the Anatomy Department of Edinburgh University! But not for you, dear reader, to have revealed to you the secrets of hopeful young doctors-to-be as they cut into dead flesh. Yes, they discover with scalpel and forceps that big nerve trunks that used to carry live messages to and fro, lie alongside arteries that pulsated, when living, with the red fluid of life. Yes, they learn how the atlas vertebra, if displaced, pressurises or even ruptures the spinal cord, so that paralysis of all body regions below that level, or even death, ensues. They find that pressure on a carotid artery in the neck can cause unconsciousness. They learn hosts of medical secrets, which it is better that you never know!

Just know that for 5 or 6 years the student learns to palpate the human body respectfully; learns to use all his senses with the aid of instruments and microscope to discover the hidden things of the body's cellular minutiae, and of the bad bacteria that so wickedly attack it. The use of forceps and other medical paraphernalia are revealed to him, and if his mind discovers that the Latin and Greek learned at school are now quite invaluable, so much the better. He learns also of medicines, poisons and chemical reactions. He learns about human reactions too.

Any former experience of mine in the realms of anatomy was limited to taking beetles from the killing bottle and in my entomological enthusiasm displaying them on bits of white cardboard. Sometimes a big oil beetle found on the footpaths of the Gower coast would need a little dissection. The abdomen was removed, emptied and stuffed with cotton wool; then stuck back on again! I also chopped up an eel that I had caught, Mother having declared that if I wished to consume the same I should cook it myself. Yummy!

But those six years of study were different; certainly many days and evenings of hard slog. And at last the day of mounting apprehension when requested by an eminent professor to listen to the 'lubb-dupp' heart sounds of some mighty blacksmith, and pronounce on the size of his heart and the reasons therefore.

"I think his heart is rather large, sir."

"Yes indeed, but why?" - "I'm not sure, sir."

"Have you asked his occupation? No? Well ask him."

"He says he is a blacksmith, sir."

"And what is his weight? Look at the chart."

"Sixteen stone, sir."

"So, are you learning anything?"

And thus it was, that having in six years acquired some knowledge I could decorate my shoulders in due course with a stethoscope. Great was the help that I had received from the care and tutelage of the E.M.M.S. in this grounding in medical missionary work. Their guidance in spiritual help was only matched by the practical experience available to me in the Livingstone Dispensary of Edinburgh's Cowgate, for which the Society was responsible.

My appointment to the post of Resident Physician to that establishment was, after graduation in 1941, an honour indeed. Six months of work there caring for the needs of the sick and poor of the Cowgate and Grassmarket areas was of great value to me. The job entailed supervising the dressing room of the dispensary, and also the work of students from the University who came there to 'do' their 12 maternity cases with a midwife's assistance. If trouble arose I was the trouble-shooter! On one occasion the two chaps out on a 'case' sent a message - 'the patient is having a fit'. Up to the High Street 7th floor flat in post haste, climbing the many stairs with my 'midder bag'. Oh dear, we had a case of eclampsia on our hands. So out with the ever-handy chloroform bottle and the 'rag' mask and sprinkle drops of the gentle anaesthetic onto the lint until fits ceased and the patient slept. In the meantime one of the students had phoned for the ambulance. Up that winding stairway came two competent men with a stretcher, loaded the patient onto it, and, with myself trying to find space at its head to drop further chloroform onto the mask, we all wound our way cautiously down those seven flights of stairs and into the ambulance. Finally the hospital was reached - the Royal Infirmary naturally - and I could deliver my patient to more experienced hands. Hopefully she would later be the proud mother of a lovely baby.

It was very useful experience. There followed six weeks as a locum to a G.P. in Irvine while the E.M.M.S. discussed with the military authorities my future fate. The latter agreed to release me provided I was rapidly shipped to Africa!

At last, with controlled excitement to board a 12,000-ton vessel, the *Andalusia Star*, and venture into the dangerous waters of the Atlantic Ocean in 1942. This was an end to the beginning, and the beginning of what was, to me a great adventure in Christian service.

Apprehension mounted again, as we voyaged unaccompanied northwest, keeping watch in turns for the telltale periscopes that spelt 'fear'. A rapid streak in a huge three quarters of a circle around those submarine infested waters, twice crossing the 'Line' as the equator was called then, (perhaps now?) and by skilled navigation and some elementary luck, no doubt, reaching the safe haven of Freetown, Sierra Leone.

A six-week stay at the home of kind, elderly Rev. Diamond, Methodist Minister; breakfast in the café opposite his house, serenaded in the morning sunshine by a tiny bird whose little song, repetitive almost *ad nauseam*, I still remember after 60 years!

I had the opportunity of a temporary job in the local hospital's operating theatre, where I learnt the mysteries of performing D's and C's, not having had hospital experience before leaving home. Wartime caused difficulties.

Then to the Bight of Benin by freighter carrying on deck a couple of steam engines destined for the railway system of Nigeria. We travelled eastwards every day. Calm seas under a blazing sun provided enchanting entertainment. Flying fish rose in little shoals out of the water, flitting speedily above it for twenty yards or so, hopefully escaping the jaws of predators below the surface, barracuda perhaps? Tiny fish suddenly broke out of the gentle swells, their 'wings' and bodies gleaming silver in the sunshine, a joy to behold.

And then I saw a sight wonderful and quite astonishing to me, untutored in the natural world beyond our shores. Several dolphins, sleek, huge and powerful, leapt from the water in a great forward arc of movement, diving and leaping repeatedly as they kept pace with, or easily outstripped our vessel. They displayed their smooth and graceful art to the delight of all on board with time to watch these charming masters of the waves.

At last, overnight, we turned 90 degrees to port and in the morning there appeared a long dark line on the horizon. The line rose gradually, extending east and west to the limits of vision, indicating, far behind, the beginnings of the enormous landmass of Africa.

The line developed, rising higher, becoming more distinct. Tiny protuberances changed into trees in long lines, great leaves waving in the on-shore breeze. Some were coconut trees, with big bunches of fruits, some were feathery casuarinas. Now, among them, and separating the tree clusters, appeared white buildings along the shore. Finally there came into view the long rocky moles of a great harbour lying beyond the disturbed shallow waters of the bar. Within it could be seen another freighter and a passenger ship at their moorings. There was an easy entry into calmer water and shortly, a careful and skilled approach to the wharf where ropes were thrown and hawsers fixed. We had reached our goal, the township of Lagos, Nigeria.

The gangplank was lowered. Not without emotion I walked down and took my first step on to the shore of Africa. No Methodist folk had arrived to greet me, but some Anglican people who were meeting their own members greeted me and whisked me away to their headquarters on the Lagos Marina. I was most kindly welcomed with a cool drink and gracious enquiries about the voyage and my health were made, as also was a telephone call to the Methodist Mission to apprise them of my arrival.

Shortly afterwards a kit-car rapidly entered the compound and screeched to a halt scattering gravel as it braked. The door was flung open and Bill, short, square, purposeful, with a happy smiling face and a vigorous manner jumped out. Bill Mann was our Mission accountant and had at one time been an auctioneer. He walked quickly with short, jerky steps and greeted me with a clear voice and a strong handgrip, a friend indeed.

The Dream. A New Hospital?

Thanking my erstwhile hosts I joined Bill in the car to be shot out of the compound on to the Marina. There followed a quick visit to the wharf to collect my luggage and bicycle, loaded into the car by labourers who responded with some alacrity to the staccato commands of my vigorous companion. We zoomed along the Marina to the Methodist Mission where I met the Chairman of the Nigerian District, Rev. Waterworth and his wife. He was our superior in the Mission hierarchy. He and his wife welcomed me graciously to the District.

We soon sped off again through thronged streets, with horn blaring and people scattering, over the bridge from Lagos Island to the mainland. We quickly ate up the seven miles to Bill's bungalow that was stepped back a little from the road to Yaba, partly screened by bushes and small palms. It was a charming little house with a delightfully charming and welcoming hostess, Bill's wife, Dorothy, standing at the open door, smiling and with outstretched hands. Peace, quiet words of welcome, a cool drink, and I felt instantly at home.

Later came a toddle round the compound talking quietly with her. There was the firm impression of a kind, gracious lady who loved her little garden with its hibiscus, bougainvillaea and tobacco plants, and who cared tenderly for her vegetable plot where carrots, beans, and even cauliflower were kindly encouraged to grow in the sandy soil. Soon there was the rapid tropical switch from light to dark. A soak in an old tin bath was refreshing, and an excellent meal of fish from the lagoon followed. After dishes were cleared, out came the Bridge cards and a three-handed game was taught to me, ignorant though I was. The vigorous hot breeze of daytime had dropped, and bed called. It was certainly very warm and humid under the mosquito net over the camp bed, but sleep came at last after the long day.

Morning light with the returning breeze was welcome. After breakfast we returned to Lagos, Bill to his office and Dorothy to introduce me to Kingsway Stores where commodities, unseen for years in wartime Britain filled the shelves and made my mouth water! There were such precious things as tins of pineapple, peaches, apricots, guava, and electric torches, carbide cycle lamps, and many household articles now only too scarce at home. I looked in admiration and envy! Afterwards she left me to browse and to savour the strange newness of Nigeria, its capital and its people.

Lagos - A First Impression

A cacophony of sound assailed my ears as I stood on the shore at the lagoon's edge. Before me lay the quiet smooth water stretching away to a palm covered island in the distance – the low lying bar of land, which for many miles fronted the ocean along Nigeria's shore affording protection to the lagoon and main land. Behind me lay the market whence came the noises of humanity.

Ilesha Pepper Market

The vast collection of shacks and stalls, roofed with corrugated iron sheets rusting in the alternating attacks of tropical rainstorms and fierce sunshine, covered a large area along the waterside fronting the township of Lagos. It was peopled by the milling figures of women, talking and laughing, young men strolling among the laden stalls, happy faced and untouched by the argumentative fury around them, greeting each other with a friendly handclap and eyeing the girls who, in small clusters, whispered and giggled under the sharp eyes of their mothers. And if occasionally a young lady gently sidled off, unnoticed by her mother's vigilant eyes while their owner noisily negotiated the proper price for her wares, well, it added to the fun and to the sparkle in the bright eyes of the girls and boys, and perhaps a new romance would be budding.

Small children happily toddled near their mothers, nude in the warm afternoon sun, while their siblings slept peacefully on their mother's backs securely wrapped in the efficient African method and undisturbed by mother's noisy screeches and gesticulations. Older children played tag or some such, in the way of children world wide, tolerated well by the adults as they dodged between laden stalls and laden people. Often they were called to order by parental stallholders and given odd jobs to keep them occupied, or for the older ones, to help their harassed mums.

Here and there small groups of men gathered, seated on the ground around low tables, sucking or chewing nuts or playing the ubiquitous game involving a wooden board having circular depressions containing small units for counters. These were transferred rapidly in ones or twos into other depressions, the players taking turns. I waited, fascinated and uncomprehending, and have never since understood the rules of the game. It kept the men happily occupied during the heat of the afternoon, while their wives attended to the business of acquiring an income – and spending it.

From reports of the fields of war, and from the deck of my ship while scanning the waves for a tell-tale periscope of a submarine, it was good to be at last on the shores of Nigeria and to share in the peaceful, happy voices and actions of its people. Tomorrow I would travel by boat to Badagry with some of them.

And my mind would be transported to the wicked former days of the trade in slaves and their misery. It felt good to belong to a people whose forebears had put an end to slavery and through wise government, decent trade and the Christian gospel had been foremost in giving a chance of better life to the people of Africa.

CHAPTER 2

I Find Africa

I stood, gazing out to sea, at the top of a vast sandy beach shelving steeply to the breaking waves. On either side the foaming water of crashing seas was visible in a long line as it swept up the steep beach whitening the sandy shore and swiftly retreating. Wave after wave slowly advanced, curled in grandeur and mightily fell. Sometimes a fish was seen in the wall of water perilously defying its imminent breaking.

Behind and above me rose a long line of palm trees, curving forwards and upwards over the heated sand, and bearing clusters of coconuts, huge fronds waving in the steady onshore breeze. The long narrow island on which I stood was covered for miles east and west with these trees, and behind me leading through the trees shade lay a long narrow path, sandy and well trodden, coming from the lagoon beyond.

It was the ancient path by which slaves were brought, bound by their fetters, from the mainland of Africa to be incarcerated in the holds of the infamous slave ships that transported them to the Americas and islands of the Caribbean in the west.

Far out to sea I saw, in my minds eye, such a ship, large of sail, tall and menacing as it pointed its prow towards Africa's shore. Almost I could hear, mesmerised as I was by the sound of pounding surf, the glinting of waves and fierce heat of the morning sun, with vivid imagination, the cries and moans of the helpless captives as they were urged forwards towards an unknown future.

Only two days previously I had disembarked from my comfortable cargo ship and had taken my first steps on Africa's shore at the port of Lagos. In contrast to the slaves experience I was met, welcomed and driven to a friendly house of future colleagues, whence I would proceed later to my place of work, namely the Wesley Guild Hospital at Ilesha.

The next day, a party of some 50 African and European missionary folk were to go by motor launch westwards along a lagoon to the port of Badagry, old headquarters of the slave trade. They would hold a service after traversing the slaves' path that I have just mentioned.

Would I like to join them? Yes, indeed! Thus I found myself squeezed warmly among the happy chattering folk all dressed in their Sunday best robes of many colours enjoying a pleasant boating excursion along the 20 miles of quiet lagoon, past my first sight of the dramatic roots of mangrove trees to the centre of that most infamous trade. The launch was covered with a substantial roof, and while the sensible African folk, mostly of the Yoruba tribe, remained in its shelter seated on backless forms, I with several others – mad English in the midday sun – climbed up to the roof and exposed our delicate epidermises to tropical sunshine. Thank goodness for the anti-malarial mepacrine which taken internally, kills the parasite in its tracks and incidentally offers quite good protection against the sun's burning power.

Reaching Badagry township we were guided to a double storey house in the town deemed suitable for such self-same Englishmen. But we all felt it would be pleasant to establish our camp beds and mosquito nets on the roof of the launch and sleep in the open air, so we made the needful preparations. Kind ladies of the local Methodist Church provided an excellent supper. We were seated at a long table on the wharf beside the water where, by candle light, hurricane lamp, Tilley lamp and a torch or two we tucked in avidly to an excellent groundnut stew, consisting of meat or chicken cooked in oil prepared from groundnuts (peanuts to the uninitiated) with yams or potatoes and vegetables – very tasty.

We beat the mosquitoes into our netted camp beds, and after reading by torchlight, slept peacefully under moon and stars, sung to sleep by the distant sound of Africa's drums and the song of the cicadas.

A morning wash was effected somehow and razor scraping of chin stubble followed by breakfast in the early sunshine on the wharf. We had oranges or grapefruit, banana and guinea corn cereal. After such pleasant introduction to the day a further excitement arrived to enchant us. A large canoe beautifully adorned with floral decorations, obviously intended for VIPs, paddled alongside. We happily availed ourselves of such lavish courtesy, stepped aboard and were comfortably conveyed across the lagoon to a long, very slim island covered in palm trees. We enjoyed the little trip of 200 yards, or so, only learning later that our first class transport had been intended for the chairman of the Methodist District and his Senior colleagues and not at all for us very junior and lesser mortals – oh dear!

Under the coconut palms we walked the old slave trail to the ocean beach, among the palm fronds and coconut husks that lined our path. I stood at the top of the beach and gazed out to sea...

The sun beat down, the palms waved overhead, the waves crashed and the foam swept up the shore. But there was no tall black ship, and the cries and moans of yesteryear were replaced by a hymn of praise from 50 African voices of the launch, as they gathered to celebrate the landing of the African Christian missionary, Thomas Birch Freeman, 100 years previously. The chairman and his retinue arrived, somewhat late, by canoe *ordinaire*, and led the service of memory and thanksgiving. Afterwards our steps were retraced along the old trail of sad memories. Thoughtfully we all boarded the launch. Quietly it slipped away from the old slave capital, passing long roots of mangroves and the long island of coconut trees, finally to reach the more civilised modern capital of Lagos. Tying up, disembarking, listening to the stories of the oldsters and looking forward to the future, I joined our accountant's car to streak madly through the crowded streets of Lagos to his home seven miles away on the mainland. "Time for a rubber before chop," said Bill, and the cards were dispensed rapidly. Bill and friends were avid addicts of Contract Bridge.

I learnt that my journey to Ilesha and the Wesley Guild Hospital, which was to be my mission station, would be by road, courtesy of Rev. Nelson Ludlow and his wife Dr Joyce F.R.C.S. who had been, prior to her marriage, one of the Wesley Guild Hospital doctors. Both were charming personalities. He was the missionary at Ilesha, a quiet, unassuming and extremely capable man running the churches and schools in his extensive area with great sincerity and expertise. She, after leaving the Hospital to become a wife, took to the task of starting up village dispensaries in the region, much aided by her husband, and staffing them with nurses trained by the Hospital.

A few days wait, while Nelson and Joyce collected stores from Kingsway and United Africa Company on the marina, gave me more waterborne fun and games in Bill's *Bunty* – heroine of many yacht races in Lagos harbour, catching fish for the fridge or to sell in the market; jack and barracuda were always welcome. Heaving the heavy fish from their watery habitat, and using oars at times to propel us homewards if the breeze failed at evening's sunset, we loved it.

Then to load up the kit-car and climb aboard to commence our 185-mile journey to Ilesha and the hospital of my dreams. To Ibadan first, along 110 miles of tarmac road, single track only, when nearside wheels would veer to the laterite road edge on meeting an oncoming vehicle. A warm ride via oil palm, banana and coconut plantations; via small villages in the bush clearings where women stood at open air stalls and tables selling heaps of oranges, bananas, cassava and yams.

Lagos to Ilesha, 185 miles

In the villages goats, sheep, pigs and chickens nimbly scattered out of our way; ducks however slowly led their broods of ducklings across the dangerous highway as if aware of the unwritten law that guaranteed their safe passage. The driver of a heavily laden lorry would always come to a halt for such a charming procession.

Beyond Ibadan where we stopped for a meal with the folk of Wesley College, the road became dusty as our tarmac gave way to a laterite surface – good old Nigerian soil that binds together in a useful, if rough and often corrugated surface. We were now passing some open country where farmers were growing yam, cassava, cocoa, bananas, 'Indian' corn, oranges etc. Later in the season after months of burning heat there would be dry vegetation very subject to fire, causing vehicles to accelerate through the smoke and flame. But in September rainstorms were a regular occurrence and plants were still green.

To Ile-Ife, capital of Ijesha land; then we passed more farm clearances and came into the region of tall trees that had stood for many years, oft supported by great triangular bracing roots, with high bush up to 20 feet, never allowing us distant views of road and country. At last our vision was gladdened by the sight of housing and more tarmac road leading to the spreading buildings of a large town. "Ilesha," said my senior colleague and his wife, "here we are, home at last." And the mud walled, cement coated walls and galvanised iron roofs of the town quickly implanted themselves in my memory as 'Home'.

Ilesha is a large town in southwest Nigeria where in 1942 there lived 30,000 Yoruba people. The main approach road and central road were of tarmac. Around a very large and grassy square were sited the big Council Hall, the Palace of the Owa, King of Ilesha, and the Police Office. Opposite were the Red Pepper Market and other stalls. The United Africa Company, John Holt Company and many other trading folk with shops and stalls lined the main street on both sides. There were Anglican, Methodist and Salvation Army churches, a Mosque, and the Apostolic Mission and other religious bodies such as Cherubim and Seraphim all established to care for Ilesha's spiritual needs.

Houses lined side streets of hard packed laterite – the reddish brown Nigerian soil. Most houses were built of big mud blocks, sun dried, cement rendered as owners could afford. Some belonging to more prosperous trading people were of sand-cement blocks. Most roofs were of corrugated galvanised iron, often of red- rusty appearance. Doors and window frames were of the very hard iroko wood.

Ilesha Town

The Hospital was at one edge of the town near a swampy area. The European compound with District Officer and other folk of managerial status was on the other side, up a hill. The westerly prevailing breeze came from that side to the town, and from town to Hospital. Storm clouds would assemble over Imo, a 1,000-foot mount, tree covered, to the east, so that the violent storms travelled from east to west, the other way. Nearest towns are Ile-Ife, 20 miles towards Ibadan, and Oshogbo, 20 miles on the other side of Ilesha. Such was to be my home for the next ten years.

CHAPTER 3

Finding More of Africa

Evening was approaching rapidly and little palm oil lamps were lighting the stalls, bush lamps were hung from handy nail fittings, and here and there more powerful Tilley lamps illuminated the faces of the stallholders. Through the town square, past the big Council Hall and the Red Pepper Market, past the Mosque, turn left into Otapete Road with a big Methodist Church on the right, half a mile to go and soon the headlamps shone on the gate and the sign above proclaiming 'Wesley Guild Hospital'.

Around the gateway were huge bunches of palm and banana leaves decorated lavishly with hibiscus flowers and bougainvillaea, and from houses near by we heard cries of "Welcome to the new Doctor!" Through the gate, past the night watchman clapping gaily, past Outpatients and Child Welfare Departments, under the spreading branches of a great 'Flame of the Forest' tree, through archways of palm leaves and more floral decorations, noting the electric lighting of pathways and buildings, to halt beside the bungalow of my future colleague.

A delightful welcome from Leslie Crosby and his wife Miriam, a hearty "Thank you" to my capable driver and future friends, Nelson and Joyce Ludlow, who then took off to their own house in the town. A long cool drink and subsidence into a solid iroko chair well lined with cushions to give welcome relief after the bumpiness of miles of corrugated laterite road.

I found Leslie to be a charming man offering a most hearty, welcoming smile with immediate outstretched hand; a little overweight but vigorous withal despite his excessive tiredness. An old Kingswood and E.M.M.S. student, after hospital experience he'd been posted to Ilesha by the Methodist Missionary Society in

1937 to join Dr Hunter, the Superintendent since 1929. Fond of music, he trained the nurses in singing with customary energy, besides the medical lectures to them on top of all the medical, surgical and maternity work. He urgently needed the fresh air of old England. Not very long married, his house was kept in apple pie order by his wife Miriam, a delightful and competent ex-teacher.

Female and Children's Wards
Wesley Guild Hospital

I was introduced to the guest room and the bathroom with a tin bath and a 4-gallon tin of hot water heated on the kitchen fire. I changed into long clothing in order to frustrate the mosquitoes, and enjoyed an excellent meal prepared by Miriam's cook, in what we in this country would regard as primitive conditions, concrete cookhouse, ancient iron stove, iroko table and a very smoky fire, but it worked well in expert African hands. Much conversation of home, conditions in wartime, lucky escapes from enemy submarines, many sadly not so lucky, bombing of towns, fighting on various fronts, and of course, the inevitable stories of sadness. Seated in the comfort and warmth with food and light, and sleep to come not threatened by sounds of war, we felt fortunate. The sadness of this land I had yet to meet.

"Time for the night round, John, want to come?" said Leslie.

The two of us set forth up the path, under the welcoming arches, past the big mango tree (fruit very turpentiney, hardly worth eating) past the tall singing casuarina tree, laden with pine needles that murmured in the gentle breeze of the night. We passed, on the right the engine house, source of the hospital's light and power. Here the 1½ k.v.a. diesel of Lister's vintage drove a reliable generator with its regular thud, thud, thud, soothing to sleep the fractious children of the medical staff, and later their weary parents, nurses and sisters. We continued walking on past the laundry room and then came the hospital's big kitchen, with its fires out for the night, and the big 10,000-gallon water tank sunk in the ground. We passed the lovely hedge of plumbago with its tiny blue and white flowers over which by day the humming bird moths hovered, darting from flower to flower, poking their long proboscis into their hearts to extract sweetness. And so on to the Female Ward.

It was quiet. Its ten beds were occupied with sleeping folk, and there were two spare beds in a separate room. There was a table centrally for the nurses' work and where records were kept and a single electric light bulb giving fair, though not generous, illumination. Nurses on duty, neatly attired in pleasant uniform, rose to meet my colleague and shyly said words of welcome to the new doctor. All was satisfactory, she reported, and my colleague checked through the small pile of charts neatly arranged on the table. We said, "Goodnight." And nurse smilingly wished us "A happy night's rest, Doctor."

We hoped so, and Leslie led the way upstairs to the Children's Ward. Here some 20 cots in the ward and cots on the veranda were occupied by kiddies in various stages of recovery from injuries and infections. Nurse was bottle-feeding a baby on her hip and mentioned the condition of two or three children who were very ill, noting further instructions from my colleague after he had assessed their condition. The mothers of those were allowed to stay beside them, and slept on the floor beside the cots. "Call me if you need me, nurse," said Leslie. Sometimes he had an undisturbed night's sleep... As we descended the stairs outside the ward the brilliant silver light of a nearly full moon shone upon us and all the buildings, outlining a charming picture of a caring institution in Africa's bush land where any ill of body or mind could be looked after, irrespective of colour, race or creed, and if unable to afford the small fees, treatment and care were free. I felt privileged to work in such a place.

To the Male Ward, some 20 odd beds, occupants quietly sleeping, and nurse preparing medicines or injections. All was in order she reported, and again the shy welcome to me. Leslie pointed out several chaps with recent operations, fractures, chest infections or typhoid and enquired about a case of tetanus in the side ward. "Sleeping at last," was the significant reply, and we quietly passed his room to view the mothers in maternity. Here we found ten happy mums either awake and breast-feeding infants, or snoozing after childbirth with their treasures beside them. "Always a happy ward," said Leslie. "All OK nurse?" The reply indicated that all was well, and one woman would probably give birth during the night. "Another job for Sister," was his comment as we wished nurse, "Goodnight."

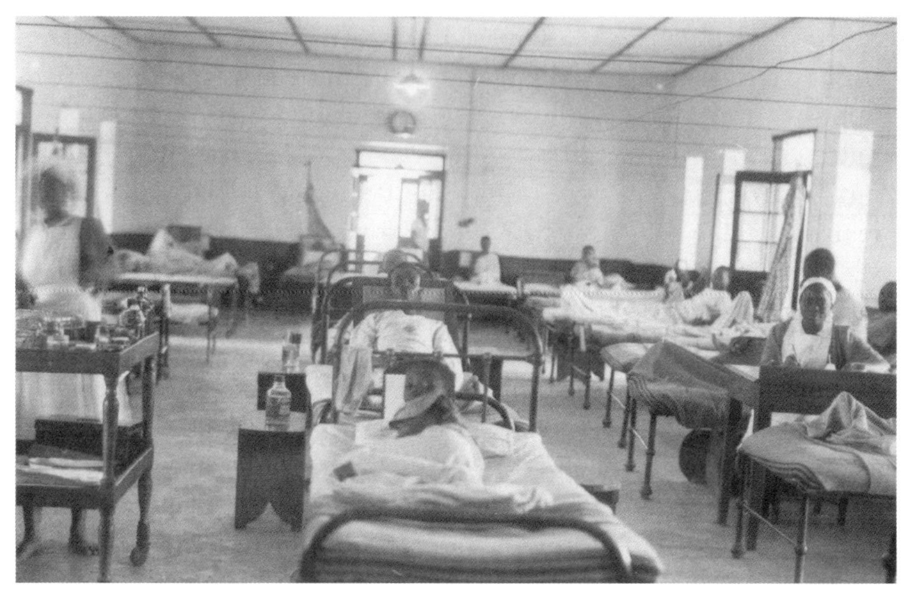

Male Ward – WGH Ilesha

On our way down to the house we called in at the engine house. Leslie checked the diesel fuel supply in the tank on the wall and reduced the voltage from 110 to 100. "It saves the oil a bit," said he, "and reduces our bills. I'll introduce you to the Operating Theatre tomorrow," he added, "sufficient unto the day…"

A cool drink awaited us, and we prepared to rest. Light shone over the pathways, outlining palm leaves waving, shadows long on the short grass, drums beating rhythmically in the distance, the engine thudded happily, and the moon shed its lovely light over the town and its people. We slept.

Getting Down to the Job

Did I say, 'slept'? Well yes, indeed I did, though sleep was somewhat slow in coming. The day had been full of new experiences, new faces, some with the pale faces of Europeans, some dark with pigmented skin of the Negro people of Africa, but all with smiles, happiness or curiosity. There had been many miles of travel through thick bush, past many villages with their mud-walled houses and thatched roofs, past crops of cocoa, maize, oranges, bananas, cassava, yam, tomato and plantain. It was all so peaceful and pleasant, so very far removed from the appalling violence that was behind me.

In contrast the sounds of the African night can be quite fascinating. Under a brilliant silvery moon, riding free in a velvety black sky attended by vast numbers of shining silver stars, sounds seem needless and intrusive. But sounds there were. The cricket orchestra, the frogs croaking, the whisper of the casuarina needles stirring in the light breeze combined to form a charming background of noise. The drums of Africa carrying mysterious messages merged with this gentle murmuring din and with the steady beat and hum of our lighting system acted as a delightful soporific. I relaxed and, covered only with a sheet, sleep came at last.

And dreams? Assuredly! A vision of my lovely Barbara's face swam into view with her great curl of brown hair, uniquely curling forward, and an upper incisor tooth pushed a little forwards by its fellows in a most enchanting fashion. So I slept and dreamed, lulled by sweet memories and sounds of the African night.

Near to dawn came a weird distant screech, high pitched at first, then falling in cadence and slowly fading away. Again it came, and yet again, an eerie scream. Thoughts of what tortured body lay behind such an awful cry were rampant. Stories of rituals, of secret societies of Africa, of the leopard society with their great claws tearing, of the appalling habits of old tribal customs of torture, murder and even cannibalism came to mind. What secrets were still hidden in the dark of the bush, what fiendish rites of pain? Horrid thoughts crept into my waking but drowsy mind as I listened, waiting for dawn to relieve mental torment.

Soon and quickly came the light to bring relief, and sense normalised as quiet clanging of the triangular iron bell of the lepers' compound across the road called those patient folk to Morning Prayer in their little chapel. It was built with their own often-deformed hands, frequently helped by the hands of my doctor predecessors assisting in the building. The light, and these thoughts reminded me that prayers with our European sisters whom I had yet to meet, and with the Nigerian nurses were at 7 o'clock in the Prayer Room of the sisters' house. I rose and was ready in time, though still more sleepy than normal. Leslie played the tiny harmonium for the morning hymn and a third year nurse read a prayer from the Anglican service book.

Then to breakfast in the sunshine on the Crosby's veranda; they had a good cook. Perhaps he knew a thing or two about planting a dose of 'native medicine', a sleep-making variety, in the evening meal. Certainly I had slept well, (until woken by the awful scream) perhaps designedly so, for I discovered that my much prized and treasured portfolio case, a precious gift (certainly not one to be purchased by an impecunious doctor) had disappeared during the night. To make a complaint on my first day in the Wesley Guild Hospital would, I thought, be unseemly, and my host never heard about the episode. I kept quiet, albeit rather sadly.

Shortly Leslie introduced me to the Operating Theatre, a goodly gift from Sir Francis Ream, and then to the Outpatients' Department and Sister Louie Trott. She was in charge of the Outpatients' treatment room. Slim and straight, height about 5 ft 2 ins, and the possessor of a charming 'Zummerset' brogue still present in her delightful friendly voice from old youthful days in the Ilminster region which was her home. Quick and efficient in action, vigorously instructing her nurses as they undertook patients' dressings and soaked their leg ulcers in antiseptic baths prepared in large kerosene tins. Louie had charge also of the main theatre where she ruled with a firm hand and voice. No funny goings on were allowed, strict discipline was essential.

Well, we've got as far as the Outpatient's Dept. This was the first building inside the Hospital gate, usefully planned with a good waiting hall, doctor's consulting room, dispensary, nurse's treatment room and small operating theatre. And here I met the VIPs – to wit our dispenser, Taiwo, and James and Hezekiah, our two clerks, indeed more than clerks, as you shall hear. Taiwo was older than the clerks, with a happy smile that gave the impression of the owner being far away, his head full of many concerns re bottles, pills and potions, suppositories and so forth; very busy indeed was our dispenser.

I was introduced to James Balogun, the senior clerk and laboratory technician. James, I found, to be a quiet, modest person, not very big but with an infectious smile, most likeable and helpful in many ways. After Primary School he had worked for Rev. Jones, our missionary in Ifaki, 60 miles away, and with his pay had financed his secondary education. He spoke English very well and had been recommended by the church for the post of interpreter at the Wesley Guild Hospital.

Gradually the doctors had advanced him into further medical mysteries. He assisted at operations, wielded the chloroform bottle as anaesthetist and was then shown the laboratory work. The last was now his chief occupation, a valuable and reliable worker who became a friend and colleague. The junior clerk, Hezekiah, I'll tell you about later. Let's keep finding Africa…

The baby that had disturbed the sleep of the duty Sister during the night was now being handed for a feed to its happy Yoruba mother, and Leslie introduced me to the nursing lady who had attended her, and who was now busy instructing the budding midwives. She, Stella Liony, the Senior Sister and Matron of the Wesley Guild Hospital was a very pleasant, extremely competent and highly trained nurse and midwife. Born of a Danish mother and Yoruba father she felt called when attending an East-End Church to offer her services in a missionary capacity to her own Yoruba people. She was gladly accepted by the Methodist Missionary Society and arrived in Ilesha in 1922. She quickly learnt the Yoruba language, and got the local Nigerian people to send their daughters for training as nurses. In the twelve-bed Hospital she performed wonders making a tremendous impression among the people of her chosen land, and continued to do so for twenty-five years. She set up the Wesley Guild Hospital Training School, respected throughout the country for its training of female Nigerian nurses; also the Midwifery Training course for the Government's Grade 2 Certificate. By that time the bed capacity of the hospital had of course increased up to 65. In 1922, when Stella first came to Ilesha, maternity work had barely begun. When she retired in 1947 after severe illness the number of deliveries recorded at the Hospital was 560.

How Wondrous is an Effective Health System

How expert its medical and nursing staff! How efficient its technical and clerical staff! How helpful its dispensers, laboratory folk, porters, telephonists, X-ray, physiotherapists, ambulance and engineering staff! Together by day and by night they try to ensure the care, diagnosis, treatment and comfort of human folk who need their help; how wonderful the management of all these experts to make good the smooth running and operation of all the many concerns of the service.

Even a small hospital needs a modicum of such personnel. Even a hospital in the deep African bush country needs to be properly run. When funds are low, fees charged very low, accounts to be presented accurately at the year's end along with a complete hospital report on the medical work accomplished, the work of a single doctor and matron can become excessive. When working solo for 365 days and nights, and being responsible for all these matters the lone doctor can become extremely weary. Leslie Crosby had coped with this for a whole year until I arrived to give a hand – and I needed to be taught!

From Stella's maternity instruction to the nurses we walked towards the Outpatients' Dept. Suddenly a lorry came round the corner of that department and stopped outside the Female Ward. A patient was being off-loaded onto a wheeled hospital stretcher. Leslie asked a few questions, the answers being interpreted by the ward porter. "It may be a strangulated hernia", said my colleague. "Will you go ahead with the outpatients John, while I sort it out with Sister." He told me the clerk's name was Hezekiah and I made my way to Outpatients.

Hezekiah and I took to each other at once. Tall and straight, brown but a much paler brown than the local folk, his smiling eyes assessed me, his features more Caucasian than Negro, he stood behind the doctor's desk and welcomed me with a strong hand clasp. Many, many times were we to meet with such mutual regard during the next ten years. Son of a local chief, member of the Otapete Methodist Church, Scoutmaster of the local troop, and, besides being clerk and interpreter, he was also the doctor's operating assistant in the main operating theatre. Whether by day or by night he was always pleasant, always reliable and very good to have around. He became a very good friend to us all.

Hezekiah and James Balogun were indeed Christian gentlemen. To call them friends was a privilege and an honour. It was no wonder that during the leadership at our new hospital of my later friend, Dr Andrew Pearson, the post of Hospital Manager should be gladly handed to Hezekiah Awodiya.

I sat at the desk and the first patient was brought in. "Worms," said Hezekiah after interrogation. I wrote on the card. The next patient, "Worms," said Hezekiah. I wrote. Third patient, "Guinea worms." – next – "A swelling in the left groin, doctor." Hernia, I wrote after examination. Yes, he would like an operation, - right, next Thursday morning. Good. And so on, and on, and on!

Shortly Leslie Crosby came to join me in Outpatients, and we continued until all were dealt with. One or two had been admitted and the others were waiting for the Dispenser to supply medicines and tablets.

The rounds of the hospital wards came next and Sister joined us as we proceeded to each patient in the Female, Children's, Maternity and Male Wards. At the end of this routine round Sister led us to her office where a very welcome cuppa was waiting.

Theatre Sister joined us and announced that all was ready in her department. A message to the Male Ward brought the patient on a trolley covered in a red blanket and we entered the theatre to scrub up.

Leslie demonstrated the technique of spinal anaesthesia, skin swabbing, towel arrangement, and then came the method of dealing with a strangulated hernia.

"You are being plunged in at the deep end, John," said my colleague.

"Thank you Leslie, I shall need a lot of this."

"Well I hope to be on the high seas very soon, so Joyce Ludlow will come and provide further education for you." Joyce Ludlow had left her work at the hospital a few years earlier to take her F.R.C.S. and was later married to Nelson.

My colleague operated with care and precision. Cut, clip, swab, and dissect. The tight constricting band of tissue causing the trouble was divided, and we waited to see if blood circulation would return to the squeezed section of gut. The patient was lucky, and we rejoiced too. The tissues became a nice healthy pink. Circulation of blood had returned properly to the threatened piece of intestine. It was gently returned to the abdominal cavity. Leslie then taught me the business of hernia repair that stood me in good stead in the years to come. Stitch up and apply skin clips and dressings.

Back to the ward for the patient, and it was time for grub. "That was our most frequent major emergency," said Leslie, "a useful introduction to the Theatre."

So it was Leslie to his bungalow, and me to sample the offerings of my cook whom I had yet to meet. I wondered what would be the next emergency. No sooner had I finished the banana fool than it came, dramatically…

CHAPTER 4

Screams

Screams from the Hospital, agonised shrieks, howls of terror approaching rapidly. Slapping of bare feet on sun baked laterite and swiftly up the wooden steps of my bungalow. What fearful catastrophe had happened? Was it fire, was it flood, was it food? I rose to meet nurse, screaming and holding her head on one side, shaking it uncontrollably. I realised it was an ear trouble – otitis media can be most painful, but not that bad surely.

I fetched an auriscope from the office; I told her to hold her head still, and a quick peep in the auditory canal – ear hole to you – showed the fearful cause of the turmoil. A tiny black ant was scrabbling about on the eardrum frantically seeking an escape route.

"Come on nurse, back to the Theatre," and as fast as I could I followed the distressed girl. I filled a 10cc syringe with warm water from the sterilizer and injected it into her ear as she bent over the sink. The ant, washed out, went down the plughole. Relief was immediate and nurse subsided sobbing on the anaesthetist's chair. Two of her colleagues, greatly disturbed, gathered round to comfort her and hearing the cause of the commotion soon burst into laughter. What, no sympathy for *le pauvre fourmie*?

More shrieks! This time from the Nurses' Home. What frightful disaster now? Again the rapid pattering of bare feet as a nurse sped to my bungalow and raced up the steps. A perfunctory knock and "Please Doctor a bad snake in the Home". This sounded serious; snakes in Yoruba land were poisonous until proved otherwise. "Anybody bitten nurse?" I enquired. "No, Doctor, not yet."

Nurses for Confirmation

Picking up the little .22 sawn-off gun left behind by friend Jonah from Ifaki when going on furlough, I quickly followed my young guide. In the Home several nurses stood clumped together pointing at a bookcase against the wall. "It's underneath, Doctor," they told me, clutching each other's hands. I knelt down and surveyed, cautiously, the space beneath the bookcase, raised up on 2-inch legs. A little snake, maybe as long as an English slow worm, was huddled against the wall. Taking careful aim with the gun muzzle, pushing it towards the snake, I pulled the trigger. Alas, poor little snake, but of course, you never know!

Screams and shrieks of course, do not necessarily denote mayhem or tragedy impending, imminent or presently active. There are juvenile screams of joy as a famous pop idol emerges onto the stage singing, yelling, dancing or contorting his body for public delight. Happy yells of approval or howls of derision will greet the popular politician or infamous rogue, and glad shrieks of excitement show appreciation of agile clowns or dare devil acrobatic performances.

Even in hospital excitement can be fun when somebody throws a party. Kekere was our driver, mechanic and post boy, a cheerful little chap, hence his name – willing and active. He collected mail from the Post Office and posted our letters to our loved ones. Above all he was famed for his driving skills and loved to demonstrate his prowess on the Hospital's Oldsmobile. He drove it with skill and sometimes abandon! One day Kekere celebrated his birthday and invited all the garden boys and houseboys off duty to help in the fun and games.

At midday they all escaped for food and siesta. Some siesta. Kekere's house in the town was the centre of drumming, shuffle dancing, singing and imbibing. The palm wine, pretty potent stuff, was poured out with a liberal hand into coconut cups; guests lost some of their control, speech became slurred, movement and wild gyrations leading to joy becoming unconfined! At 3 p.m. the Hospital bell for afternoon work session was ringing and workers began to drift back to their jobs, but with a difference! Peter, my garden laddie, attacked the grass with alcoholic fury swinging his 'cutting grass' with unaccustomed vigour. Already short, the green stuff fled in all directions from his onslaught. Our Hospital gardener, never known to indulge in the English language if he could help it, actually burst into lines of Shakespeare dredged up from his classroom days of yore. William, dear and slightly mournful soul, whose normal habit was the dreary singing of 'Art thou weary, art thou languid' – (and he was usually both) was stimulated into cheerful activity, laughing and smiling and wielding garden implements joyfully until the end of the stint.

Off-duty nurses

One could not help sharing their happiness. But, surpassing all the outpourings of birthday fun there arose from all the areas of the Hospital screams that meant not terror or fear but rather joy and uninhibited fun and delight. For Kekere, loosed from his normal proper and respectful behaviour was chasing round the wards, Outpatients and Theatres, kissing and cuddling every uniformed girl who with wild but happy protests was glad to be the object of his passionate fervour! The screams and yells continued until Sister and I, brought back from our dreams of, respectively, the green grass of Ireland and the survivors of the Himalayan ridges and couloirs, hurried to restore order amidst the heated disorder created by our birthday boy. We could not be cross in the midst of the fun. We dispatched Kekere to walk (not cycle) to the Post Office for the afternoon mail, if any. The giggling in the Hospital took some time to subside. Happy nurses!

So now you are going to remind me about that dreadful scream in the night. Alright, – but just a minute, I think Dr Crosby wants to take me to meet the folk in the Lepers' Compound. "This way, John, we go through the gate behind all those mighty bougainvilleas and past those lovely white frangipani flowers with the wonderful scent." We passed through as described and crossed the Ilesha to Esaoke road to the door of the Leper's Compound standing opposite.

Leprosy folk and chapel

We entered, meeting almost immediately the senior occupant, Mr Balogun. He was a very well built and strong individual, about 5ft 6ins, carrying farm implements in a purposeful way. Leslie introduced me, one of their number interpreting, and I learnt that all two-dozen of the company were busy on the farm's land where they were practically self-supporting. Another old chap came, smiled and said that his name was James. He was of happy disposition always, but sadly was rather badly damaged by the disease. His nose had sunk in; his fingers were deformed with loss of the terminal phalanx here and there. Feet were afflicted in similar fashion. It was his duty to present himself to the doctor every Saturday a.m. to receive a few pounds from Hospital funds to enable food such as meat and so on to be bought at Ilesha market. "Do they eat eggs?" I enquired. "Oh yes, the Sister taught us" they said. "We have our own supply," and they indicated a well-built hen house from which a brown hen was emerging clucking cheerfully as if to say, "Jolly well laid!" Small chickens busily scraped and pecked away nearby. A fine young cockerel was in attendance, proudly possessive. Suddenly in my mind, the penny dropped! That agonising scream, that terrifying noise of the night became clear - you get the message? Cock-a-doodle-doooo!!

I felt that I had found Africa!

A Good Teacher

What a surprise. Not a palm-leafed roof over a bamboo structured area serving as a sitting room, bedroom or operating theatre, with a hurricane lamp for illumination, and dripping leaks everywhere when the rain bucketed down. Not at all; a real house that could truly be called a home. A theatre in the hospital, well designed on modern lines. A lighting system that reliably defied the long dark nights of the tropics and coped with dim and awkward places when storm clouds darkened the sky; that was indeed a surprise amidst the mud walls, tin roofs and palm trees of Ilesha.

The generating plant had much to cope with - hospital wards, theatres, staff houses and the main roadway to the Sister's house bordered with the ubiquitous palm trees. Lighting was adequate, if not brilliant, and the engine most reliable. Not that occasional problems did not occur. After all Africa was different…

I was a light sleeper. One night there had been a heavy rainstorm causing me to use my umbrella as I went to do my night round of the hospital. On return I had entered the engine house and reduced the voltage slightly. It was good to get back over the soaking wet tennis lawn to the shelter of my bungalow from the continued downpour. Thus to bed with a book, diving under my mosquito net, nice to have electric light.

I heard the click of the gate to the tennis lawn but not the gentle fall of the nurse's wet bare feet on the concrete way to my bedroom. A knock – "Please Doctor," - "Yes nurse," - "Please doctor, the lights have gone out, but the engine is still running." A short pause - "Alright nurse," I said, "I'll come over and see; is the night watchman lighting the bush lamps?" - "Yes Doctor, and Sister is in the hospital". I looked at my watch. It was 1 a.m., too bad.

I drew on mosquito boots and a light dressing gown. The rain had stopped. I entered the engine house and confirmed nurse's statement. I knew nothing of diesel engines, except to feed them with the necessary fuel oil, and leave alone. Up to the hospital where I found Sister faithfully supervising lighting and ensuring that any needful attention was being given. "You'll need Momodu," said she, - "he's our engine expert." Sister knew everything that a new young doctor needed to know, and told me where the expert lived. I hastened to the garage that was in the Sister's big mansion, and underneath one of the bedrooms, on the ground floor. I opened the gates, climbed into the car and found the ignition key in place; reversed, and with lights switched on made for the hospital gate. The watchman was trying to light a Tilley lamp. "Towards the town," Sister had said, "Look for a big double storey house on the right side, about half a mile." She was right, there it was, and all the rooms were lighted, with the sound of Yoruba music and the beat of a drum. Lots of humanity present, evidently a party – someone's birthday perhaps? Palm wine with a liberal hand maybe!

I stopped, sat in the car and shouted, - "Momodu." - no reply. Again, louder. No reply. And again - just sounds of happiness! I pressed the Oldsmobile twin horn, and a face appearing at the window, poked out. "Wash the matter, why you blow horn?" said the owner. I explained that I was the hospital doctor and that we had engine and lighting trouble. "All right Dokita I come," said he, and in due course, staggering a little, come he did. Momodu himself.

I drove back to the hospital. I did not need to show him the engine house; he knew it from previous adventures with the oddities thereof. He passed by the engine, throbbing valiantly, and went straight, more or less, to the switchboard, to pull out the two big fifteen amp fuses. "Oh ho! Fuses blown," said Momodu, and showed me the burnt remains. "You get fuse wire, Dokita?"

Well, as it happened I had noticed when looking around the mysteries of the engine house a small roll of silvery wire on a shelf. I offered it to him. "Oh ho!" said he again, "that's OK." And he cheerfully wrapped about fifteen strands of wire around each fuse. After breaking the wire he plunged the fuses back into position. "Now," he said, "we will see," and he pushed up the two big switches.

Light blazed forth, all 110 volts of it! Engine house, hospital, staff houses and pathways under the palm trees, all came to life again. Not brilliant but adequate.

"So what was the matter Momodu?" I inquired. – "Ah well Dokita, it has been raining, very much rain. Your electric wires go from pole to pole to your houses. They go under the palm trees.

The trees have leaves, very big leaves. They get very wet, very heavy. They bend; bend down, more and more. They touch overhead wires and poof! Out go lights; the fuses have burnt out."

"I see," said I. "Thank you Momodu. But why are the lights on now?" He took me by the arm, and directed my gaze upwards to the palm leaves. Rain had stopped and leaves were beginning to dry and lift again. They were well away from the wires.

"You savvy, Dokita?" I savvied.

Over the years I learnt a lot from Momodu. He, and experience oft repeated, were good teachers!

CHAPTER 5

A Bush Interlude

Nearly sixty years have passed since a senior missionary colleague, Rev. Nelson Ludlow in fact, faced me saying vehemently, "I feel you should not do this and I strongly advise against it." My reply? - "Oh I'm sure that all will be well you know. After all it's not far, and we have excellent transport."

"None the less" he said, "I believe it is a very unwise idea, and I hope you will revise your proposed plan." The argument became very heated. At last he retired from the verbal battle, which I, a recently qualified doctor, knowing everything of course, and being slightly arrogant, felt that I had won. I therefore made arrangements as planned.

And the plan? To take with me on the doctor's monthly trek through the African rain forest to visit outlying dispensaries one of our hospital's junior missionary Sisters. I saw no problem. My companion would be Sister Louie Trott, a very experienced traveller who had been transferred to our hospital from the Indian subcontinent in 1940.

The propriety of such an adventure through the Southern Nigerian bush was far from my thoughts, but evidently, in retrospect, very much uppermost in the mind of my senior colleague, wise in African ways and well versed in the thoughts and emotions of both the Yoruba people and of female missionary staff.

Thinking only of the trek ahead, on a sunny, very hot day in the big hospital Oldsmobile recently serviced in Lagos, packed with cases of bottled medicines and supplies, we set forth on the 85 mile trip on rough and dusty roads, over ruts and potholes. Every 20 miles we stopped at a village dispensary and tended a small group of patients collected by the resident nurse. At the third stop we also visited the house of a missionary whose hospitality was already arranged. There was a hearty welcome and evidence of some surprise at seeing the lady passenger, but a welcome for her also and his assurance of accommodation in his capacious double storey house. A meal and a cold drink and a rest were soon to hand. Then down to the dispensary in the compound to perform a minor operative procedure and to treat a number of patients late in the hot afternoon.

A good chat and story swapping followed that evening, with a night's rest, sung to sleep by the songs of the hosts of crickets in the bush around the house. Mosquitoes and fireflies silently tested our nets.

Next day, after a cheery "Goodbye" we came to a 15 mile stretch of bush road, switch backing over steep ups and downs, round acute bends, over two plank bridges spanning small streams, making sure that our front wheels met the planks accurately. Another dispensary stop followed by a further stint to our last call. The patients were again folk selected by the nurse as requiring a doctor's attention. Children with Yaws, covered in scabby sores needing intravenous injections, folk with worms, malaria, dysentery, measles and whooping cough, all potentially dangerous. We did our best and it was time to leave for the return trip to the hospital that night.

During the last 20 miles we had noticed that the car was reluctant to climb hills, and needed more accelerator. Now we felt that the car was not happy, and again required more petrol to climb the hills that were short but steep. Back at the mission house for a cup of tea and a pow-wow with our host, a well experienced traveller on Africa's bush roads. We decided to continue and hope for the best. We bade him "Farewell" and drove on.

The hills were frequent, the car groaned over them, and soon darkness fell. We eyed each other with apprehension. What if it broke down? A night in the bush with all its awkwardness was foremost in our minds, and with each rise in the road our anxiety mounted. Sister became edgy, and I, with little knowledge of motor mechanics, was worried indeed. Another hill with a village just behind it; the engine slowed. I floored the accelerator, but the car stopped 20 yards short of the top. Daylight long gone; only starlight relieved the blackness, but the car's lights were still operative. To push the heavy vehicle was beyond us. We looked at each other helplessly.

Our clerk volunteered to walk into the village for help. Off he went in the dark. We tried to be cheerful, but doubts were paramount and we feared the outcome. In the bush round about crickets chirruped furiously. We waited, and waited. No drinks, no biscuits. At long last a small company of men appeared in the headlights. The clerk had experienced difficulty. To his door knocking had come the reply, repeatedly, "Go away, you be thief man, I no open door." At last the story of the doctor in trouble had been accepted and enough strong chaps offered to push the car over the hilltop. Thankfully after the push we were able to coast down to the chief's house in the village. Relief flooded our hearts. Surely he would have a car and some petrol to spare, surely...

The chief was a charming gentleman, courteous and helpfully inclined, but his car was unusable and he had no petrol. He spoke excellent English having spent time in our country. He would send a runner into Ilesha town next morning and a mechanic with a car would soon arrive. Meanwhile perhaps the local school-teacher could be of help. More relief calmed our nerves, until the teacher, a kindly chap, showed us our sleeping quarters. A large blackboard was set up on trestles in one corner of the 30 by 20 ft.

schoolroom, and another in the opposite corner; somewhat primitive beds but better than the floor. There was a bowl of water and a toilet of sorts outside. We ate a sandwich that we found in the car, provided by our missionary host, and a banana or two offered by the teacher, and were grateful. In some trepidation we drank a coconut cup of un-boiled water.

We lay on the blackboards in our clothes, without benefit of mosquito nets. Our muscles ached, our thoughts worked overtime, but we were grateful for the kind mercies provided. The crickets chirruped, but rest came to the weary and at least there were no thieves breaking in with cutlasses or leopards prowling about under our elevated blackboards. At last we slept. The mosquitoes gorged themselves.

Morning light brought a very edgy Sister. There came also an offering of bananas and eggs, the former was most welcome, the latter highly inedible. We had learnt, or rather Louie had taught me, to fill the calabash bowl of eggs with water. The eggs that floated would be full of gas, sulphurated hydrogen no less, and were thrown away. Those that sank might be edible. Few sank! The chief, most co-operative, sent his runner to the town and hospital with messages, a 20 mile trip.

At about 11 a.m. the mechanic arrived, Momodu himself indeed and our inner tension, already eased by sleep and bananas was eased further, until he said happily, "I think the Lagos mechanic cheated you, these are the old plugs and leads; perhaps the new one ones are in his pocket!" Anyway he managed to start the car - Hurrah!

We reached the hospital in time for a wash, a good lunch provided by the understanding Sisters, and a full explanation! The Sisters had coped with the outpatients and had left a few minor operations for my attention.

Some weeks passed and the memory of the journey faded. Then there came a sequel. The Nigerian police, while investigating the disappearance of a number of children from the village of our night's sojourn, had arrested the helpful and nicely spoken Chief. He was charged with the ritual murder of the children. He was tried. He was convicted. He was sentenced to death. He was hanged. In future days I listened to my senior colleagues with less arrogance, and more respect.

Police Palaver and My Nicest Post-Mortem

"The Coroner is on the phone, Doctor," said my receptionist, in 1953 or thereabouts, or "the coroner's officer is at the door," said my wife. Queries about reports, further details and other matters needed attention. Patients with genuine, living complaints, had to wait a little longer.

Inquests would follow and somehow the needs of our patients would be squeezed into a day's routine. Coroner palaver is not a doctor's favourite cup of tea, but the law requires compliance and medical practice needs must accommodate.

Relatives of the deceased abhor such matters and fear the publicity. But to ensure that there has been no ill will, no abuse or law breaking, and that any suspicions are properly aired and dealt with we must all submit to the grinding of the law's mechanisms.

It was rarely so in the Nigerian forties, but on occasions police sometimes required examinations of dead bodies to be made by a competent medical man, and the appropriate form filling to be completed. Thus it was that when a certain village chief became aware that a corpse had been found in a hollow tree within the area of his jurisdiction he felt it necessary to pass on the information to the police authorities.

The corpse, being headless, would perhaps be difficult to identify, and investigation would be needed urgently and an offender apprehended.

And so it came about that late on a hot afternoon, while examining patients in my consulting room, there came a message that would both divert my mind and bring quite an interesting alternative to the normal hum-drum of a doctor's life in an equatorial hospital.

Knock, knock! - "Please Dokita," came a quiet call from the rear doorway behind me. The door stood open for ventilation's sake. Four other doors kept the flow of air, and patients, in and out of the consulting room in the Outpatients' building. One was to allow patients in from the waiting room, one to the dressing room for the treatment of sores, wounds and such like; one to provide access to the Dispensary area, and one to the Examination room. I was well served, so too the patients. I turned round to find the 'small boy' from my house anxious to address me. He was the messenger and factotum (dogsbody) to the house steward.

"Yes, Isaac, what is it?"

"Please Dokita, there is telephone call, it is sergeant for police," he replied.

"Alright, Isaac, tell him I'm coming." Isaac departed at a run and I turned to complete the care of the patient sitting at my desk, and to write the appropriate prescription for her. "I'll come back to see the others, Hezekiah" I said, and proceeded through the back door to my bungalow, about 100 yards away.

"Hallo Sergeant, Doctor here, what can I do for you?" The Sergeant replied with the customary polite Yoruba salutations, hoping that I was well, that my wife and children were well, but I was obliged to cut into his charming array of greetings and repeated my query, "What's the matter, Sergeant?"

"Ah yes, well it's a matter of a P.M. Dokita; we need you to do a post-mortem please."

"I understand, Sergeant, tell me more, please."

"Yes well, there is a body Dokita."

"Yes of course, a body - where?"

"Ah well, it is in the bush. It is 15 miles along the Ife road. You turn left. There is a village."

"Yes Sergeant, 15 miles, Ife road - turn left into a village."

"Yes, ah, the body is in a hollow tree, Dokita."

"This is becoming quite interesting, Sergeant, any more details?"

"Well, yes Dokita, there is no head."

"Well, well, and you want to know the cause of death of a body that has had its head chopped off! Surely, Sergeant!" I said with heavy sarcasm.

"Yes Dokita, but there are the forms, you know, they have to be filled up and sent to the police headquarters, there is the bureaucracy."

This was undeniable and since a fee of two pound ten shillings was payable I gave in to pressure and agreed to comply with police wishes. I returned to the consulting room to see the remaining folk who had patiently waited. This was an afternoon surgery, and normally quite small, about a dozen people who had missed the morning, much bigger, crowd of outpatients. I told Hezekiah what was afoot and he attended later to the supply of post-mortem instruments. These did not of course require pre-operative sterilising, and I just hoped that they were boiled after use. I informed Sister of the proposed expedition and requested a pair of stout rubber gloves.

The hospital car, the long-springed Oldsmobile was brought into use and H and I set forth for our trip into the bush.

Following instructions and surviving the heavily corrugated dirt road, we finally reached the village.

We enquired the whereabouts of the headless corpse in the hollow tree. Villagers, as usual, were know-alls. They enthusiastically directed us. "The path leads this way, - you have to walk."

"How far?" - "About one mile, then there is a river."

"There is a bridge?" - "No bridge." H and I looked at each other and groaned inwardly.

"How far beyond the river?"

"About one mile along the bush path."

Hezekiah and I regarded one another solemnly. I looked at my watch. It was 6 p.m. In 30 minutes it would be dark, and starlight and a 'bush' lamp would be our only means of illumination. The bush lamp was what we know as a small 'hurricane lamp'. Discretion would certainly be the better part of valour, and with one accord we turned towards the car. It was good to find the hospital electric lights welcoming us home. I bade H, "Goodnight" and repaired to my house to telephone the police. "Hallo Sergeant, it is too dark, we have not found your body". Suddenly a dose of inspiration enlivened my thoughts, "Sergeant" I said, "why don't you arrange to have the body collected and bring it to me?" - "Ah yes, Dokita, why I no think of that?" - I could guess the answer! "Telephone me when you have the body" I said, and so it was agreed. The body in the tree was five days old. The shade temperature was in the upper eighties! Two days passed and on a fine Saturday morning the Sergeant phoned.

"We have your body, Dokita."

"Not my body Sergeant, yours."

"Yes Dokita, of course, what shall we do?"

My mind suddenly presented me with a vision of a procession down the hospital drive towards the mortuary, 50 yards from my house, conveying on a galvanised iron roofing sheet the Sergeant's latest horror, probably crawling with black ants. Inspiration followed rapidly again. I remembered the visitors' or strangers' cemetery on the other side of the town, beyond the town wall, and beneath the tall trees that denoted the borders of Ilesha town.

I spoke to the Sergeant and told him where to meet me.

"Aha yes, Dokita, I meet you there."

"At high noon, Sergeant."

"At 12 o'clock, Dokita."

At the appointed hour Hezekiah and I stood beneath the tall trees beyond the town wall, waiting with our box of instruments. A patter of bare feet on the dry leaves whispered, became louder, and a little procession appeared. A uniformed prison warder led the procession. Behind him two prisoners in prison garb followed, one behind the other, carrying on their heads a corrugated iron sheet over which was spread a piece of native cloth covering a not very large object. Gilbert and Sullivan came to mind, "To make the punishment fit the crime, to make the punishment fit the crime". The Sergeant followed, swinging his cane of office, and at a word from him the prisoners' burden was laid at my feet.

Hezekiah and I regarded each other across the concealed object. We bent down. Each took a corner of the cloth and turned it back a little way. Our eyes met. Truly there was no head. We pulled a little further. Four eyebrows rose in surprise. "Right off H," said I. We removed the cloth. Our surprise was complete. Before us lay, in good skeletal order, all the bones of the unfortunate victim, picked dry and clean by numerous little denizens of the forest; remaining attached to each other for the most part by means of dry ligamentous tissue. It was a remarkably clean anatomical specimen, and not very odoriferous. The ants and their colleagues had performed yeoman service. It was quite the nicest post-mortem examination that I had had the luck to perform.

The only sign of injury was a cutlass wound, one inch long, at the medial end of the clavicle. The Sergeant got his report. Bureaucracy was satisfied. In course of time the little fee was paid.

CHAPTER 6

My First Operation Solo

A few weeks after my arrival and before Leslie Crosby was due to catch the boat for home he and Dr Ludlow F.R.C.S. were going off one morning to Ibadan for a meeting.

It had to happen. It was inevitable. It was also something of a shock, and I felt the beat of a pulse in my neck as I realised that a very major experience faced me, for which I felt totally unprepared.

My day had begun normally and after waving goodbye to my two senior colleagues who were driving the long, hot, dusty 75 miles to the meeting, I started morning outpatients. I broke off at 9 a.m. to join Sister for a hospital round. From the Children's Ward with its tiny ill-nourished scraps of humanity to the Female Ward where apprehensive glances had now become smiles, I passed the Operating Theatre to Maternity, where happy mums were breast feeding eager offspring, quietly passing an isolation room where a tetanus case was mercifully asleep at last. Then to the big Male Ward where medical, surgical, and orthopaedic patients swapped stories and admired the neat uniformed figures of nursing staff, who, being young, were not unaware of the obvious admiration. I paused with Sister at each bed *en route* to discuss treatment. Back to finish outpatients and then enjoy a cup of tea in Sister's office with a slice of sponge cake from the expert hands of her cook. We envied her that cook.

Several minor operative procedures in the Outpatients' Operating Theatre followed with an inspection of big ulcers, of a guinea worm that protruded from an ankle and was being wound, a little more each day, around a thin stick, carefully, of course, to ensure that the worm did not break. I incised an abscess or two, and put Plaster of Paris on a fracture. Back to see Sister again and inquire if any other items needed attention – if not, lunch was on the menu.

As we spoke a lorry rattled round the corner of the Outpatients' Department and stopped outside the little approach to the main Operating Theatre. The driver descended with two others and from the back of the lorry unloaded an ill man off a bamboo stretcher, then onto a wheeled hospital stretcher brought by two ward 'boys'. A little convoy of stretcher and patient, ward 'boys' and relatives moved down the corridor to the Male Ward. I waited for the nurse's knock on the office door.

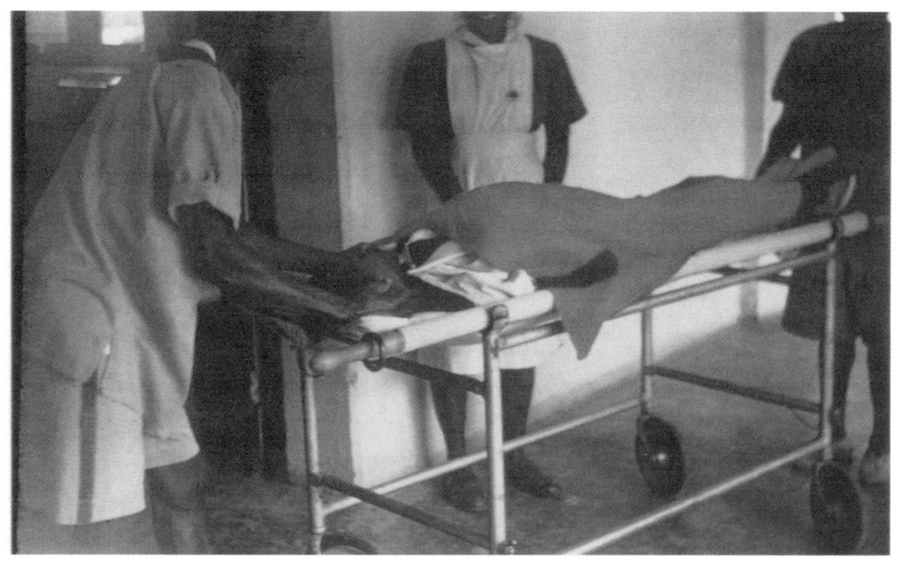

Operation pending

"Please Doctor, there is a new patient. He complains of abdominal pain and there is a big swelling in the abdomen." Temperature, respiration and pulse rates followed. "Thank you, nurse. I'll come and see him."

Sister and I went along the corridor to examine him. I confirmed nurse's report. His swelling was painful to touch, his face fearful, and his pulse slower than expected – perhaps from a surfeit of native medicine. I ordered morphia and atropine for the patient. He needed help urgently. I could make no diagnosis; so 'look-see' was obviously needed.

Sister Liony and I returned to the office and regarded each other. She was a wise lady of wide experience and, like me, would be thinking of the two doctors now far away. Plainly this was a human being in need of urgent help. We had no X-rays. Scans had not been invented. I had never before performed an abdominal operation, solo. I thought of the old Professor of Surgery who had uttered the dictum – "He who openeth the abdomen should be capable of dealing with any abnormality he may find therein". I felt very inadequate. The pulse beat in my neck I took a deep breath and said, "Will you please prepare the theatre, Sister." She replied, "Yes, I think I'd better."

The relatives were waiting for me and anxious to tell their story. Two weeks before, Abraham was working his farm where he grew yams, cassava, maize, tomatoes and other edibles. He had cleared a big area of bush, 10 or more feet high with older bigger trees, dug out roots, chopped branches for firewood, made log fires, dug and planted. His family had taken home big bundles of firewood. Many were his bonfires.

One day he felt some discomfort in his tummy but told himself, "That's a bad worm," and worked on. He walked home that evening, and next day walked back several miles to his farm and carried on with ground clearing and planting. The discomfort had grown to a pain and his journey home was slow and painful. His wife went to see the medicine man in the village who gave her a concoction of leaves, boiled and not nice to taste. There was no improvement. There was a painful lump in his mid abdomen, and they sent for the medicine man. He came, felt the lump and elicited a grunt of pain from the patient. He pronounced his opinion – "This is a very bad worm, you must have stronger medicine and rest." And he went away, and sent a stronger medicine. Painful days and nights passed. The medicine did no good and made him vomit. Poor old Abraham was certainly in serious trouble.

Some folk in the village had experience of help from the missionary hospital twenty miles distant. "Why not go there?" they said. Relatives said they would help with money for a lorry and hospital fees, and after some days the journey was arranged. A stretcher was made, a length of strong native cloth tied at each end to a stout three or four inch bamboo pole, and the patient was carried to a pick up point where the lorry would pass. A long wait, and it came, laden with folk with their loads, livestock and impedimenta. The driver demanded his fare and somehow the poor man was bundled in to endure the extremely painful, bumpy ride, on a rough road littered with potholes and corrugations.

I warned the relatives that their charge was a very ill man and the outcome of the operation was very uncertain. But they were glad that some positive effort should be made. I retired to my bungalow for a light lunch. My big textbook of operative surgery was soon in my hands and I read, and read, and read…

There was a knock at the door, "Yes nurse," – "Please Doctor, the Sister says the theatre is ready." I proceeded to the Theatre. The patient was already on the operating table. A message had been sent requesting the presence of Hezekiah, and he had already arrived to act as assistant at the operation. I explained to him the problem. This was to be our first major operation together.

We 'scrubbed up' thoroughly and noted that 'A' was now more comfortable and sleepy after the morphia and rest time. I had had good experience of performing spinal anaesthetics over the past few weeks, and, when the patient was made ready, I injected a little local anaesthetic into the skin, and then carefully pushed in the long spinal needle. When drops of clear fluid emerged from it I applied the 10ml. syringe and pushed the plunger, placing the measured dose of anaesthetic into the spinal canal to anaesthetise the nerves. Nurses altered the slope of the bed to ensure that the heavy solution would reach appropriate nerves. I turned away and donned rubber gloves, cap and sterile gown, returning to the table that was now level. The patient looked relaxed and was on the verge of sleep. Pain was absent when I checked. Apprehensions and emotions settled, no nerves now, it was time for action. I looked at Sister, eyebrows questioning. She nodded. I lifted the scalpel.

Keyhole surgery would be useless. An incision of three inches or more was essential. The scalpel was sharp, the instruments efficient, and soon muscles and tissues could be gently pushed aside and the membrane lining the abdominal cavity was revealed. Lifting the tissue with forceps, I made a small cut and extended it up and down, and the offending lump became visible.

The intestines were intact and in good order, being pushed aside by the swelling that arose from the back of the abdomen. It overlay the big main arteries and veins, and by touching its surface the powerful pulsation of the abdominal aorta could be felt. What could it be? Not solid but fluid certainly. Could it be an aortic aneurysm? Of such I had no experience but knew that a small prick or cut in its wall would result in a fountain of blood, with dire consequences.

I was no further on. I had found a big cystic swelling five or six inches long and four inches wide pushing forwards and full of fluid of unknown nature. What to do? Perhaps just carefully tack its surface all around the edges of the peritoneum, the lining membrane mentioned, and close the incised wound with some big stitches. Then if my returned colleague wanted to see it, with just a whiff of chloroform, cut a few stitches, and he could easily look for himself, consider and decide. I took a needle, threaded it with 'catgut', and stitched very carefully, attaching the surface of the swelling to the whole edge of the wound. Several big silkworm stitches bringing together the abdominal wound edges, a suitable dressing, and adequate binder and the operation was over. Hezekiah had been a great help and I thanked him for a good job.

Back to the ward bed for 'A' where nurses later on propped him up efficiently. When I looked in to check on him he was awake, still feeling no pain, smiling and raised both hands in grateful salute saying, "Adupe O, Adupe O" – the Yoruba "Thank you". I checked again in the evening, he was still awake and smiling, saying, "Adupe O" His relatives at the door of the ward were equally enthusiastic though I gave them fair warning that he was still in much danger and the outcome was doubtful. I refrained from adding that I really had no idea what was the matter with him; a further dose of morphia was given a little later to ensure his comfort.

My colleague returned after his long and busy day at about 10.30 p.m. and I gave him a full account of my first solo major emergency. When he had rested for a while we went up to the hospital together to do the night rounds. A check in the Female Ward when nurse welcomed him back, and he touched hands with one or two patients still awake; upstairs to the children's beds and cots where nurses reported on some of them who were very weak. Coming down the outside stairs the brilliant silvery light of a full moon charmed us on our way to Maternity where all was at peace, and then to look at our male patients. Nurse reported, "He's still awake, Doctor." And so he was, still smiling, still saying "Adupe O" with hands raised in salute. My colleague felt his pulse, considered, and decided to let well alone – no interference.

We visited the hospital engine room, reduced the voltage, a nightly routine, and after talking about his meeting and my patient for a while we bade each other good night.

The next day it was still "Adupe O", and he could drink water. Next day again he was happily repeating "Adupe O" and his relatives were smiling too.

On the third day as I entered the ward for the morning round Sister called me to his bed where, behind screens, she attended to the wound dressing. "I think you should see this, Doctor." Two nurses were present, one holding a large kidney dish at the side of his abdomen. Sister was pressing gently on the other side, having removed three big stitches. From the open wound was pouring, like lava from a volcano, a river of thickish white-yellow pus. Sister, nurses and patient were smiling. "Well," I said, "so now we know!" "Yes indeed," said Sister, "best abscess for a long time!"

I retreated to other duties passing relatives who clapped their hands and again echoed the patient's "Adupe O". The big retroperitoneal abscess drained well, recovery was swift and healing of the wound began and proceeded satisfactorily. In time he was able to get up and move about the ward and verandas, still saying "Adupe O." whenever I passed by. Before long a lorry was found to return relatives and patient to their village. He brought me quite a lot of patients after that. I concluded later that really I couldn't have done better if I'd known what I was doing!

So what of my assistant at what had been a very major operation for two young people to perform? He had assisted well indeed and was to do so at many more serious procedures. The son of an Ilesha Chief, Hezekiah Awodiya was a very fine young man. He deserves more than one paragraph. Read on...

The Scoutmaster

Hezekiah had told me that when off duty at the hospital he was the Scoutmaster to a troupe of scouts. Of upright carriage, tall and youthful, his skin was of a brown hue, less dark than that of many Negro people, his eyes dark and steady and the whites clear. A ready smile illuminated his face as he spoke, telling me of his proposed campfire and night under the stars with his young scouts. Evening had approached and the light had gone rapidly. I had watched his vigorous figure cycling away to his home and passing beneath our widely spreading flamboyant tree. I felt a strong desire to visit that camp and view the youngsters of Africa in their scouting discipline.

The Doctor's efficient team

My evening meal finished, I bade the cook and steward "Good night" and collected the carbide lamp from my storehouse. The hot flame gave a brilliant light to my path as I stepped out into the soft air of a warm tropical night. I passed a row of tall sunflowers leading to my favourite Frangipani tree, fragrant with perfume. Thence under an arch of Bougainvillaea to a gate in the wall of the hospital compound and through the surrounding thick bushes to the road outside. Busy by day with the passing feet of villagers journeying to bush farms miles away from our town, the road was silent now save for the light breeze gently rustling in the nearby palms. The hospital's leper settlement lay on the opposite side of the road among the trees where the ring of an iron triangle called the patients to evening prayer. My lamp threw a beam far along the dry, red, laterite road. I walked the short half-mile under silver stars that seemed to hang suspended against their background of black drape. Tall palm trees bordered the road, their huge leaves drooping and dark beyond the beam of light. Shortly I took a side turning on a path leading into the thick bush and winding around tall trees. A snake some three feet long slithered across the path and I waited while it moved away. The path led along to a clearing and I paused, extinguishing my lamp.

Before me the light of a vigorous campfire revealed a charming scene of good order and quiet discipline. Some twenty youngsters of the Yoruba tribe sat cross-legged on the ground in a double semi-circle before the fire. A blackboard and easel stood to one side, and beside it the tall figure of the Scoutmaster, immaculate in scouting uniform and hat, pointing with his cane to the orders on the board. The flickering flames were reflected in twenty pairs of eyes as they listened to their tutor's every word. Carefully he went through the arrangements and duties for the following day, dealing with questions and ensuring that each boy knew his job. Arrangements had been carried out with precision. Six palm-leaf covered shelters had been erected. A pile of firewood was neatly stacked, cooking pots stood nearby, and a small food store hung from a high branch. The whole area had been cleaned, weeded and swept, as if for the Chief Scout himself.

To the boys, Hezekiah was indeed Chief Scout. There he stood, quietly confident in command, quickly issuing orders, teaching Scout law and instilling the discipline that a boy needs for success. Tonight the son of an important chief in the township respected and honoured by the boys who displayed their trust in him. Tomorrow, clerk and interpreter in my hospital, chief assistant at the table of the Operating Theatre, in all his work the lives of young and old were in his hands, and on his broad young shoulders responsibility sat lightly and was faithfully borne.

A sense of pride came over me and with a feeling of deep humility I stepped forward into the light of the campsite and gave the Yoruba greeting for "Good work. Well done".

Who Helps Whom – A Story for Children

Hallo girls and boys! Isn't it nice to have Spring back again! Winter was pretty awful wasn't it, wet windy, cloudy, icy and snowy in some places. O.K. for snowballs and sledging, but miserable when it thawed, with the garden sopping wet and boots to be cleaned before Mummy would let you into the house. The cars needed washing often, good for pocket money of course but jolly cold on the fingers. School journeys were wet and dismal. Horrible wasn't it?

How would you like to live in an African country with hot sunshine day after day, a warm breeze and palm trees waving their huge leaves overhead? At the seaside lovely warm waves breaking and swishing over hot sand, little crabs by the hundred scuttle away and quickly bury themselves out of sight in the sand when you go in bathing. But even in hot sunny Africa girls and boys are poorly sometimes and need a nurse or doctor to help them.

Hundreds of stories there are about doctors and nurses going out from our country to help African children.

Here is a different story - the other way round.

It was a glorious sunny day both in England and Nigeria, a very big country in Africa. But the wind was very cool in England, while quite hot in Nigeria. Two little boys four years old, Johnny in England on the sands of Cleethorpes, a town in east Yorkshire, and Taiwo, 2,000 miles away on the dusty ground of his Nigerian village called Ifaki, had been playing all day.

In late afternoon both went home and told their mummies that they were very tired. Johnny said he'd a pain in his chest when he breathed, and had a little cough. He was hot and breathless. Taiwo said his head hurt awfully and so did his arms and legs and back and tummy. He was very hot too. Their mothers were worried and sent for doctors to come and see them.

"Pneumonia he's got" said the English doctor. "Give him this medicine, and put hot poultices on his chest three times a day." He put his stethoscope in his pocket and went home.

"He's got a bad worm in his head" said the African medicine man. "Come to my house for medicine for him." And he also went home to chop up leaves to boil them for making medicine.

Taiwo and Johnny were very ill for days and days and their mummies nursed and looked after them day and night. Their dads were worried too. At long last they both began to get better and were eating again. The English doctor said that Johnny's heart was bad, and advised the parents to go and live in the warm south of England. But Taiwo had troubles too for he could not move his legs. Not at all! He had to shuffle about the house on his bottom and hands. Life was very difficult for him. The years passed.

Johnny went to school and university and became a doctor. His heart got quite better. Taiwo however could never walk again. But he did not give up. His father was the village blacksmith, and when Taiwo shuffled on his bottom and hands to his father's workplace, just a palm-leaf shelter with a fire made of palm-nut kernels, an anvil and heavy tools, he learned to help his dad who taught him all he knew. He made the palm kernel fire, pumped the bellows to make it hot, used the hammers little and big, and from his hips upwards he became strong and powerful but his legs were tiny and could not move. Although disabled he became the village blacksmith, succeeding in due course his father.

Johnny went to a mission hospital in the Nigerian bush country, and learnt to operate on people and give them new hope in their lives. Taiwo, learnt to repair people's cooking pots and farm tools, so that their work was easier.

And one day they met.

At the edge of a good sized town called Ilesha stood the Mission Hospital where John worked. Once a month it was the doctor's job to go by car 85 miles up country visiting dispensaries on the way, taking lots of bottles full of medicine, syringes and injections to treat folk at the dispensaries.

On a hot sunny day the hospital car was loaded up with boxes of supplies for the dispensaries, and John began his journey. On a road made of African laterite soil, quite firmly packed to make a hard surface, the sun shone through the trees and huge bushes on either side making a pleasant dappled picture on the road. But it became very hot. A figure appeared in the distance, a big man pale of face and wearing the white robes of a priest. John stopped the car and offered him a lift, which he accepted gratefully. Some miles further on there were potholes on the road's surface, not yet repaired. The car struck the edge of a hole very heavily, on account of the man's extra weight. There was a loud crack, and the near side of the car sank down several inches. John found that the mainspring of the car had broken in half, something a doctor was unable to repair, and not the kind of repair he was used to.

Very slowly they could drive on to the next village. The priest had now reached his destination, and John attended to the folk at the dispensary there, giving injections and medicines. Then he asked for a strong piece of wood called iroko, very hard wood, too hard for white ants to eat. With a piece of stone he managed to hammer it in between the leaves of the spring to support the broken mainspring. The car could now drive safely but slowly for 20 miles to the house of a missionary outside the village of Ifaki. The doctor doing the round of the bush dispensaries called there every month for a meal, rest and chat with Rev. E.J. Jones, a missionary of many years standing, since 1923 in fact.

Jonah welcomed us and he listened to John's tale of woe and sympathised. He sent for an African mechanic from the village who came and took off the spring. The two pieces of spring were balanced on the head of a ten-year-old boy, and we all walked down to the village stopping at a mud-walled house. Did I say 'we'? Well, you'll have guessed of course, that I, the writer of the story was the Johnny and doctor with the broken spring. We knocked on the strong iroko door. The door opened, and to our surprise the owner was sitting on the floor. Looking up he asked in his own language what we wanted. We explained.

He invited us to follow him, and he shuffled on his bottom and his hands to his palm-leaf covered place of work. There we saw a small fire, a big anvil, a heavy hammer and a pair of tongs. His helper, a small boy of 9 or 10 years, pumped the bellows of the fire until it was white-hot. Taiwo, for of course it was he, was the strong village blacksmith for Ifaki and district, unable to walk, but with powerful hands, arms and shoulders. He plunged the ends of the spring into the fire until they too were white hot, and then hammered and hammered each one on his anvil until they were the right shape. Then he held them together firmly, made four holes in them, and hammered four rivets into the holes, tightly. When satisfied he poured cold water over the repair and offered the spring, now wonderfully strong again to our mechanic.

We gladly paid his price and thanked him for the excellent job that he had done. The mechanic replaced the spring underneath the car, and tightened everything thoroughly. All was well again! So it was that Taiwo and I met in the bush village where I was helping the people of his country, and he, badly crippled by his childhood polio, refused to give in to his disability, and helped me to do my job.

I never saw Taiwo again. I wonder if he, like me, nearly 50 years on, is still alive. I wonder if he still mends people's pots and pans. I wonder if he has a strong son to do the heavier work of repairing the springs of lorries or doctors' motorcars? I hope so.

CHAPTER 7

The Rise and Fall of Moses, and his Resurrection

Southern Nigeria is a huge region of tall trees and thick high bushes, coconut and oil palms, all watered by frequent tropical storms of furious intensity. It is a land where the traveller, penetrating these forested areas, can never be allowed a distant vision; so dense and high is the abundant foliage.

There are populated areas where trees and bushes have been cleared away for the building of villages and towns, and many areas cleared by farmers for the purpose of growing crops. In such places there are parcels of land, presided over and owned by important chiefs and African businessmen, maybe leased for a fee to the foreigners, merchants, gold miners, big trading establishments, mission stations with churches, schools and hospitals who wish to settle there.

Certain crops are carefully preserved. Coconut areas on the coastal regions, cocoa plantations up and down the country, groundnut farms in the north, and everywhere flourish thousands of oil palms, all of which contribute to the nation's wealth. There are, of course, the crops of local food produce such as yams, cassava, 'Indian' corn, tomatoes, bananas and red pepper grown by the small farmer for his family and local trading in village stalls and town shops.

The palm oil trees in any land are the property of the chiefs who own the land. One such area existed, with others, some miles from the township of Ilesha, a populous town of some 30,000 people.

At the time of my story the area chief was preparing to harvest his crops of oil nuts that were present in big collections called 'bangas' at the tops of palm trees. He employed a number of men, expert in tree climbing, to perform this task, and he sent one day for a man named Moses, giving him orders to service a particular area, climb the trees, throw down the big 'bangas' of nuts, these to be collected by a small labour force and brought into the storehouse in the town.

Moses duly prepared and sallied forth walking some miles to the stated region, carrying his rope and a suitable cutting instrument. Having identified his area he set to work, climbing, cutting and throwing down the nuts. Now these trees have a very rough bark, occasioned by the breaking off of very large leaves, maybe eight feet in length, or more, spectacular when raised in youthful exuberance to the heavens, but when old, breaking at their base and leaving a hard woody stump. The fierce high winds of tropical storms often cause them to crack and fall and the stump is left with hard sharp edges.

The method of climbing is to throw the rope around the tree, and then round the back of the climber. Fixing it he leans back and literally walks up the tree. The rope used by Moses was not the immensely strong Terylene rope of modern times, but rather a bit of liana culled from forest vegetation; perhaps he learned from Tarzan! Previous use had worn some of the fibres on the sharp edges of the leafy stumps. I am reminded of a former friend who endeavoured to climb a palm tree, without benefit of a rope, but slipped and badly grazed his legs on the way down to *terra firma*. As Moses proceeded up the tree, his rope, already frayed, but unnoticed by him, suddenly broke, and Moses crashed to the ground. He gave a loud shriek, with further yells of pain as he writhed on the ground and tried to rise. He had seen others with broken bones and soon realised that his right femur was indeed broken. As Moses lay in pain, trying to ease himself, he knew that he was miles from his village, and could not hear any neighbouring workers within calling distance. Nonetheless he yelled for help, and yelled and yelled. It seemed a long time before he heard an answering shout. He called again and he was answered; call and answer repeated, until a man appeared out of the bush and offered to help him. His helper quickly understood the situation, tried to straighten the leg, very painful for Moses, and told him he must go and get help. Off he went and soon found a friend and while Moses, of course, lay alone in great suffering they shouted to him that they would soon come back to help him.

Together they returned to the village where they spread the news. The village women searched out a goodly length of strong native cloth, and the men cut a length of three or four inch bamboo. The cloth tied to it by its corners made a useful stretcher, according to traditional usage. Returning to the injured man, they gently pushed an edge of the cloth under him and each taking one end of the bamboo, raised it and carried him home over the miles to the village. Already counsels wise and unwise had culminated in a decision to get him to the Mission Hospital some twenty miles distant, for native medicine, as they knew from experience, would be useless. Nonetheless he was given a dose of a painkiller, and then they took him to the road through the village, and hoped for a lorry that was bound for Ilesha.

Eventually one came, greeted with joy after hours of waiting. It was crowded with folk seated on forms with their loads of goods and produce, live fowls and maybe a dog or two, not to speak of babies on their mother's backs. The driver stated his price, which was agreed, and everybody crowded together to enable Moses, poor chap, to be lifted up and deposited on his stretcher on the lorry floor amongst them all. Such was a common occurrence among the lives of local folk, but to a patient in great pain from the rough bumping over the corrugations and potholes of bush roads of a hard sprung vehicle designed for inanimate loads, the agony must have been quite frightful.

Reaching town most of the passengers and impedimenta were offloaded, and the lorry moved on to the gates of the Wesley Guild Hospital. Through the gates, round the Outpatients' Department, to halt on the road between the Female Ward and Sister's office, opposite the slope leading to the main corridor. Two ward boys appeared with a wheeled hospital stretcher and Moses was transferred and wheeled more gently past Sister's office to a bed in the Male Ward. Relatives followed.

I was discussing a matter with Sister and we noticed the little convoy and waited for nurse's message. "There is a new patient, Doctor," said nurse. Complaint, temperature and respiratory rate followed. "Thank you, nurse I'm coming," I replied, and went with Sister to inspect the casualty, and listen to the relatives' story for they had come also, piled into the lorry.

The damage was self-evident; the thigh swollen and painful, the leg two inches shorter than its fellow. His pulse was slower than expected. I inquired about native medicine dosage, for experience suggested that some of these medicines could slow the heart rate, sometimes dangerously so. However he seemed in fair shape despite the damage and journeying experiences.

I ordered morphia and atropine, and Sister prepared the theatre for an anaesthetic and the normal splintage arrangements under chloroform anaesthetic. Traction was applied to the leg, and the bones were moved into apposition, a Thomas' splint was applied, and a sandbag weight to maintain the traction. He was peaceful under the anaesthetic given by Sister.

While still asleep Moses' leg on its Thomas' Splint was raised up and slung from a wooden beam, called a Balkan Beam, over the bed, beloved of hospitals in those days and effective in reduction of swelling by encouraging the fluid to return to the circulation. On my night round later I greeted him and ordered another dose of morphia. He seemed easier and looked content.

His relatives had gone to town to find lodgings, so they were happier too.

The tension in the Theatre relaxed. No new emergencies occurred. Some satisfaction was in order, but alas it was short lived. The next day, after morning prayers with the nursing staff, Sister spoke sadly, "You know Moses, bed 14 with the fractured femur?"

"I do indeed," said I.

"Well I'm sorry to disappoint you, but he has taken off his Thomas' Splint." Consternation!! Comment seemed superfluous.

"I'll come and see," I said.

Moses did not look happy and was obviously in pain. The leg was again two inches short and the thigh very swollen. I gave him a lecture about non-interference, interpreted by the senior nurse, and Sister arranged another Theatre session complete with 'rag and bottle', as we called chloroform anaesthesia. A couple of ward boys (porters) were called to pull the shoulders at one end and the leg at the other so that reduction of the fracture could be effected; another Thomas' Splint, a profusion of bandages to immobilise everything, and leg and splint swinging from the Balkan Beam as before. "That'll fix him," I said. And so for a couple of days it did.

And then? Sister was rather gloomy after morning prayers. "I'm afraid he's had another go, Doctor, he's taken it all off again." I felt gloomy too, as well as somewhat wrathful. We addressed the patient in no uncertain terms, not forgetting to tell the relatives so that they, in their own way could reinforce the message. They would doubtless estimate that with a longer stay in hospital the costs would escalate!

There were plenty of tasks awaiting my attention and I got on with them; pneumonias, abscesses, osteomyelitis with pieces of dead bone to be extracted, the Female Ward and Maternity problems, desperately malnourished children and so on but the matter of Moses' leg was niggling me, and I remembered that I had in the store room a seven pound tin of Plaster of Paris. I found Sister busy instructing nurses about attending to a wound dressing. "How about a plaster spica from his tummy to the ankle?" I said. "That should do the trick, but you'll need lots of big bandages, so I'll get the night staff to make a good supply," said Sister. The bandages, four inch ones, were spread out yard by yard on Night Nurses' table. Sprinkled liberally with Plaster of Paris and rolled up ready for use.

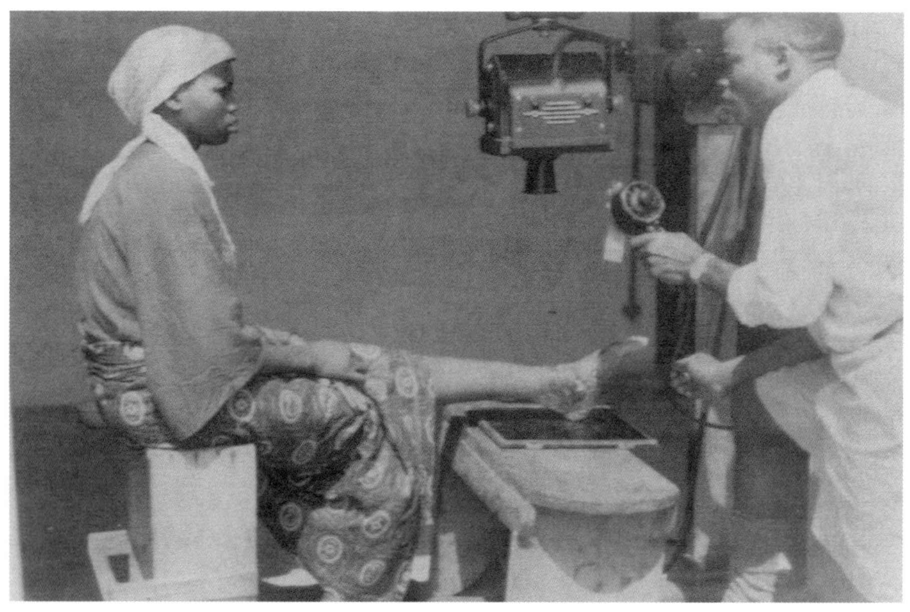

X-Ray for an ankle

Another Theatre session, more rag, bottle and chloroform and more tugging by ward boys. A large dish of water, bandages dipped in, squeezed gently one after another, and then bandaging began; slapping them on wet, round and round the lower abdomen and pelvis, thigh with fractured bones in good position, and right down to the ankle joint.

"That will teach him," said my assistant, and happy smiles surrounded the unconscious patient. The plaster soon dried and Moses was returned to the ward and made as comfortable as circumstances allowed. No doubt his relatives at visiting time would emphasise the rule of 'no interference', and we felt grateful that, at last, the trouble with Moses was settled. And for ten days it was!

Then peace was shattered as a message from Sister was brought to me. "Dear Doctor, Moses has got his plaster off!"

Alas Moses had defeated us again. A little explanation seems necessary. From our knowledge in England of plaster casts the idea of the patient removing one would be laughable, but in the damp tropical atmosphere of Nigeria the plaster taken from its tin would draw to itself moisture from the air that would lessen the powerful hardening process when subsequently used for a cast.

Moses had scraped away till he'd found the end of the bandage and pulled and pulled and pulled! To blow him up might improve staff morale, but it wouldn't help the patient and it was help he needed, and help that we missionary servants were there to provide in Christ's name. For a few days I spent spare time, when available, in browsing in a textbook of operating orthopaedics and admired the expertise of the surgeons. If only I had been able to work for a while under such expert teachers, but in wartime, and being rapidly pushed a year after qualifying into the depths of central Africa, such luxury was of course denied. Suddenly there came to my mind a picture.

During my first furlough I took a job in Ipswich hospital evading flying bombs and stitching up casualties who watched the explosions from bedroom windows. In Theatre one day an orthopaedic specialist was operating and I was his assistant. He was performing an arthrodesis of the knee for a patient with severe arthritis of the joint. Having opened the joint and cleaned away a lot of roughened cartilage and bony abnormalities, he chiselled out from the front of the tibia a peg of bone about three inches long and a quarter of an inch wide. This he pushed into the medullary cavities of the tibia on one side and femur on the other and straightened the joint. Hopefully when healed this would make a solid, welded, rigid joint adequate for the patient's future locomotion. The picture took life vividly in my mind and I thought – "Why not?" – and told Sister, informing the patient that we could help him again.

Back to the Theatre; more anaesthetic. Forget the splint and bandages and plaster, just take a scalpel and chisel and hammer, no spanner required! More vigorous traction by ward boys. Skin of thigh and lower leg had already been prepared the night before, thorough cleansing, twice swabbed with Bonney's Blue, Brilliant Green and Gentian Violet and covered with sterile dressings to deter germs. "Ready Sister? Hope the knife is sharp!"

An extensive slash down the outer side of the thigh, forceps to bleeding points, carefully separating the muscle bundles to gain access to the injured area. Already much callus (soft bone formation) had formed around the fractured ends of the bone and this was penetrated and partly moved. An onslaught on the tibia with the hammer and chisel followed, and a satisfactory peg of bone, three inches by a quarter inch, prized out. Very firm pulling of the leg and shoulders by our assistants enabled the peg to be inserted into the broken ends of the femur, and they came nicely into apposition. Mopping dry, checking for bleeding, tying off bleeding points and repositioning of separated tissues followed, with a drainage tube inserted and long rows of stitches, not forgetting the tibial wound. Dressings and bandages and back to the ward, and remembering adequate pain killers.

"Alright Sister? That'll fix him" – "I don't think he'll wriggle out of that," she replied. He didn't. Moses' recovery from the operation was greeted by the ward full of patients with applause and a fair amount of ribald chaffing and with witty jokes. He found that he had become a popular hero among his fellow patients, and any of them sufficiently mobile were glad to help ease his discomforts.

Nursing staff kept a close eye on both his pulse rate and his itchy fingers, and were not slow to reprimand him for previous naughtiness, delivering lectures at the drop of a hat, with dire warnings regarding future interference!

Moses first ventures into weight bearing were indeed painful, but he persevered, encouraged by the helpful attitude of both nursing staff and other sufferers in the ward. The latter took delight in quoting to him a variety of Yoruba proverbs equivalent to 'He that is down need fear no fall' and 'more haste less speed'. All such fun was delivered with good-humoured laughter, and the more able of the patients would gladly offer Moses a hand when needed. He continued to make progress with dogged determination, and earned the admiration of all patients and staff. In six weeks he was hobbling about the ward with a couple of sticks. Soon afterwards he returned home with his relatives, and perhaps the villagers threw a celebration party!

Would he ever climb an oil palm again? Well, with a gentleman of such determined character anything might happen. Maybe he would get a Christmas present of a stout Terylene rope!

CHAPTER 8

Kwashiorkor

It was a hot and drowsy Sunday and the hospital was quiet. The morning ward round had found the condition of patients satisfactory, save for several rather ill, small children whose treatment seemed to be on the right lines. No emergencies, no palavers.

I'd had a hot half-mile walk to the morning service and endured a harangue in Yoruba that I took to be the sermon. My mistake, it was the week's notices! The sermon was even longer and came later, equally incomprehensible. Men and women listened earnestly and babies slept on their mother's backs.

My eyes strayed to watch, outside the window, the expert plaiting of a child's hair by her mother. A hot walk back to my bungalow where, as a special treat, my usual diet of goat's meat had been changed to a pleasant dose of bush antelope. Then banana fool as was customary.

No urgent messages. Peace reigned. Just right for the post-prandial siesta. I relaxed and drowsed into a half sleep. But wait! A sharp knock on my doorpost followed by steps on the veranda. Eyes opened, I beheld Harold Gibson, a young missionary whose station was the outpost village of Imesi-Ile, 25 miles distant.

"Hallo Harold, nice to see you. You look hot!"

"Hallo John." Harold sank thankfully into a chair. "It was a long ride."

I found him a long glass of orange juice and noticed his bicycle outside the gate, a further jug of juice and a little nourishment, after which we would chat.

Imesi-Ile was a village in the bush, far from English folk and Harold had been stationed there to learn the language, and under the tutelage of an African pastor to discover the way of running Christian worship in the deep bush. He was a sincere and devoted chap and would be much appreciated.

But it was a medical matter that was troubling him. It was not his own health that had inspired him to force his cycle pedals round and round on the long ride up hill, down dale, potholes and rough surface notwithstanding, under the midday sun blazing all the way. After a little rest he said, "There is a little girl I'm very worried about, and I feel that she is very ill. I wonder if you could come and see her. The parents won't bring her here. They are very afraid of ill wishing."

It seemed that she was seven or eight years old. She had been ailing for a long time, treated by her granny with a brew of native medicine against the wishes of her young parents; but granny was all-powerful and they were obliged to submit to her instructions. She was becoming pale and weak. Arms and face were thin, eyes sad, hair becoming reddish. Legs had become very swollen, feet grossly so, and the abdomen was becoming huge like a drum. It was a well-known story medically; the child was plainly very ill. The name of the condition was Kwashiorkor. When the mother ceases to breast feed her child at about 2 years old, the latter subsists on a cornflower (cassava) diet. This food is ground to powder and mixed with water, a milk substitute. The mix consists almost entirely of carbohydrate, and extreme protein deficiency and other dietary essentials may result. It is often fatal, along with malaria and dysentery accounting for the very high death rate in African children.

I told Harold that I would certainly come to see her, but that he must have a meal and a good rest first. My small pantry provided cold food for him, and while he put his feet up I went to arrange things with Sister.

Pyjamas, dressing gown and mosquito boots were soon packed up with toilet articles added. The hospital car was soon ready and we packed the bicycle into its cavernous boot. On the road to Imesi-Ile I was glad to be borne in comfort, and certainly Harold welcomed the change. I had brought my faithful Raleigh cycle to Nigeria, but a single trip of two miles to the Apostolic Compound to visit the Eltons in Ilesha was quite enough to convert me to motor transport.

The road wound through bush and forest trees, up and down, the car occasionally putting up huge clouds of varicoloured butterflies that were sunning themselves on the warm road surface. Sometimes a sleepy snake, similarly occupied would slither out of the way. It must have been a hard cycle ride and I appreciated the love and dedication of my friend as he had endured those 25 miles in order to beg for help for the little girl of his village.

We arrived in daylight and I was shown the village with its little church, the school and the dispensary. After dark the schoolteacher took us to the house where the child lived; a mud-walled, stoutly constructed job with galvanised iron sheets for a roof and a wooden shutter or two for windows. A palm oil lamp served for light rather inadequately, so the teacher brought his bright Tilley lamp.

The father and mother brought in their precious seven year old, unclothed, and shivering, more from fear than cold. She stood before me obviously terrified. To conduct a physical examination would have been most unfair and was not necessary. The diagnosis was quite plain. The awful protein deficiency, kwashiorkor, was perfectly clear. Only a lengthy stay in hospital with all the care at our command could offer any hope. To continue as they had been doing, with the inadequate diet and native medicine, would quite certainly cause the child's death. I stated my case; the teacher interpreted, and the parents hesitantly looked at granny, afraid to speak. Granny objected most vigorously. The palaver became quite heated and went on and on, a real ding-dong. The parents began to push for hospital care for their little one and at last, suddenly, granny gave way. She said in effect "alright she can go" and added that she would go too, to see 'fair play' perhaps. And it was agreed.

The meeting broke up. Harold's cook provided a good meal and after a long chat with story swapping we retired for the night. I dossed down on Harold's camp bed under a net. The crickets and distant drums lulled us to sleep, but not before my mind had dwelt on the seemingly interminable argument in the shadowed room of the mud walled house, where words were batted to and fro over the matter of life or death of a very sick child. Thankfully good sense had prevailed. Now to win the real war...

Early next morning a hurried breakfast, and a hasty farewell to Harold, a lonely intrepid figure in a difficult situation. I'd promised to pick up granny and the kiddie outside the village, and found them waiting there in the bush beside the road, for it was important not to be seen by the villagers for fear of ill wishing.

And so back to the hospital, for the child to be introduced to the ward with other children of her own kind. A warm comforting welcome by Sister and the Yoruba nurses, a cot with mattress and a blanket, and a nourishing drink which we hoped her body would be able to absorb, not just swallow. Granny sat beside the little girl, and tended by a young nurse, she soon relaxed and slept.

The days and weeks passed. Treatment in those days consisted largely of milk feeds, spelt Klim of course, being the only available milk powder, with added simple foods and such vitamins as were in Sister's store. Gradually improvement began and granny began to smile. As the weeks went by the patient tried smiling too and attempted little games with the nurses. Very shyly she started speaking and later getting out of her cot and tottering over to see another patient.

Progress became quite quick now as her diet was made richer and she was actively playing with other little poppets, all of them recovering well. Her mother had been able to follow us, but the father needed to work of course. Mother and granny were delighted at the improvement. The nurses gave the girlie a new name, 'Olu Funmilayo' which translates as ' Joy come down from Heaven'.

So Olu became a pet patient, and after 7 or 8 weeks she was walking and running. She could be discharged. Dietary advice was given to the mother and granny. They came to say goodbye, granny falling on her knees in the concrete corridor and repeating many times "Adupe O, Adupe O", the Yoruba "Thank you". Olu's father had also arrived to take his daughter home, so now all three, hand in hand, pottered away down the road to the market place in Ilesha to catch a lorry bound for Imesi-Ile.

It felt very good to win a war. Harold's cycle ride had paid off.

Lumps and Bumps and Fear

A very pleasant young man was Joseph in his mid twenties, 5ft 7ins tall, well built and dark eyed. An Ijesha of the Yoruba tribe, he greeted me with the customary polite Yoruba greeting, "I hope you are well. I hope your wife is well, and your children, etc." I responded suitably and enquired what I could do for him. He looked very well and I discovered that he was a teacher at a near-by school.

He came straight to the point. "Doctor, I want you to take off my leg." I was surprised, stunned in fact, and sought further enlightenment. It appeared that he lived in a village 10 miles distant, had been to college in the big city of Abeokuta and was clearly well educated. He had heard well of our hospital.

His leg had troubled him for years and caused him to drag it and limp. He realised that it would not improve and that there was no cure. With some difficulty he pulled up his trouser leg and offered the limb for inspection.

The leg below the knee was hugely swollen, the skin thick, pitted and oedematous; likewise the foot. The diagnosis was not in doubt. As he well knew, he had developed elephantiasis. The word accurately described the wretched appearance of the limb. Huge, heavy and awkward it most certainly was. No wonder that he wished to part company with it.

He would like a wooden leg he said. Obviously he had done some research, and had discovered that there were Italian prisoners of war in Lagos who were skilled in making such prostheses. Would I please do the operation and arrange for appropriate after care.

We had quickly realised that our African folk were not tolerant of unusual lumps in their anatomical arrangements, and to be asked to remove fatty lumps was not unusual. This was! Most unusual!

The condition is caused by blockage of the lymph vessels - tiny vessels through which the clear body fluid is returned to the circulation. Once again the mosquito is the cause of the trouble. It bites a person already infected with a minute worm called filaria. On sucking up that person's blood and lymph fluid some of the filariae are taken as well. They lodge in the mosquito's salivary glands. There they develop becoming larger. When the insect bites another person it injects a small drop of saliva to prevent its victim's blood from clotting while being sucked up, and in go the filariae! Very cute isn't it?

The wee pests will now live in the lymphatic vessels of their new host, multiplying sufficiently to cause blockage of these vessels. If the vessels affected are in the leg the fluid, unable to return to the circulation of the blood system causes the leg to become swollen. Complicated isn't it? The name of the unpleasant invading filaria is, you really must learn this, Wucheria Bancrofti, so that's even worse - don't you agree? And this is what had happened to Joseph, poor chap. Death to mosquitoes!

Medical science had found no solution to this trouble, and Joseph's request would certainly relieve him of a very uncomfortable condition, and was therefore reasonable. I agreed to help and asked to see him the next week. That would give me time to look up matters in my textbooks of surgery and orthopaedics and instruct myself regarding the technique of leg amputation! It was one thing to watch the process as performed by the eminent surgeons of Edinburgh Royal Infirmary, but quite another to be faced with the demand 'do it yourself'. I spent an evening or two reading. I felt it necessary to pop up to the theatre, open the glass instrument case and examine the condition of the amputation knives and saw. The use of such instruments was rather infrequent.

So, did he have his amputation? Yes, of course he did. I'll spare you the details dear reader, the scalpel, the sawing, the forceps, the catgut, rubber drains and silkworm sutures, but he survived the experience very nicely; healing was good and he departed home with an improvised crutch or two. A happy man was he!

In due course he visited the prosthesis experts in Lagos, and returned with a useful artificial limb to be offered work as a clerk in our hospital. He proved an excellent additional member of staff.

Well, the Yoruba people are not alone in their dislike of abnormal lumps in their anatomy. The wen, common enough also in European areas, is detested. As also the fatty lump, lipoma, and pleas to remove them were common. A wen is a lump containing a collection of oily material, the secretions of sweat glands. If glands are blocked by sweat and dust the material forms a lump. It often occurs in the scalp. The task of removing them was easy, a wen being extruded from a scalp incision like a pea from a pod.

The lipoma requires a little more of dissection and persuasion. One woman was the proud owner of a large such growth extending from the right shoulder to the mastoid region, and, on removal, weighing all of a kilogram. She was grateful indeed when the horrid object lay in a kidney dish instead of deforming her natural body outline.

Other lumps there were, one in particular deserves mention. A woman in her late forties attended outpatients one day with a large goitre. This is a swelling of the thyroid gland in the front of the neck that grows overlarge in an endeavour to produce enough thyroxin for the body's requirements. What is thyroxin? Try an encyclopaedia... This essential commodity needs iodine for its manufacture, and in some areas this mineral is lacking, as in Derbyshire here at home. The lady pointed mournfully at the disfiguring lump and begged for a cure.

The only answer of course was a chopping procedure. She had already experimented with native medicines to no avail naturally, so we explained about the proposed operation, briefly mentioning that it would be risky, and she, greatly trusting, was happy about it. For me a few deep breaths, and again recourse to my surgical textbook was very necessary before venturing with scalpel and forceps into so vital an area. After all there were large veins, furious arteries, nerves of speech and other useful structures, not to mention tubes for air supply and the passage of food.

Refreshing my knowledge of the neck's anatomy, so efficiently and minutely described by Dr. Jamieson of Edinburgh took up several hours of spare evening time, between games of Monopoly with my colleague and our wives.

The day came to give the lady the promised relief. Anaesthetic by Sister, theatre instruments checked, staff all attention, and we could begin... A nice curving incision along a natural neckline, the scar to be easily hidden later by a necklace (of local gold perhaps?) and careful dissection avoiding important structures. Quite a number of small blood vessels cut and caught with forceps were sutured with catgut, and always there were more bleeding points awaiting capture. It's a sanguinary area. Using a Spencer-Wells forceps on one of them I was at once rewarded by a rasping air intake under the anaesthetic mask, the stridor of vocal cords in trouble. I released the instrument hurriedly and breathing returned to normal, thankfully. The forceps had, in the little lake of blood where lay the cut end of the small arteriole, picked up the branch of the recurrent laryngeal nerve. This controls the vocal cords in the voice box. All thyroid surgeons are well aware of its proximity and do their best not to meet it!

After that episode all went according to plan and the large offending tumour was removed and placed in a kidney dish to await investigation or disposal. The patient was returned to the ward with a neat dressing and bandage, and awoke later, very pleased to be minus the object of offence.

We found our dark skinned patients a most grateful people, unfailing in their "Thank yous". After all they had no National Health Service and paid, in part at any rate, for their treatment. Often they borrowed money to pay their little bills, and gradually repaid over months to follow. When the bill for a hernia operation and three weeks in hospital, all found, equalled their monthly income such a matter could be serious. Does that make a difference to the gratitude expressed? Maybe advance payment by general taxation is preferable? The debate continues...

There were lumps large and small, some painless and some very painful indeed. Jiggers, little beasts that penetrated unprotected toes, were often left to our houseboys to deal with, most expertly I might add. A little antiseptic to follow and all was well.

On board ship, returning from furlough in England we had stopped at Freetown. A clothes wash had taken place, clothes drying on lines on deck thereafter. A week later when nearing Lagos my wife and children noticed small lumps on tummies and arms, unusual but not really painful. They were beyond my medical understanding. A fellow missionary, a lady, hearing the mild complaints volunteered her services, which were gladly accepted. "Oho", said she, "tumbo fly" and taking a piece of lint or some such, she squeezed the little bumps. To our astonishment a maggot was delivered from each one, and the resulting hole rapidly healed up. Apparently tumbo flies in Freetown had laid eggs on the clothes while they were drying on the line. Tiny maggots had emerged, burrowed into the wearer's skin, very painlessly, and derived nourishment from her until ready to emerge. Clever little chaps - what fun!

There were other lumps. A little swelling in the ankle region would break open and the head of a long guinea worm would pop out to find fresh oxygen, food, water or whatever. This was quite a long fellow present in the subcutaneous tissues, and often long enough to reach into the upper thigh. He was persuaded to come further by the simple expedient of tying his head to a matchstick, or small piece of wood; each day the stick would be turned around once or twice. Hopefully after a week or two the whole worm could be thus extracted... However should the treatment cause the worm to break, killing it, an abscess would soon form, maybe several abscesses along the whole length of the worm. This length would be a septic area for a long time unless treated. Where there is pus 'let it out' was the principle to be followed, and the scalpel would be used liberally.

The tapeworm of course is an internal parasite living within the intestine, and may attain three metres in length. It produces eggs that pass to the exterior and may be picked up by pigs, goats and sheep. Suitable worm killer will abolish it, but thorough cooking of meat is needed to prevent human re-infection.

There were lesions of the skin of course. Not exactly lumps pushing up beneath it but more flat areas of nastiness that portended trouble. The dirty yellowish lesions of the 'yaws' disease, occurring more in children perhaps, especially affecting the face were most unpleasant and disfiguring and could lead to other more serious troubles. Fortunately, weekly injections of a preparation containing minute doses of arsenic were effective as a cure. Later when penicillin was available this was the treatment of choice. Often in tiny malnourished children the veins in the arm were very small and collapsed, needing patience and a good technician to make them visible at all. Our excellent assistants, James and Hezekiah had been well trained and were experts at making veins stand up and be counted.

Following a dose of measles there was sometimes trouble. Against measles our patients had little resistance and it was a serious infection, sometimes fatal and always extremely debilitating. Occasionally a small lesion would occur on the face, spreading rapidly and deeply into the cheek substance. It could penetrate the whole thickness of the cheek causing a hole through to the mouth, ever spreading and enlarging like a cancer. Hence it was given the name 'Cancrum Oris', a dreaded disease. It was extremely difficult to treat and often fatal.

Occasionally a patient would appear, apparently in normal health but with an expression of anxiety and indeed fear on his face. A friend, usually his wife, would point fearfully to a pale patch of skin on his back or elsewhere. This might be insensitive to touch, heat or cold. Fingers or toes might also suffer loss of sensation. The patient feared the diagnosis; leprosy was undeniably the cause, greatly dreaded by everybody. While nowadays curative treatment is readily available and segregation unnecessary, this was a different matter in the early 1900's. The patient was feared and isolated by all people and treatment was by injections of chaulmoogra oil. My predecessors at the W.G.H. had taught the leper patients in their compound next door to us to administer their own injections. Nearly all were now 'burnt out' cases (disease arrested). They were a very cheery little crowd of two-dozen or so folk. Many of them had suffered nasty losses of toes or fingers, often with nasal loss and facial deformity. But daily they gave thanks in their little chapel for what life was left to them. Our little leper community were very self sufficient, working on their patch of land and growing vegetables, and as has been mentioned already caring for poultry, eating their eggs, and admiring their cockerel!

In these days new drugs taken by mouth for three years cures the disease. Surgical treatment by experts is undertaken for deformity. Hope is restored, and there is much cause for thankfulness.

This and That

A variety of happenings which separately would hardly warrant a chapter of a book, might well be worth a mention as illustrations to the scene of medical life near the Equator.

A tsetse fly for example flew into the car one day when I was off on my monthly travel to the dispensaries. It chose to alight on my right arm that did most of the steering, and rapidly bit, helping itself to a dose of my good blood. A most painful bite it was and for a moment the car veered to one side, recovering quickly as I assisted the fly's departure, using the other hand, vigorously!

This fly can, of course, transfer the dangerous little trypanosome, a protozoan, to both humans and animals, causing serious trouble or death. 'Sleeping sickness' could be the result, and this nasty little brute, when infecting animals such as cows, certainly produces a fatal outcome. Hence no dairy milk was available in Nigeria, except from a herd of cows in Lagos that were carefully protected in a mosquito-proofed enclosure. For some weeks after the bite I remained rather anxious about being unduly sleepy, but there were other things to worry about, such as meeting in ward rounds diseases of which I had little knowledge and less experience. So I forgot the trypanosomiasis, but remembered the bite!

"How long before the theatre will be ready, Sister?" There was another patient afflicted with a sudden peritonitis of the lower abdominal region, possibly due to a ruptured typhoid ulcer, who had been ill with a high fever for about three weeks and had now been brought in for help. "About an hour Doctor," came the reply. Just time to drive the 20 miles to the railway station at Oshogbo where our Senior Sister would be arriving by train from Lagos following her furlough in England.

It was a very hot and bumpy ride by car, the dry laterite road being badly rutted and corrugated transversely due to the passage of many lorries with their human loads.

Sister Liony, the lion hearted and wonderfully dedicated lady of mixed parentage, African and Danish, whose skill and nursing discipline had been the driving force in establishing the nursing reputation of the W.G.H., was waiting at the station with her luggage, and we were soon homeward bound.

Two miles from home the engine began to beat irregularly, (we diagnosed 'auricular fibrillation') juddered briefly and stopped. Evidently it was telling us that enough was enough. Far too late for digitalis and no facilities for intravenous injections of heart stimulants, so we looked at the dashboard! One look was enough, and that was the operative word, or rather, not enough. My mistake. Sterile towels, gloves and instruments for the theatre were essential naturally, but I should have used some of the sterilising time to fill up with petrol. Oh dear! And the day was hot, very hot for a two-mile walk, and the patient was waiting...

But we were lucky. An army car, manned by two English soldiers drew up beside us on noticing our plight - useful to have a lady on board. They responded willingly to our plea for help, producing a stout rubber tube and a gallon petrol can. My first lesson in sucking up petrol and siphoning it into a can was learnt in Africa's burning heat, and we were most grateful. I still remember the clever little trick!

We reached the hospital in time to return Stella to the welcoming arms of her colleagues, and to exchange the siphoning tube for the intravenous saline and the scalpel and forceps. The patient was 7 months pregnant and had been very ill apparently for some three weeks in a nearby village. She was fortunate to survive the illness and subsequent operation.

Yes, it was a burst typhoid ulcer. A purse-string suture around it, pulled tight, was enough to close the hole, and some reinforcement with a patch of omentum stitched over the damaged area made assurance doubly sure. Talking to the relatives of this woman patient had been informative. They all collected water from the spring not far from the hospital gates. A little stream, dammed by a wall of cement block, about which more information elsewhere, was their drinking water supply. This led to the suspicion that the water was typhoid infected. We talked to the lady, on recovery, and to her relatives about the boiling of water. I understood that the pregnancy ended normally under the care of our Sisters. Memo: Talk to the Council about that spring!

Phantom of some Anxiety?

The morning Outpatients was progressing as usual. A man and woman of the Ibo tribe entered. He had some English of sorts, something to do with a pigeon...? "She get child, Sah." Said Hezekiah, translating with a smile, "she is pregnant, Doctor, she says 6 months". She willingly stretched out on the examination table and revealed her swollen tummy. It looked about right for six months, and she seemed very happy. Aged about 30 I thought, with no previous pregnancies. Unusual. Did I detect a slight note of doubt in her husband's attitude? His voice sounded somewhat strained, and his face looked concerned.

I felt the swelling. It was softish, not firm. I tapped it all over - hollow, not fluid. I applied the foetal stethoscope and listened. Bowel sounds only were heard. There was no foetal heartbeat. There was really no doubt about it; this was a phantom pregnancy. Such may occur in the case of a woman longing earnestly for a baby to fulfil her womanhood. I was obliged, however reluctantly, to give my verdict.

My opinion was met with vehement protestations "But there is six month swelling! She never see her time for six month! You must be wrong!" Hezekiah looked sad and helpless; he didn't like it either.

"There is a way to be certain," I told them. "If we give her medicine to put her to sleep the swelling will go away, and you will see there in no pregnancy." I explained to Hezekiah the neuro-muscular phenomenon resulting from the patient's intense desire for a child. Other family members were brought in and we talked to them. All agreed to the proposed anaesthetic. So again the rag and bottle technique, with ethyl chloride sprayed onto a mask. The patient took deep breaths and as consciousness was lost the abdominal muscles all relaxed, and the abdomen was flat once more. Husband and family members were all suitably amazed, and accepted the explanations, trying to understand. The patient awoke and was tearful, naturally.

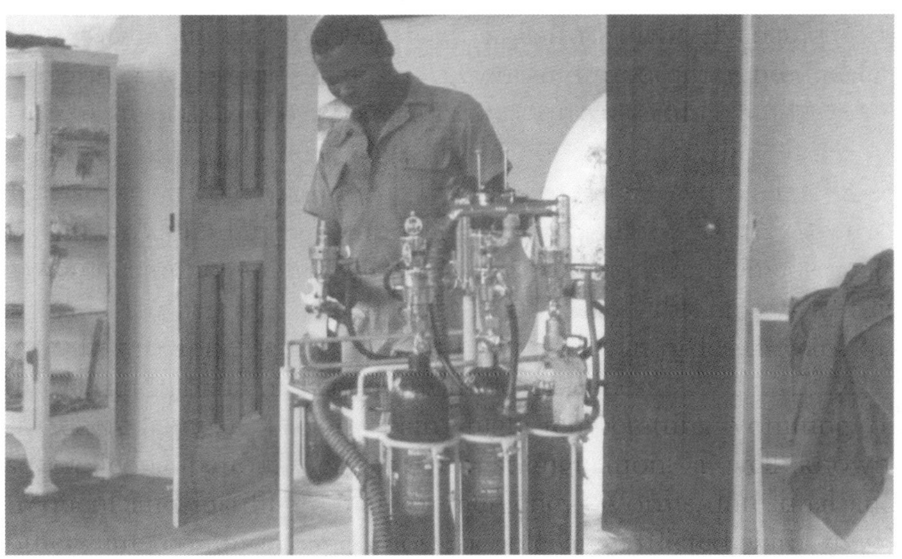

Simeon, Theatre Nurse
with anaesthetic machine

Afterwards it would be our job to try and find out reasons why. This was not an easy task in those days, and of course the first suspicion would be that the fallopian tubes had become blocked by an infection, probably of gonorrhoeal origin some years previously. Lots of enquiries to undertake without modern facilities and not having the medical expertise necessary for such an exercise. It looked like yet another case of quite tragic unfulfillment.

*_*_*_*_*_*_*_*_*_*_*_*

"What about the surgical instruments doctor? Were you very short? How did you cope?" Such were the questions often asked when we returned to this well stocked country, where hospital theatre cupboards overflow with modern surgical instruments and impedimenta. But at the Wesley Guild Hospital our surgical supplies were really very adequate, updated by the diligence of my predecessors, and were mostly of stainless steel and in very good repair.

There were naturally a few difficulties, especially in wartime. A scalpel blade would expect long and frequent use. When the operator complained about the toughness of the Yoruba skin it was time to ask our expert James Balogun to try his well used expertise with the steel blade on a piece of suitable stone!

If in the engine house an essential nut were lost and could only be retrieved by a long Kocker's forceps, then that was where the engine house benefited from its proximity to the operating theatre. In like manner if one needed to drill a hole in the tibial tubercle in order to fix an extension device for obtaining suitable traction for a fractured femur, then recourse to the engine house was necessary to obtain a drill, suitably sterilised of course. Any part of the drill difficult to sterilise was wrapped in sterile towels naturally. Should it happen that just prior to an operation the sky clouded over darkly portending rain or an electrical storm, when our mechanic laddie was collecting the post, or driving any of the ladies shopping in town, then it was only 40 yards for the doctor to run quickly to the engine house, turn the heavy flywheel, release the valve lifter, and the theatre would be brightly lit as desired. No problem!

To inspect an ear hole, (auditory meatus to the professional) the old-fashioned head mirror with a central viewing hole was quite efficient, magnifying glass extra of course, rather a clumsy combination, but it worked.

The episode of the visiting doctor's worn out plugs which illustrated the usefulness of the plug spanner came into our ride to Ile-Ife, when Sister had persuaded me to go and admire the American hot water system at the Seventh Day Adventist hospital. Admiration spawned an idea in my mind. Of course improvement on their system was imperative. Bigger and better must be the British job. So two 44-gallon drums were connected together by a one-inch pipe and laid on iron bars with room for a roaring fire beneath. These were then enclosed in a big fireplace structure consisting of four walls surmounted by a concrete roof and chimney. On the roof there stood upright two more 44-gallon drums connected to each other and to the drums below; a generous quantity of hot water indeed. The nurses dignified it by the name of Powell Boiler No. 2! A four-gallon boiler previously invented had been No.1 of that ilk! The sisters were now happy, and morning coffee in their office was a cheerful time...

*_*_*_*_*_*_*_*_*_*_*_*

Intestinal infections are very common in the topics. Along the horrid little agents responsible for such troubles is the amoeba. Not, dear reader, the little chap beloved by our budding schoolboy biologists, pushing out his pseudopodia here and there, but the tropical resident endued with more evil intent, by name Entamoeba Histolytica. This plaguesome fellow has long been known as the cause of severe dysentery and intestinal damage in those whom it attacks. On account of its ravages a doctor predecessor of mine at our hospital had been forced back to England, leaving the fine work he had been doing at the W.G.H. This was Dr. Beaugie who when not medically busy arranged the extremely useful piping and plumbing system, to the joy of us all.

Other complications can occur in the course of an amoebic infection. A woman was admitted one day with fever and pain in the region of the right lower ribs, with an enlarged and painful liver. A day or two for observation and investigation, and the diagnosis was certain, an abscess of the liver. Mention has already been made of the advice of our Edinburgh surgeon, 'where there is pus let it out'. She was brought into the theatre; an injection of local anaesthetic into the skin and a little cut made between two ribs. A suitable sized trocar and cannula was pushed into the underlying abscess. A very satisfactory flow of pus resulted and over some days it gradually drained away with eventual healing. Treatment of the amoebic infection was of course essential and this continued until the patient could be pronounced, hopefully, cured.

Amazing the things that happen!

CHAPTER 9

Emergencies – Little and Less Little

Often in the course of an Outpatient session there would appear a man in distress with a finger or thumb into which a collection of bacteria had entered, from some minor injury, small cut or prick from a sharp object. Happily multiplying they could rapidly cause an abscess in the terminal pulp of the digit, very painful and incapacitating. A minor operation was the remedy and on his record card the words, 'for op.' told Sister in charge all she needed to know. In my early days at the hospital a nurse would select the needed instruments and take them to the hospital kitchen. Cook would accept them, put them in a pan (when one was empty) add water and leave it on the kitchen stove to boil. The patient, poor chap would wait, unhappily, finger throbbing germs multiplying.

After Outpatients and hospital ward round, various minor procedures and examinations, not forgetting to attend to the needs of the carpenter (more screws, please), plumber (we need pipe connections for our one inch pipe), mechanic (I go get petrol for the car, sah?), I could retire and await a call from Sister. Time passed. Time for another letter? Better send Sister a note about that thumb operation..... After a while came a nurse with the message, "Sorry Doctor, cook went off duty and the fire went out!" Mmmm! Job for the hospital manager to sort out – where is he? I found him, in my bathroom, looking at me from the shaving mirror! The sterilisation arrangements for minor operations in Outpatients changed for the better, rapidly! Later, as you will read, steam sterilisation was installed by a friendly engineer and we had heat at the turn of a tap. What! In the African deep bush? Why not? What's all this about third world hospitals? They go forward too!

Freed temporarily from the urgency of medical matters lunchtime followed by a siesta combined to bring needed relaxation. All hospital workers not immediately needed went off to rest, those living near by, to their own quarters. Only a few essential ward staff stayed at their posts. The others, persuaded by the heat of the midday sun, snoozed gladly. My eight-foot front veranda was furnished with two strong iroko chairs nicely padded, and a long couch to match. In comfort I could gaze eastwards to Mount Imo, whence might come a cloud over its top presaging longed for rain.

Beyond the entrance lay a ten-foot dais at the same level surrounded by wooden planks raised up a foot or so and providing excellent seating for a variety of lizards. These delighted in sunning themselves, and in their orange and dark blue colour were a joy to watch. Sturdy chaps, some ten inches in length, they would lie parallel to each other, two of them head to tail, whacking each other with strong vigorous sweeps of their tails. Like jousting knights in armour they provided good entertainment until one decided to grant victory to his opponent and scuttled off. The victor would raise himself up and down on forelegs until, becoming soporific no doubt; he subsided in the hot sun.

Beyond lay the well-tended lawn of the Sisters' house with its lovely flower borders and surrounding path. On my right a great tree rising to a hundred feet or more, trunk entirely bare of branches, crowned at its top with branches and leaves that rustled in a quiet breeze by day. To the right of the path a thick border of bougainvillaea, red and green and spiky, acted as backdrop to a lovely scented frangipani tree, bare of leaf but lavishly decorated with brilliant small white flowers enchantingly perfumed; perfect clothing for the compound wall. A gate led through the wall to the roadway outside, and beyond it to the lepers' compound. Some two dozen of them occupied small houses and lived and worked at small farms, attended 6 a.m. prayers daily at their little church, gave each other injections of hydnocarpus oil, and were a wonderfully cheery crowd of patient sufferers.

Leaving the theatre one day a man approached leading by the hand an elderly woman who dabbed her eyes with a cloth. Said he, "Sah, this woman get worm for eye." They had come quickly through the hospital gate, followed by the clerk who was writing on an Outpatients' card. On gently pulling down her lower eyelid the trouble was obvious. Under the clear conjunctival membrane that covers the white part of the eye, a transparent filarial worm about one and a half inches long wriggled slowly, perhaps like the ant seeking an escape route.

Back into the theatre and the lady was laid flat on the operating table. "Cocaine eye drops please nurse, also a pair of small scissors and small toothed forceps." Very shortly came a tray with drops and instruments sterilised and ready for use. A few drops to the eye acted in half a minute, pick up a little fold of conjunctiva, snip a tiny hole in it beside the worm, and collect the latter with small-toothed forceps. A drop to the eye, and on the eye a pad for an hour or two to keep out the dust while the conjunctiva quickly healed; an easy worm and a satisfactory minor operation.

I'm reminded of another occasion. On board a 22,000-ton ship travelling home at the end of my first tour in Ilesha, a fellow lady missionary mentioned at breakfast one day that her eye was very irritating. A quick peep at the offending orb, and behold – she too was the proud possessor of a filaria! Breakfast finished we went off along the vast decks of the huge ship to find the hospital.

It was 1944 and the decks were crowded with troops returning to the fray in the European theatre of war. We kept enquiring and finally found our quarry, a very fine hospital Operating Theatre with a peaceful staff including a delightful young doctor who took a look at the eye and its occupant. "Oh lord," said he, "what ever is that? I can't do anything about that!"

"Well I can," I replied, "if I can borrow your Theatre for a few minutes," and we were invited to be his guests. Very shortly afterwards the patient felt much happier and the young doctor was most grateful for his further dose of education. We reached Gourock with no further medical excitements, the only mishap occurring when, during a day's stay at Gibraltar we were waiting for a convoy coming through the Mediterranean. Some gung-ho chappie doing a bit of firing practice from land managed to pop a small shell straight into the carpenter's shop, somewhere near the water line! Rumour was that the ship's carpenter, returning to his shop after temporary and fortunate absence, was quite displeased! Repair effected, we caught up the convoy with no trouble during the night.

A worse emergency with which we had the misfortune to deal originated from the belief in, and customs regarding, the world of spirits. I hasten to aver that in no way am I knowledgeable in this regard; I mention only what I have understood on hearsay. The African beliefs and ways regarding spirits are indeed far beyond my comprehension. I have been led to think that after the death of a family member it was the custom in our area to give the spirit of such a person an occasional 'outing' or entertainment. This took the form of an evening party where relatives would gather together and take the spirit for a little shuffly dance around the town. A professional drummer or two (depending perhaps on the cost) would be hired to join the procession. A Tilley lamp or two would provide light; perhaps a photograph of the deceased would be carried, and a hunter or one able to manipulate a Dane gun would be included. Off would go the little crowd clapping hands, dancing a little to the drum beats, and occasionally the gun would fire. Through the streets of Ilesha they processed, a merry little party, happy to provide a little fun for the spirit of their relative.

It so happened that on one occasion the gun which normally would be fired upwards, unloaded of course, went off, perhaps accidentally, while still pointing down and forwards, sadly towards the calf of the man in front, causing a nasty wound. The hospital was not far away and two strong chaps brought him into the Male Ward. The report went to Sister, who promptly examined his leg and ordered the theatre to be prepared.

On that evening I was the sole doctor in the hospital and was suffering a bad attack of malaria, rigors and high fever with other unpleasant symptoms and unable to help in any way. However, Sister was well used to attending to injuries of many kinds, and proceeded to cleanse and remove damaged tissue from the patient's leg, doubtless liberally dosing the wound with M & B powder and giving him tablets of same to take. He refused to stay in the ward despite persuasion, and was told to return in the morning.

I heard this next day after my fever had reduced and I was improved but feeble. The patient did not return. We had no address and could obtain no knowledge of him, but hoped he would soon turn up.

Five days later a kit-car arrived with the poor man desperately trying to survive a massive attack of gas gangrene. Although no bullet had been loaded in the gun the wadding which compressed the explosive gunpowder had entered very deeply, unseen at the time of original treatment. The resulting infection had spread far up the thigh and involved the abdomen. Morphia in very adequate dosage was our sole resource, and of course to save him was, very sadly, beyond our means. I believe his relatives understood. During the night he found permanent peace.

In those days gunshot wounds were thankfully very rare, - would it were still so!

Emergencies, Sad and Happy

This was an acute hospital. No case could be denied admission when needed. Yes, there were other hospitals: twenty miles in one direction lay the American Baptist at Ile-Ife; twenty in another direction the government hospital buildings at Oshoqbo; fifty miles towards the Niger at Akure the Church Missionary Society operated a hospital with sisters and nurses but no doctor for some years; seventy five miles back towards Lagos another government institution at Ibadan. The population in towns and bush villages over so many square miles was huge, and the illness incidence enormous. If beds were full a message to our hospital carpenter could produce a wooden bed quite quickly, a mattress or blanket or two from Sister's store and such a minor emergency was soon solved. Where to put it? Well if the centre of the ward was already taken up the Male Ward had eight-foot verandas, so why worry! All that the doctor in Outpatients needed to do was to write T.C.I. (to come in) on the patient's record card and sister, carpenter, ward 'boys' and nurses quickly found a resting place. What! Ring up the ward and ask if there's a bed? You must be joking!!

Non-urgent cases were admitted within a week, while the urgent received immediate admission. The sixty-five-bed hospital often expanded to ninety and often the staff pondered the possibility of finding further accommodation, but that story comes later.

To such an acute hospital would come, as well as simple cases, the most serious and advanced cases of illness, medical, surgical, obstetric or paediatric. Particularly there came, only too often, small children very seriously undernourished usually aged two or more when their mother had ceased to breast feed them, and in place of breast milk was substituted a diet of watery corn flour with its gross lack of necessary protein and other nutrients needed for a growing child. Sadly cure was often beyond our skills, and cases which, in a modern hospital with all its wonderful facilities and staff experience might well have turned the corner and blossomed into new life, could only be watched as they passed into unconsciousness, never to recover. Such cases defied our utmost efforts. Kwashiorkor was a dreadful condition where the child was unable to absorb into its system the milk (Klim from a tin) that was our main standby in those days. (ref - Chapter 8)

Too often in my light sleep at night I would be roused by the quiet patter of nurse's bare feet on the concrete veranda of my bungalow even before her door knock sounded and her voice gently called, "Please Doctor, bed 'X' in the Children's Ward has stopped." While putting on my mosquito boots to attend the ward in response, and trying to recall the details of the little patient, there came to my ears the wailing and keening of the mother as with the dead child strapped to her back she hurried away from the hospital. There was no action that nurse or I could take, and of course to charge the parents a fee for services rendered was quite out of the question.

I pictured the scene in the ward. In sad exhaustion the mother would at last be sleeping, on the floor beside her child's cot, where the desperately ill kiddie would be quietly slipping away. Nurse, doing another round to check on the condition of her little patients, would be feeling an absent pulse, trying again, noting that the breathing had ceased, and realising that death had claimed yet another of the tragic sufferers from kwashiorkor. There would be the waking of the sleeping mother, the agonised cry that would wake the mothers beside other cots, and their dumb watchfulness as the mother placed the child on her back supporting its limp body with a length of stout native cloth tied around her own body. There would follow her hurried footsteps down the stairs from the ward, making a rapid exit through the hospital gateway; there was no reply to the night watchman's greeting as the wailing woman retraced her sad and lonely journey, this time with her hope denied, to the mud-walled house that was her home. The last act, the charge nurse giving to her junior the necessary message to the doctor on call.

Other children almost equally ill were cared for in the ward, and we could only try our limited best for those surviving, and their mothers hoping… I thanked Junior Nurse and dismissed her.

Rest and sleep were essential for efficiency in the next day's adventures in healing. I removed my mosquito boots, but sleep was a long time coming, delayed by the bad experience. But it was good to remember that little charmer, Olu, who had survived the dreadful condition and had returned home successfully.

The sounds of the night were those of the throbbing diesel engine and generator delivering light to the compound, wards and houses, the merry chirping of crickets and the croaking of frogs, and I found these quite soothing in the warmth of the tropical night.

Happier Noises and a bit of Fun

My brain mercifully blanked out the other noises which perturbed one often. Noises above my head bringing visions of slithery snakes in the roof, rats and mice or other unknown small denizens that seemed to be skittering about over the ceiling boards. I often wondered sleepily how to deny them their cosy habitat. Despite the noises and visions sleep took hold and prepared my nervous system for the following day.

By its light I conferred with Diamond, my cook and factotum, and with my 'small boy' Isaac, general-purpose houseboy. They offered little advice, but to my mind came inspiration - why not lead a trail of black ants into the roof, and let them deal with the squatters and plaguesome little beasties that disturbed my rest? Cigarettes were a curse but the tins that housed fifty of them often came in very useful, and shortly Isaac was commanded to collect in such a tin as many ants as possible (bites permitting) – he was not pleased! These to be placed up in the roof, we hoped they would pass the glad news of unlimited fodder to their fellows in one of the black trails that crossed our compound. Alas nothing happened, and there were other things to do. The noises continued…

It was Thursday morning - operating morning and the Theatre was ready. A couple of hernias to begin with followed by a laparotomy (a look inside the abdomen to see what was the matter), all performed under spinal anaesthesia. A carefully calculated push on the long spinal needle between two lumber vertebrae into the spinal canal, the tip of the needle to penetrate the membrane of the canal whence drops of spinal fluid would emerge through the needle to tell the operator 'needle in place'. Injection of needful anaesthetic solution, and all was ready for the operation to commence. These procedures were followed by an operation for osteomyelitis where a piece of dead bone had caused a big abscess, now burst and draining pus – a duration of many months. Here a bit of hammer and chisel work was useful, the piece of dead bone was removed and the wound packed suitably, often with iodoform impregnated gauze. Usually a native 'doctor' had made many small incisions in the skin; if only his courage had produced a deeper penetration through the muscle layers as well he might have effected a cure. We were late in finishing, only to be faced with the arrival in a lorry of a man stabbed in his front chest during a fight! The wound appeared superficial, but investigation revealed a deeper penetration, touching a lung.

Fortunately there was no serious invasion of air into the chest cavity and just careful cleansing and suturing under a light anaesthetic took care of the injury. None the less it was 3 p.m. by the time gloves were off, and the bell for the afternoon gardening session was ringing. On my way to my bungalow for dinner I noted the garden 'boys' were all assembled around a palm tree throwing stones up at it. Enquiring of Diamond I was told, "Very bad snake for top of tree, sah, boys go kill him." I replied that I would bring my gun after 'chop' (food). Goat's meat, yam and green stuff of some kind followed by banana fool revived my inner man, and in due course I went off to join the battle.

The snake in question appeared to be about 3 – 4ft in length, and was peacefully snoozing, entwined around the highest leaf of the palm tree. A shame to disturb him! I was assured that he was "very bad snake, sah". Generally speaking the snakes of Nigeria were all assumed to be 'very bad' until proved otherwise, especially if a little 'dash' (money) was offered in exchange for the heads thereof! The hospital carpenter was busily employed watching the gardeners' efforts. "Sam," said I to him, "go and fetch a ladder, put it against the tree, climb up and shake that leaf until the snake falls down. Then I will shoot him."

Sam regarded me with disbelief. "Go on Sam" I said, "Do not fear." Reluctantly he moved off to collect the needful. The barrage of sticks and stones continued. I loaded my .22 sawn-off rifle with a little cartridge, armament lent to me by my missionary friend, Jonah. He was going to Wales on leave after two years battle against mosquitoes, snakes, ignorance and the teacher training college which he ran 60 miles away in Ifaki in the bush.

Sam returned slowly bearing the ladder. Slowly he placed it against the tree and, turning, looked at me. "Go on Sam, shake him down," said I. Sam fixed the ladder, shaking his head sadly. (How crazy can these Europeans be?). He climbed with exaggerated care, stopping well before the top. “I not fit reach palm leaf,” he said. “Oh, come down,” I replied, “I’ll go up myself.” Sam descended willingly, and grasping my little gun tightly I took his place going up higher till within eight feet of the unsuspecting sleeper. I raised the gun and pulled the trigger. The snake leapt up and fell, among the big palm leaves at my feet twisting and slithering. I frantically sought in my trouser pocket for another cartridge trying to maintain a precarious balance on top of the ladder.

The snake was more concerned with nibbling at the skin holes where a tiny pellet or two had entered rather than taking revenge with a bite on my bare ankles. Unmindful of the enemies below, he overbalanced and fell to the ground. The garden ‘boys’ with heavy sticks gleefully despatched him, ending the episode, and held up the snake by its tail, noisily congratulating each other and exclaiming about the dangers of so venomous a reptile.

The carpenter looked at me with intent, saying nothing, shaking his head, and carted the ladder away. The garden ‘boys’ returned to cutting the short grass. I returned to my bungalow stowed away gun and cartridges, vowed to have more sense in future, and retired for a late siesta after the day’s adventures. To distract my thoughts I picked up a Western novel given by the Red Cross, and after a page or two slept, hoping mosquitoes would do the same.

No Emergency this - a Planned Job

You will have noted that I mentioned travelling homewards on a large vessel when a bad worm had provided some entertainment, a happy adventure! This journey occurred at the end of my first tour in April 1944. I was full of joyful anticipation of course, planning to meet my lovely fiancée, and this time marriage was uppermost in my mind! Come on that wedding ring!

Our ship, the *Queen of Bermuda*, could easily outdistance any submarine still at large in the Atlantic but she kept with the convoy from the Mediterranean, and, after leaving Gibraltar made a comfortable and uneventful journey to Gourock. I joined the telephone queue to announce my arrival, caught a waiting train and rattled south to Wellington, Salop, to find happiness long awaited. Six weeks later at Thorpe St. Andrew, Norwich, the ring was happily positioned and the name of the game was honeymoon, minus scalpels or spanners in our eager hands. Refreshment from the tropics, enchantments in England!

Two months later found us in Ipswich where I had acquired the hospital job, the object being to improve my surgical expertise. (My diary notes: Barbara being a bit sick. I wonder why?) My return to Ilesha early in 1945 was, once again without my beloved wife, extra passengers not being allowed, even if in utero! Alas! We had confessed to the pregnancy and her passage was cancelled. I travelled on a French ship where I tended to speak Yoruba words (what little I knew) and on reaching Lagos my old schoolboy French returned and puzzled the Yorubas! It was not until a year or more later that my dear wife and baby daughter followed me into the harbour at Lagos. I drove them with the greatest care the 185 miles to our Ilesha bungalow. For months I had practised the art of driving with utmost smoothness, gently braking, smoothing out the bends and avoiding potholes. It paid off. We arrived home happily. The busy emergencies began again next day, so it was me to the theatre and my wife to cross swords with our cook! The Crosbys left Ilesha later in 1945 and we moved into the senior doctor's bungalow. This was the original one from the days of Dr. Stephens and his successors, and was shipped out in pieces in those early days. The wood was deal and needed careful watching lest white ants attacked it. Raised on six-foot iron stanchions it was fairly safe, most of the time!

The rainy season (our summer) passed, autumn came with its alternating showers and more showers and sunshine… and then… the storm... and its complication…

CHAPTER 1O

Storm and Strangulation

From the shade of my bungalow veranda I gazed sleepily out over the lawn of the sister's house with its well-tended dahlias and canna lilies. Beyond lay the wall of the hospital compound, built of stout mud blocks, well drained, coated with cement that cracked in the blazing heat. Over it hung on both sides great bushes of bougainvillaea, stretching long thorny arms up and outwards in thick meshed defence work over the cracking wall fabric, covering the bareness with verdant foliage of dark green, richly decorated with its small magenta flowers.

Outside it lay an earthen road of reddish-brown laterite soil, beaten hard by the sun, traffic and the passing of many feet. It led to a large village, fourteen miles distant, giving access to small hamlets, farms and clearings in isolated areas of near virgin forest.

Along the road small boys of six to ten years or so pattered softly, carrying headloads of firewood bundles from their father's farms to their homes in the town. Women, bare of foot, erect of habit, strode sedately past carrying laden baskets full of farm produce accurately balanced on thick plaited hair, a coil of native cloth on the head helping to poise the heavy load. They called greetings to other travellers as they all passed to and fro, turning their heads with loads in expertly balanced movement of long practice, to continue conversation until beyond earshot of each other. They and the children formed an important transport system from farm to town, working on their farms in early morning, carrying produce home 'ere darkness fell.

Men travelled the road more in an organising and protective role, working on the farm by day, sometimes sleeping in the bush at night if far from home. Stick in hand they followed their small convoy of women folk and children, but seemed less purposeful than the women with their striding tread and graceful carriage, conveying family goods and chattels.

My vision lifted beyond the walking, tired folk, over the green bush beyond to mount Imo, raising its tree clad summit into the eastern sky, and I sensed that many hopeful eyes of hot, tired people would be glancing in that direction. The hot red-brown soil of Africa was baked and cracked by week after week of unremitting heat; the dusty leaves of bush land tree, the browning grass, the cracking long black seed pods of the 'Flame of the Forest' tree, all spoke of dry heat, and from every solid object in the sun's full glare heat radiated, and still the sun beat down.

Bulking hugely in the east stood mount Imo a thousand feet above, its slopes lit by the afternoon radiance; its thickly bushed top indicating the path whence might come the longed-for rain. Parched ground, dry leaf and branch, and weary man and beast, longingly, in the late afternoon, watched its dark summit. Would a cloud appear? All watched, all hoped, all waited.

On such a day, the work of morning done, the road beyond the wall hushed in the afternoon heat, my wife, Barbara, and I rested on the veranda, while our eldest daughter of eighteen months idly played on the mat-covered concrete. Our eyes lifted from time to time from book or knitting to scan the mountaintop in the east. Was there a small promise? We hoped and waited…

A tiny, formless patch of white appeared over Imo. Like a bit of froth upon the tree line. Rising, rounded, small as a human hand it seemed, and the cloud grew and gathered shape over the summit of the mount.

Hope sprang in thousands of hearts, and the oppressiveness of the day increased but could not quell the rising tide of glad expectation as the cloud gently swelled and rose.

Storms had passed to the north or south of Imo occasionally in the weeks past, waxing in dark threat. But they had ignored the pleas of man and beast and baking soil, and had passed on either side of the town. Their winds had driven dust into eyes and faces, and their dark cloud had blanketed the sun's light and heat, but there was never a single drop of cooling rain. Quickly the disturbance had moved on, hopes had faded, groans had been uttered and the sun's fierce heat had returned. But now – a cloud, central over the hill – surely – at last…

There was a patter of feet on the concrete steps of the veranda, and knock, knock on its doorpost. "Yes, nurse, come in." "Please Doctor. There is a new patient. He complains of pains in the abdomen." There followed a brief description of a groin swelling, with the patient's account of his trouble, and Sister's report of the pulse rate, temperature and respiration – "All right, thank you nurse. I'll come and see him at once."

I looked eastwards. The cloud was growing. Brilliant white in the sweltering sun, mushrooming from its dark bed above the mount, pregnant with living force, bellying in several areas, it was urging forwards and upwards, and spreading sideways in tightly formed clusters of cloudlets.

I passed my small 'boy', Isaac, on my way to the Male Ward. Flat of foot was he, and clumsy of hand, but an expansive smile spread over his face; he too could read the signs in the sky. "We get rain soon, sah," was his happy comment. A garden 'boy' Peter, lazing with his cutting grass in the shade of a casuarina tree, spied me and the eastern sky at the same time, looked again at the sky, smiled as I passed him and swung his implement with renewed vigour, not that there was any grass worth cutting.

I joined Sister at the patient's bedside and examined him. I spoke to the relatives with the aid of my chief clerk and interpreter, Hezekiah. "How many days has he had the swelling?" – "Three days," they replied, and there was a look of doubt and sympathy from the good clerk, whose knowledge was now wide, and feelings very human. A strangulated hernia of three days duration did not suggest a happy prognosis, and I had to give the relatives the usual warning, out of the patient's earshot. They responded gloomily as befitted the occasion, but agreed to operative surgery, and Sister busied away to prepare the Theatre and to issue the necessary instructions to the nursing staff.

I took the opportunity to visit a few rather ill folk in the maternity, female and children's wards. Sister joined me and we stopped together to appraise the sky.

"We shall get a soak this time, Doctor," she said, "better remind the 'boys' to disconnect the water piping to the tanks." I took the hint from one older and more experienced in tropical life then I, and called the hospital gardeners to give the order. The first rain would wash a tremendous amount of dust from the corrugated iron roofs of the hospital buildings, and not until this was washed away would the gutters and pipes be connected to carry clean water to the underground concrete tanks. We had finished our store of 30,000 gallons a few weeks previously, and water was being carried from a good well in the compound and pumped up by semi-rotary pumps into roof tanks above the ward ceilings. The carpenter came at my call and agreed to inspect the roof gutters after the first fury of the storm was over and I would join him when I was free, for stopping major leaks was important to our water supply.

I rejoined my wife, Barbara, to await the approaching storm and the completion of the preparations in the Operating Theatre. There, four burner pressure stoves burning kerosene would be roaring beneath the sterilizer full of bowls and instruments and rubber gloves in cotton bags. Nurses would be busy swabbing trays and trolleys with antiseptic and getting ready the trappings for major surgery, too busy to look at the sky.

The cloud was bigger. We stood to watch it develop. From a cluster of cotton-woolly mushrooms brightly shining above the mountain it had spread far up into the sky. It had developed into pillars and battlements of cloud, rounded shoulders and tops reflecting the golden glory of sunshine, and dark depths revealing a hitherto unseen menace of future storm. Fast grew the outer shining castellated defence works, and deeper grew the dark shadow within the walls. Tier upon tier of towers, walls and battlements rose upon each other, fiery shouldered and inky centred, and now bright flickers of fire flashed soundlessly within the structure. Dark swirlings of cloud angrily moved in the centre, and greater shadows were cast by the huge crags of the outer towers. Thus far the cloud had just grown mightily above Imo filling a huge sector of the sky above and behind the mountain. Suddenly a change was apparent. The cloud having risen and bedecked itself with all the trappings of battle, now like a huge knight in armour bestriding a mighty war horse, darkly threatening without, furious with wrath within, flickering with wild stabs of lightning and growing distant thunder, began to rush forward.

Gathering speed it advanced across the sky obliterating three sectors of the heavens, throwing out long grey outriders of cloud rack on flanks and centre. The awful shape darkened further with menace, throwing away those sunlit edges of fiery beauty, and blotting out the sun itself with a dark mantle.

Now came the sudden rush of black cloud overhead, and a sudden breeze stirring the dust of garden paths, rapidly changing to wind of increasing power, bending the compound's bushes and trees and slamming doors. Hurriedly we sped round the house closing shutters and noting that the mountaintop had vanished behind heavy rain. Hardly had we done so than the preparatory raindrops, which raised the dust and delighted the nostrils with the smell of damp earth, changed to a fury of rainfall full of threat and force, hammering on the roof with roaring voice and filling garden gutters to overflowing. A mighty flash streaked through the gathered darkness and a fearful crack of thunder assailed our ears and spread across the heavens rumbling mightily. 'Ere it died away a further tremendous flash and thunder crack battered our senses, to be repeated time after time over the next hour as the vast electrical storm swept over and around us. It stabbed the trees and ground with streaking sparks of millions of volts, while the rainstorm drenched all nature with its weight of water. Damage to trees, fences and 'tin' roofs, road blockage from fallen trees, ditches full of fast flowing water were the norm. Drivers of lorries caught by the storm would form queues behind huge trees collapsed across the narrow roads. The hospital water tanks would benefit as roofs and gutters overflowed with the deluge that poured through pipes into the welcoming empty concrete structures.

Gradually the enormous fury of lightning, thunder, wind and rain began to subside, as the storm moved away. The time between lightning flash and thunder crash lengthened. The carpenter and I sallied forth with boots, umbrellas and spanners to adjust rainwater gutters, for the rain would continue for some hours and water must be saved. Dark clouds were replaced by lighter ones, and small patches of blue would soon appear. The edges of retreating cloud would again be tinged with gold, and suddenly watery sunshine would illuminate the scene. Damage and survival would reveal themselves.

Broken branches, drooping palm leaves, injured roses and a welter of leaves, seedpods and garden bric-a-brac would await order or repair. Very soon a gentle mist of water vapour would arise from the steaming ground in the renewed warmth of Africa's sun. I returned to my house pondering the wonder of nature.

My thoughts were disturbed by a patter of feet on the veranda. A gentle knock and a quiet voice, "Please Doctor, the Sister says the theatre is ready." – "Thank you, nurse. Please tell her I'm coming." So it was on with mosquito boots and light mac, and I sallied forth up the road to the hospital. Light rain still fell; the deep gutters beside the road which we called 'kotos' still ran with a welter of rain water fed by the dripping grass and trees and overflowing gutters. The water music tinkled happily until I entered the theatre, there to be replaced with the roar of the primus stoves beneath the sterilizer.

All was ready, Sister with 'rag and bottle' of anaesthetic, nurse with trolley of instruments all laid ready for use, and Hezekiah scrubbing up. I joined him, scrubbed and gloved and gowned to approach the table on which our patient lay, quietly asleep under Sister's ministrations. I checked for warm moist swabs of gauze, which I knew would also be ready, and took the scalpel.

The cut. The forceps to bleeding points, the relieving of the tight band that constricted the loop of gut, all were routine. Then gently to ease the small loop of intestine out, lay it on a warm moist gauze pack and cover with another one, applying a little pressure, so gently. Repeat warm packs, and repeat again.

Inspect. The congestion of the area of gut squeezed mercilessly by the tight band was subsiding. Blood vessels could be seen pulsing, healthy redness was replacing the dark blue of congestion. All was well. No serious damage, the little loop of gut would live! Back into the abdominal cavity it went to join its friends. Stitches as appropriate to close the peritoneal opening, and firmer ones to repair the defective inguinal 'hole' responsible for the trouble; an old-fashioned repair job that would need three weeks of patient's inactivity for healing to be certain. Close the fascial tissues and the skin and apply dressings.

Sister stopped the anaesthetic. There were smiles of satisfaction all round as the patient was lifted on to a trolley and wheeled back to the Male Ward. It was good to see the happy faces of the ward and theatre staff. Even the patient, well sedated, had seemed to smile in his sleep as anaesthetic had taken away his pain, and he had not felt the scalpel. Only the relatives looked mournful and anxious, but Sister encouraged them, and next morning they were smiling too as the object of their care and ours was now free from the condition that threatened his life.

Grass would start growing, clumps of blue and white flowers would lift happy faces to the sky, water pumps would be operated again, our patient would return to his house, our children would again play with energy beneath the palm leaf shade.

And the sun would blaze again, and our eyes would soon seek another cloud over Mount Imo.

Water

When visiting London and Bristol for tropical equipment, shirts, shorts, sandals, topee of course and the more vital protection of yellow fever vaccination, small pox and tetanus jabs, with anti-malarial tablets, (an extremely necessary precaution) there was some question whether anti-typhoid injections were considered necessary.

A story of my public health lecturer in student days was fresh in my mind. We had a small typhoid outbreak in Edinburgh. He proceeded to describe the P.H. Department's investigation of the matter.

"Patients came from a certain village where water supply was at that time drawn from wells, so we tested the waters, not forgetting the occasional privies nearby. The well belonging to one elderly dame was, we felt, suspicious. She objected to the testing. "I've drawn water from that well for 70 years" she said, "and never a day's illness". Despite protests we succeeded in testing her too, and found that she was the typhoid carrier! Some people can harbour the germ in their gall bladders without falling victim to the disease... I ordered the typhoid vaccination and got my doctor to inoculate me 'ere setting sail for Africa.

In due course when at our Ilesha Hospital a few cases occurred of suspected typhoid infection, an abdominal upset and discomfort, a temperature rising higher day by day for a week, a peak of temperature sustained for a week, followed by a gradual fall and recovery, providing no emergencies arose. But ulcers were a complication, occurring in the gut wall, and in the third week could perhaps rupture causing dangerous peritonitis. It was necessary to keep the intestine quiet, no bulky meals, only fluids were permitted. Patients felt hungry in the third week, and a nurse was stationed at the door of the ward to make sure that no food parcels were brought in.

A little chap of 10 or 11 was recovering well from typhoid. A friend or relative felt he needed feeding up, and, avoiding the nurse's inspection, managed to pass him a package of pounded yam, flavoured perhaps with red pepper and wrapped in a piece of banana leaf. He ate gladly. The result was dramatic. Junior nurse came running to my house. "Please Dr, Bed 18, Male Ward has a very bad abdominal pain," she said urgently. "I'm coming nurse," I said. I felt his tummy, quite tender. He was sweating, restless and the pulse was fast – plainly a perforation had occurred in the intestine and I asked Sister to prepare the Theatre. "I have already got the big kerosene stove going Doctor," she replied. It was not long before the little chap was asleep under the ether and the scalpel was put to work. The intestinal hole was found and closed. The peritoneal cavity was gently swabbed clean, wound sutured and bandaged and antibacterial treatment begun. He was lucky and went home with his parents who were instructed about water and the cleaning of vegetables and hand washing. Life was difficult for many people.

Bad water supply

His water supply came from a spring not far from the hospital gate. We had no means of investigating water or latrines nearby, but the Public Health Department was informed about the typhoid case, and about a few others also which had occurred in that area.

The spring ran down a slope to form a good pool, formed and partly surrounded by a wall of concrete blocks, cement rendered. In the wall were four or five holes large enough to allow passage of calabash bowls. Women collecting water for their homes would pass the bowl through the wall to collect a supply of water, tip it into a large earthenware pot, which, being filled, they would carry home on their heads with admirable expertise.

The Public Health Department became aware that germs could be slaughtered by chlorine, and felt that to treat the water with the chemical might well improve the town's health. A man was therefore appointed to stand beside the said pool, and, having an 80oz. Winchester bottle of chlorinated water in his care, to place a teaspoon of this European 'magic' into every calabash bowl of water taken from the pool.

But it so happened that the ladies were by no means enamoured of the taste of the chlorine – although how much of it was available after this medicinal fluid had stood in a convenient saucer for several hours in the hot sunshine, was debatable. Anyway they were happy to pay the Public Health representative a penny a time to refrain from adulterating their water with Public Health 'magic'! So he supplemented his income and he was happy. The spring kept on flowing, and the hospital was kept busy.

The town had to wait more years before a piped water supply reached Ilesha from below the hills of Effon, some twenty miles distant. If the pipes cracked and leaked at times, well, there was still the spring, and wells could still supply. The roads were traversed by lorries heavily laden with good Nigerian timber which might well cause damage to underlying water pipes, helped by heavy rain soaking the earth roads and hot sun cracking their surface. Anyway the rain would still come and the underground water would be replenished, and the hospital well in particular, thirty feet deep with six foot of water in the bottom, never ran dry.

CHAPTER 11

More Water

If bread be the staff of life, enabling us to exert the energy to keep our bodies on life's busy treadmill, it must be remembered that the very basic staff of life, fundamental to all existence is water. This simple fluid is so often forgotten, wasted atrociously, adulterated thoughtlessly, treated as of little value, yet feared when, in overwhelming volume, it challenges and effortlessly overcomes our puny strength, flooding our vital resources with its fearful power. It needs to be respected, treasured and stored against the day of water famine. Industry, powerhouses, transport and our homes all require it in ever-greater quantity. For a hospital water is the ultimate essential without which the most brilliant care systems are powerless.

Water in the tropical rain forest regions is a well-known commodity. When vast clouds rise and darken above the tall trees all eyes look skywards hopefully, and their owners make preparations. Electrically charged, the clouds sweep forward in spring and autumn, ushering violent storms with lightning and thunder, depositing their torrents of rain upon forest and bush, and on whole areas of land that have often endured weeks or months of baking sunshine.

Children dance, naked and joyful in the rain and lungs that have inhaled dry and dusty air painfully, now welcome the moist atmosphere with relief. Sometimes damage to buildings may be extensive and repairs will be needed, but a day or two later there will rise among the erstwhile parched grass blades a quick growth of green enfolding charming little crops of crocuses that blaze with colour and radiate beauty where had lain the horrid cracked soil and brown dust of drought.

The wit of a medical man must ensure supplies of that generous water for his hospital's future use, and make adequate provision for its safe storage. Large concrete tanks, three in number, dug deeply and covered with thick concrete roofing, stored some 30,000 gallons of water. A doctor on the staff who had been experienced in plumbing before making use of his abilities in the field of practical medicine had made good use of previous experience. Guttering to the hospital roofs, down pipes and conduits to the tanks and many yards of pipe work brought water to semi-rotary pumps fixed to the walls of the wards. Manual operation by the garden boys pushed the water up via further piping to adequate roof tanks, from which wash basins and sinks of maternity and main theatre for operations were supplied by pipes and taps.

Soft rainwater, excellent for the instrument sterilizer, hand washing, steam boilers and all cleansing procedures in the theatres was now available for daily use. It needed to be carefully used, not wantonly, hands washed in the basin, not under a running tap. The laundry, engine cooling system, baby bathing, adult needs, cook's kitchen and foot baths could now all be supplied by rain water from the buildings' roofs. Tanks also collected water from the roof of the Outpatients' building and Infant Welfare Department as well as from the Nurse's home and Sisters and Doctors' houses. These supplies lasted all spring and summer months (the latter being the wet season) and boosted by tropical storms in autumn could supply water well into the dry season. But the time came when tanked supplies began to fail and it was time to call on the main hospital well for fresh water until the rains began again in spring. This was a good 30-foot deep well, a hundred yards down the sloping compound from the hospital with a constant 6-foot depth of water.

The work of the garden boys now changed from hacking at nearly non existent grass, the ground being very dry, to raising buckets of water from the well, filling 4-gallon kerosene tins and carrying them as head loads up to the hospital. There they were emptied into a 44-gallon tank and the water pumped up manually by semi-rotary pumps into the hospital's roof tanks. The well never ran dry. There was always water. Entertainment was available from the swimming bath next to Sister's house. An excellent job, 20 foot by 10 foot, with shallow and deep ends, it was filled by rainwater from the roof of the Sister's house. Surrounded by flowering bushes it made an ideal form of cool relaxation in the late afternoon, and doctors' wives and children were frequent visitors to its inviting depths, as well as medical and nursing staff when time allowed. In the evening the local frogs would replace the humans and mix their raucous croaking with the incessant chirrup of crickets to make a nightly serenade and soothing lullaby for the Sisters seeking sleep after the work of another busy day.

After bathing sessions the doctors' children would happily spoon an evening meal into their little tummies and retire to roost in their mosquito-proof room or cots, lulled to slumber by a made-up story from Mum or Dad with the soothing noise of the diesel lighting set not far away. If ever the engine failed, which was seldom, it was noteworthy that some child would awake and express its displeasure at the dark and quietness with a resounding yell. Proper engine maintenance was important, for peace and quiet.

The parents often got together in the evening and talked or played games, medical emergencies permitting. There was no radio, and no T.V. of course, but a supply of books - courtesy of the Red Cross (largely Westerns!) and also from the same kind handout some games, the favourite being Monopoly; nice to envisage wealth in view of our meagre salaries. A game would often continue until time for the night round of the hospital, and bed to follow.

Birthday Party for James

Our steward, James had completed work one evening, and as he left for home my wife called, "Please put the nappies on the engine pipes to dry, James." He responded and Monopoly continued, houses and hotels rising and falling, £200 salaries accruing on passing 'Go' and fines following regularly. We became aware after a while of a hot smell and a whiff of smoke and assumed a fire had been lit outside the hospital wall, and played on.

"Time for night round," I said when my wife had scooped up all the hotels. She often won the game! Our colleagues returned over the grass to their home and I went up to check the wards.

Coming back I visited the engine house to reduce the voltage, and found the cause of the hot smell and smoke whiff. James had failed to drape the nappies over the hot water pipes. He had carefully placed them on the exhaust pipe – just ashes met my eyes. Immediately post-war, nappies were almost impossible to obtain alas, a major emergency indeed! We tried Sister's storehouse next morning. She was used to emergencies and failed us not. "Water pipes! Water pipes!! James," we told him.

Worm Palaver

People of light skin, yellowish skin, reddish, brownish, people in fact of all races, are continually seeking the cause of ill health. They urgently want to know and explain to themselves and their offspring the origin of illness. Ancient and modern, non educated and highly educated, all are anxious, often terrified and always eager to find out the 'Why' of suffering and, if they have no precise knowledge, to invent theories of their own... "The gods are angry," they say, "Shopona, god of smallpox, is very angry," and other minor deities of the Nigerian scene are blamed. Small wayside shrines are set up with sacrifices of chickens *et alia* as offerings to appease the gods of this or that, in order to ward off disease and obtain protection from deadly illness.

There is fear: fear of pain, high temperature, vomiting or severe constipation, hernias with strangulation, a well known, frequent and justifiably feared emergency. Worms, intestinal and others are common, and most people are afflicted with them. They are blamed for a host of different troubles, tummy pain, headache, meningitis and malaria. Medicine men, native and foreign prescribe anti-worm medicine, and the patient is often instructed to count the number of wriggly worms produced per rectum!

On a hot afternoon a little brown girl of 8 or 10 years vomits and defecates several times. She complains of tummy pains. Her mother, concerned, calls for the medicine man's help and pays the fee. He comes and looks at her daughter, and pronounces, "A bad worm troubles her." He provides medicine of a leafy origin and this is taken. The child vomits it back. The family are distracted. A neighbour says "The hospital is very near, they will cure the worm, take her there". At 3 p.m. or so nurse sends me a message as instructed by Sister, "There is a new patient Doctor, with abdominal pain and vomiting. There is a swelling in the abdomen." Temperature, pulse and respiratory rate follow.

I join Sister in the Children's Ward and greet the parents. A frightened little girl looks up at me clutching her tummy. Deep brown was her skin and shining black her hair and eyes. Anxious, yet brave, she stood erect before me, staring eyes and writhing hands revealing her fear, and to my gaze on that hot afternoon she seemed to embody all the pain of the great continent of Africa. The nurse on duty in her simple neat uniform took her hand and led her to a bed in the women's ward, while the eyes of other female patients expressed their sympathy. The child's mother, voluble and dramatic, told her story in the Yoruba language, her daughter lying still the while. The nurse interpreted, speaking the English tongue very clearly and accurately for all her 17 years and only two of them having been spent in daily contact with the hospital missionary staff. However the nurse was of the Yoruba tribe and understood the mother well. The latter's speech was quite incomprehensible to me but her gestures were most eloquent.

It appeared that a worm was biting the little girl. It had done so for several days. Its teeth were sharp. The child had vomited several times. She would not eat. Her bowels... etc. etc. Her forehead sweated, her heart pounded, and so on...

Nurse lecturing new mothers

The message came across very well and spelt that horrid word, greatly feared word, intestinal obstruction. I examined the little one gently and briefly. Pulse and temperature were raised as nurse had reported, and a lump was certainly present, nearly as large as her fist. The lump was central, in the middle of her abdomen, easily felt through the thin abdominal wall. I made little of the worm story, and quickly reached a probable diagnosis, - "Intussusception, I think Sister, she will need an operation as soon as possible." Sister gave the necessary orders and went to supervise the theatre preparation. In due course the wee girlie was asleep under the anaesthetic mask. My assistant and I were scrubbed up, masked, gowned and gloved, and the towels were arranged around the operation area. I looked at Sister applying the ether, at Hezekiah, my assistant, enquiring with a glance. Assent was given; all was ready. I lifted the scalpel and cut. Tissues and muscles were drawn aside and the abdominal lining membrane opened, revealing the offending lump.

Oh hello reader, have I lost you? What is an intussusception? Perhaps a word of explanation; sometimes, and more particularly in 6 month babies in this country, it happens that the first part of the large intestine does a bit of vigorous contracting and pulls in a little of itself along with the appendix attached and even some of the small intestine. Further contractions continue to pull the gut in and begin to be painful, until there is quite a mass of obstructed gut, and vomiting and pain spasms are frequent. It can be very nasty. It can indeed be fatal. I mention this elsewhere in my narrative.

However on this occasion I was wrong. The native medicine man was right, - nearly. In a greatly distended coil of small intestine was, not one bad worm, but a veritable 'Tea Party of worms'! All were intertwined happily together, squiggling and wriggling, held in a ball by the contracting muscles of gut wall. I placed several warm moist cloths closely around the mass leaving only a very small half-inch circle of gut wall exposed. A small nick in the gut, and then a pair of tissue forceps gently inserted to pick up a worm, three or four inches long, and extract to deposit the same in a kidney dish held by a nurse. Again, and again, and again until the tally of wrigglers in the dish totalled sixty-three! Suturing of the little hole followed and layers of stitches closed the abdominal wound and completed the job. Dressings and bandages made everything tidy.

Suddenly the Operating Theatre door opened and the Sister from the Infant Welfare Department entered. She spied the dish with its wriggly burden and exclaimed with great delight. "Just what I need" she said, and carried it off in triumph to illustrate to her children's mother's group the reasons why boiling of their drinking water and adequate cooking of food could effectively save their offspring from many of the diseases which they so greatly dread. Our little patient recovered well and in a couple of weeks or so they toddled off to their home hand in hand, after graciously thanking the caring and smiling staff.

Infant Welfare Clinic

What, another Sister? Yes we were fortunate. Sister Edith was a lovely personality with a giggly enchantment of a laugh, well built and full of bounce. No wonder that when Rev. Bill Roberts of the Ibadan Wesley College met her he promptly fell in love with her! In due course they were married at our Otapete Church, and most romantically on Christmas Day!

Naturally Edith popped off to her new home. She was replaced by Margaret Gregory, a Geordie, who took over and cared for the mothers and children with equal love and concern.

CHAPTER 12

Not a Knife—the Other Thing

Well, you've had a bit about the scalpel, rather a needful part of the surgical accoutrement, so now you're entitled to ask where the spanner comes in. Let me illustrate.

After returning to England, afflicted by too many parasites, one day I visited my old headmaster who, learning of my work in Africa said he hoped I would one day come and tell the school something of the fun of being a medical missionary. The invitation had failed to arrive, but here is some of the fun, with a spanner!

The hospital Sisters were concerned that whenever hot water was needed they were perforce obliged to request the cook to boil his big kettle in the hospital kitchen. A story had reached them from the American Seventh Day Adventist Hospital at Ife, a large town 20 miles distant, telling of how the staff there enjoyed a far more modern method of acquiring hot water, and they begged me to drive the senior Sister, Stella Liony to Ife to learn of the new method.

I did so via 20 miles of hot dusty, twisty road, through high bush and tall trees. We were welcomed with true American hospitality, and refreshed with ice-cold fruit juice (how wonderful to have a fridge!) and a generous lunch of gammon and pineapple; a happy time, with hot water demonstration and lots of medical topics for discussion. Back home to use the knowledge thus obtained and to satisfy Sister's demand for heated water. Of course we issued an invitation to their staff to visit us in return, and their doctor gladly agreed to accept.

On the day of his expected visit Africa's sun blazed powerfully, and after the morning's work, we were glad to wait in the shade of our bungalow for Dr. K to arrive for lunch. Time passed. No doctor. The sun blazed. We waited.

At 2.30 p.m. or thereabouts, a figure was seen coming slowly and wearily down the drive to our house carrying a jacket, sun helmet still in place, very dusty, very tired. Meeting him I inquired what had happened. "The car's broken down two or three miles out" he said. "My wife's stayed to look after it". In that heat!

After a little refreshment we set forth in our big Oldsmobile with a good length of stout rope, to find the car and his long-suffering wife. Carefully attaching the rope, and hoping his brakes worked and that he knew the tricks about being towed, I managed to bring them safely back and stopped in front of our garage, which was in the Sister's house, downstairs under her bedroom.

A welcome meal for us all was waiting, and a talk about mechanical failures took the place of medical topics. I inquired about his plugs. "Plugs? What are plugs?" said he.

I barely suppressed a smile, thinking of his tales of nearly 50,000 miles driven by himself in this self same car over many American roads. Plainly his undoubted medical expertise was in no way matched by knowledge of the car's very essential electrical system.

I offered eagerly to demonstrate my superior knowledge of such matters, and unearthed my tool kit to find a plug spanner. In the shade of the opened car bonnet, I removed a plug lead and attached the spanner. It was a long time I thought since that plug saw daylight, but with perseverance and a lot of power it finally left the plughole behind.

The plug was an electrical nightmare. Almost white, worn and distorted, it had finally given up the ability to produce a spark, with points nearly non-existent and a gap like the mouth of a hippopotamus. Our driver was sent to town to acquire a replacement set. He was successful and we left him to install the new plugs and start the engine. It responded joyfully. Our doctor friend was impressed and vowed that he would obtain a motor repair manual when he returned to the States. I tidied my tool kit away. What a wonderful thing is a spanner…

Sometimes a little light relief refreshes the soul in the tropics. It was always a joy to see and hear of the happiness of children playing games beneath the gently waving fronds of the oil palms. As with adults' preoccupation with the ball, - rugby, soccer, tennis, cricket or what-have-you, so kiddies love to enjoy their ball throwing and catching - or missing. Passing their play area on my way to the wards on a hot afternoon I noticed my two little girls playing ball. Catch, catch, miss, catch, miss, missed again - a poor throw that time. In excessive heat tempers began to fray. A yell of rage after another poor throw - Jill, in fury to her sister – "I'll throw your ball right up into the sky!" - Carol's lightning response - "And ask Jesus to hold it for you?"

Of course like pussycats there are two kinds of spanners. Why pussycats? Well, at one time the Sisters' double storey house was afflicted by little beasts of the rodent species, which ladies traditionally abhor. Sister wisely decided to ask for advice from the Public Health Department, and in due course the local health officer arrived and carried out an inspection. What he saw was not recorded but on reporting to Sister his words were quite definite. "Sister Ludlow" said he, "you have mice." "Yes" she replied, "you confirm my suspicions; what can you do about it?" He replied solemnly and with great emphasis, "Well, you must have cats. You will need two cats, an upstairs cat and a downstairs cat." Sister dined out on that story with great joy for years!

So with spanners, they perform day and night. There are day spanners and night spanners...

The day had been busy as usual, with O.P., clinics, ward rounds, Outpatients' theatre work, and an emergency in the main

Operating Theatre where I was able again to practise my newly acquired skill in spinal anaesthesia technique. Further rounds, time to dip into a surgical textbook in preparation for the next day's work, and when time allowed even a dip into the cooling water of our little swimming pool. Being youthful it was fun to practise under-water swimming, to do as many lengths as possible before rising for air. The bath was only 20 ft long.

An evening round with Sister, a bath and a long sleeved shirt to deter mosquitoes, and after a meal some more bookwork. The hospital night round of all the wards followed later, listening to nurses' reports, and giving orders regarding some seriously ill patients. Finally as I passed the engine house on my way back to the bungalow I popped in to check the fuel supply and to reduce the voltage, normally 110 volts, to about 100, hopefully saving fuel, as previously mentioned. I was glad at last to creep under my mosquito net, to be lulled to slumber by the regular thudding of the diesel power unit.

Outside the net hummed mosquitoes eager for my blood, fireflies flitted around the room and in the compound the fine needles of the casuarina tree played high-pitched notes, soothing and peaceful in the reduced breeze of the night. Suddenly the peace was shattered, violently. Ears, both mine, and others were assaulted by the fearful roar of the twin horns of our big hospital car, forty yards away in the garage. Did I mention that that same garage was directly underneath the Sister's bedroom! Out from under the net, into mosquito boots, down the steps donning dressing gown as I ran, across the grass to reach and fling wide open the double doors of the garage. I recoiled momentarily as the noise intensified, battering my senses. Rushing to open the car door I found that the ignition keys were in place and turned off correctly. The noise was appalling; only battery disconnection could stop the din. I hunted for a toolkit, and found it. I undid the bonnet lock. I switched on the garage light and rushed to the front of the car. Covering one ear firmly I raised the bonnet recoiling again as the full blast of furious sound assailed my being. Fumbling frantically among the tools I managed to find the right spanner. I applied it to the big notch securing the battery lead to one terminal. A few turns, a wrench; the lead came free. The noise stopped.

But after the short minute under the car bonnet my head and ears were ringing and dizziness was threatening. I stepped out into the night air and waited until calm returned to my nervous system. Bed called, and I returned to creep once again under my net. Sleep was rather delayed.

Prayers with the nurses were at 7 a.m. I played the little organ. A nurse read a lovely prayer from the Anglican Service Book. Afterwards Sister said, "A noisy night Doctor". "Short circuit Sister", I replied, "perhaps our driver hit a pool in the road yesterday". "Yes doctor, he's inclined to put a spanner in the works sometimes."

Life Differences

At home in dear old civilised (?) England a gentleman who should have known better once asked me, when I was on leave recuperating from the tropics, "These coloured people, (and he used a word which I have banned from this book - Black) when you, um, operate on them, what do they look like inside? Well, what about you dear reader? Do you wonder that too? Oh dear!

Summer is nearly on our doorstep as I write. Soon people in this cloudy land will be throwing off their shirts to catch our elusive sunshine on their pale skins. Many will fly off eagerly to semi-tropical lands, hoping to catch a stronger variety of those magic rays that burn or brown us. Often they endure pain and loss of the very layer of skin with which they hoped to emulate our coloured friends - too bad!

I told my enquirer about melanin. A brown pigment laid down in the superficial layers of the skin cells for the very purpose of protecting the skin from the sun's harmful rays. Some folk have more, some less; some become so very dark brown that for the sake of brevity and in an attitude of laziness and inaccuracy they are dubbed black.

That is dangerous rubbish, especially calculated to polarise people of different colouration. None are black, nor any white. These words should be utterly banned from use in the description of the human races. There are only degrees of darkness and pallor. Colour is confined to the outer layers of the skin, and the internal appearance is identical.

Was he convinced? Well I guess he'll still remove his shirt to acquire, hopefully, a brown tint when he returns his sailing dinghy to the water this summer. How about you?

Yes, Differences Occur

I was busy repairing a hernia in the theatre one morning when the door opened. In the doorway stood, not the next desperate emergency, but the hospital plumber complete in his glad rags and with the tools of his trade in his hands. "Dokita," he said, "I want pipe connections for 1 inch pipe, one angle pipe and one T-junction pipe. You get keys for store?"

"Sister would you kindly delve into my trouser pocket for the store keys and keep the plumber happy, and occupied".

On another occasion the carpenter needed keys for the timber store underneath my bungalow, and invaded the theatre in the midst of a plastering procedure for somebody's fractured leg. "I need 3 inch by 4 inch iroko joist, Dokita," said he.

We kept him happy too... Even the operating theatre was not sacrosanct!

Of course on my first night in Nigeria I met mosquito nets. Soon after the early sunset, darkness rushing on rapidly at about 6 p.m., long trousers and long dresses with mosquito boots up to the knees were essential, with arms to be covered as well of course. At night you must leap into bed quickly and tuck the nets well in, making sure no mossies accompany you to gorge themselves while you sleep. Ensure that you keep your anatomy well away from the net during the night. Mosquitoes can bite through the net's little holes, and they are expert bloodsuckers!

A Different Life? Yes indeed, and malaria carrying mosquitoes are not a joke, they are a deadly curse. Avoid them like the plague!

*_*_*_*_*_*_*_*_*_*_*_*

Want a drink of water? You need a lot in tropical climes. All that heat makes you sweat copiously. But wait a minute, water from where? Rainwater from gutters is collected in tanks. Water from wells may be 30 feet deep or more. Spring water trickles down sloping little hills. All safe you hope? Don't trust any of it!

So cook boils 4-gallon tins of water in a big kerosene can on his wood-burning stove in the cook house. It is left to cool. Then the house steward pours it into a large pottery container having porous candle filters through which the water passes. Germs, even dead ones are unable to pass these. Now you may turn on the filter tap and drink. Add water to your evening tipple only from the filter. A pot of tea should be safe provided that the water is boiled properly and that the teapot is adequately cleaned with boiling water.

A might complicated? Never mind, Life is valuable, make sure you keep it.

*_*_*_*_*_*_*_*_*_*_*_*

Thinking of water, remember it is a very precious commodity. Don't waste it!

Use the minimum quantity in a basin. The same goes for the Operating Theatre. No scrubbing up under a flowing tap. Just add Dettol or some such to your basin of water.

There is plenty of rain in the wet seasons. The furious electrical tropical storms in spring and autumn are very generous, but storage is limited by the size of available tanks, and the dry season is very dry indeed. As water dries out from the planks, mahogany or iroko of which our table is made, even those excellent planks actually curl up a little from side to side. They straighten out again when they absorb moisture in the wet season.

Expensive tables you think; too good for impecunious missionaries? Well at one shilling and sixpence per cubic foot (in those days) they were affordable!

The mid-morning break in Sister's office was always welcome. Popping in one day from the theatre following a hernia with complications and a laparotomy with others, I found a visitor, John Mellanby, our tame and most expert engineer and knitter of scarves, about whom more later. He was sipping tea and munching delightedly at a slice of cream sponge wonderfully concocted by Sister's treasured cook! I could not resist the opportunity and said, "John, our lights are rather poor nowadays. Would you have a look and advise please when you have finished your tea."

And John, ever courteously helpful, went with me to the engine house, wound the big flywheel and started our faithful Lister diesel. "Yes the voltage is certainly down," said John, "perhaps the belts are slipping" and he felt the driving belts to the generator, after stopping the engine with the valve lifter. "I'll tighten them up, anybody got a spanner? And if Kekere would get some rosin please..."

Our mechanic laddie, Kekere, promptly found a garden boy and demanded rosin. The latter simply walked to the big casuarina tree, scraped away for a few minutes and returned with a handful of the sticky substance.

"Now Kekere, just turn the flywheel slowly," said John, and he rubbed the sticky stuff onto the driving surface of the belts.

"Let's try that". And the engine thudded again. The belts no longer slipped; the voltage rose to 110 volts and the lights blazed cheerfully. Another lesson learned.

"That will be O.K. for tonight's emergency" said I.

John joined us for a game of Monopoly instead, and Jack Souster scooped all the hotels.

*_*_*_*_*_*_*_*_*_*_*_*

When collecting building materials for our new hospital (which story awaits the telling) we had purchased a 5-ton diesel lorry. Why a diesel? Well partly for fuel economy. Also because our amateur mechanics who loved looking under the bonnet, and messing about with all the gadgets, did not understand the lack of an ignition system - no sparks, no plugs, no leads. "Ow 'e go Sah?" So they left it alone and the engine benefited. Bully for diesel!

We would run a lorry full of sacks of cocoa for the farmers to the Lagos storehouses, and the money paid for that service covered the return journey, bringing back bags of cement, roofing sheets and timber. This was when preparing for the new hospital, of which more to come.

One morning Disu, the lorry driver, stood at my door, sad faced.

"What's the matter Disu?"

"Lorry engine no go Sah, I go fill tank with diesel but still no go."

We disconnected the fuel pipe to the engine. Only air emerged from it. Alas! The tank had emptied too far before refilling and the pipe had filled with air! Fortunately the lorry possessed a starting handle for the engine (a bit out of date now), so we reconnected the fuel pipe, fitted the handle and turned the engine. And turned, and turned *ad nauseam*. It was hard work against the high pressure in the diesel cylinders pulling and pushing in the hot sunshine - a lengthy job. Eventually a healthy thud from the engine, a vigorous roar and all was well. We were in business, off to Lagos for Disu, and for us - next patient please! With a scalpel of course!

Engineer friends tell me I should have just sucked on the fuel pipe, friends indeed! Fifty-five years too late.

Yes, Life Differed Somewhat!

Let's look at Taiwo. A qualified dispenser, middle aged, a little temperamental, quite an actor in fact, but very able none the less. We kept him remarkably busy with demands for medicines, pills, drops, suppositories and what have you. I provided him with the basic materials from the doctor's store and Taiwo weighed them, mixed them, bottled them in 80oz. Winchester bottles, calculating quantities of drugs, filling Sister's bottles for the wards and for our monthly dispensary trips up-country, counting pills and supplying all the Outpatients' requirements as they presented their prescriptions. Phew! A busy boy!

One day he emerged from his sanctum, the dispensary, holding his head and in utter despair. "Alas" said he "the doctor will be angry, but I cannot do it. Oh, my head, my head!"

I took him by the arm, and we had a good toddle around the compound, breathing deeply the warm air, admiring the floral arrangements, the plumbago hedge, the hibiscus flowers, and the bougainvillaea. At last he recovered and felt relaxed.

"I feared the doctor's anger," he said, "but his anger soon passes and then all is sweetness and light." Dear old Taiwo!

Transport was often a problem. A huge country but with a road system developing well and penetrating to the small towns and villages both east and west of the great river Niger. A Public Works Department, that, well organised, did a good job within financial limits in making the roads passable despite massive rainstorms and trees, struck by lightning or by wind, falling and blocking roads.

At Ifaki, where lived our missionary friend Jonah, was the dispensary visited monthly by one of us doctors. On one visit I found Jonah in the process of buying an old used car from one of the chiefs who lived in the village of Ijero, some 15 miles on the road towards Ikole. I had finished my dispensary clinic in good time. "I'm going to fetch this car," said Jonah, "want to come?"

So we piled into his ageing jalopy and set forth. The chief was a pleasant old chap and the business quite straightforward. The car had petrol, the engine started and ran satisfactorily, and battery appeared reasonable. But while the brakes operated well there were no inner tubes in the tyres.

"Stuff tyres with banana leaves," said Jonah, who had faced many transport emergencies during his years of service at Ifaki. So the order was given and huge quantities of such leaves and other small green stuff were stuffed as tightly as possible into the five tyres until we could stuff no more. Wheels were replaced and Jonah decided to tow the vehicle. Towrope was attached. Jonah drove and I followed in his 'new' car, steering and braking with care. Halfway home the towing car's engine stopped and refused to start again. Drama! Would the engine and banana tyres of Jonah's new purchase accept the burden of a tow? We changed the towrope and tried it. Glory be! We were again in business and reached Ifaki in triumph. I left Jonah to his new toy and returned to Ilesha, once again apologising to the Sisters for my late arrival. Alas, it was getting to be a habit. The next day Jonah arrived to search for five inner tubes for his new chariot, and I typed a letter to the Missionary Society regarding the need for reliable transport for their missionaries if their health was to be preserved. After all there was no bullock cart as in India to convey the enfeebled European, and no coolies to perform backpacking services for them!

Life Was Different.

CHAPTER 13

Battle

Discipline. Only with which can the good schemes of mice and men best be laid. Without which chaos and disorder are rampant, and unbridled folly leads to destruction and loss of life's treasures. With which the smooth running of an army or industrial concern, of an enterprise brought to success, of a household or a hospital, brings triumph over difficulty and victory to replace defeat.

My father-in-law was a Lt. Colonel seeing action in the North West frontier of India. Efficient in action, he later became, after retirement, a useful spokesman for the League of Nations and still later in his retirement took to the practice of gardening. Long practised in discipline, tidy in mind and body, careful in speech, dress and habit, he caused his garden to reflect its owner's habits in its neat serried rows of vegetables, carefully tended lawn and tidy tool shed.

Such qualities he passed to his eldest daughter, Barbara, a highly qualified nurse and my treasured wife. Her inherited tendencies she took to the hospital compound where I worked, and there established a vegetable garden. Neat and tidy were the rows of carrots and cauliflowers, with a charming plantation of pineapples showing fruit standing up nobly like the men of her father's regiment, and reflecting a sure and certain discipline.

But for aeons there had existed another discipline in the humid heat of Africa. On one occasion we had inspected our growing crops and spotted, running through the pineapples, a well ordered river of black ants. An unending trail swiftly proceeded in disciplined manner from an unknown source to an unknown destination. We gazed admiringly, and instinctively stepped over the one-inch wide river, leaving them severely alone. Non-interference with such an orderly army was certainly the safest policy. They well might have carried a banner, "We march, disturb us not." We obeyed, and went our ways to home or hospital.

Our house was a building of pitch pine and board construction raised on steel stanchions to defeat any invasion of destructive white ants that kindly refrained from climbing up ironwork. They didn't like our iroko furniture either, highly inedible to them, but gained access to my tool room and, alas, made short work of the wooden handles of my precious planes, chisels, saws and so forth. Death to white ants!

A central sitting room, open at each end for good ventilation, a visitors' bedroom and small kitchen to one side, the master bedroom on the other side with children's room and bathroom leading off it at the corners. Behind the room was an 8-foot veranda and steps leading down to a toilet, a small construction housing a useful seat above a 30-foot borehole; most useful, no attention needed, no smell and never filled up! At the other end of the house was my office, the front steps of the house beside it and behind it the small pantry with steps to the kitchen across the side road, whence came regular supplies of our cook's good food. The 8-foot veranda all around the house could be enclosed by shutters raised horizontally by sticks to provide shade and ventilation.

A narrow road, laterite surfaced, ran round the house to west and south sides, and a flight of steps from it up to our front southern veranda completed the housing arrangements.

Inside was good order and reasonable tidiness, inspired admirably by my wife, when the wiles and energies of three small children made it possible. A large houseplant gave a perch for our pet chameleon that clung tightly to it, rolling his eyes in opposite directions, most uncanny, and keeping very sedate and still. Flies and other insects he disposed of most expeditiously, with no fuss, no noise and no visible movement. They just suddenly disappeared, attached to his sticky tongue, a very long one, normally curled up in his mouth, until like a lightning flash it whipped out, collected its prey and retreated into his mouth. Prey gone, but all too fast for the eye to follow! Wonderful! Our house servants called him a devil, as he never seemed to eat.

Across the road south of the house was a spacious lawn bordered by another delightful hedge of plumbago with its tiny blue and white flowers and the humming bird hawk moths hovering above them. At the far side of the lawn a large jacaranda tree poured its lovely flowers upon the grass creating a carpet of blue, charming to the eye. East of the lawn a spacious wire enclosure provided a run for our dozen hens and therein stood the 12-foot hen house having a nesting box for each of the twelve hens! But they liked to be matey, not disciplined, and only used two or three. They taught us lots of tricks! A dear little duiker antelope 20 inches high lived with the hens, having been reared from babyhood by my wife using a pipette and a tin of Klim milk. A second baby was similarly reared and was kindly adopted and cared for by the older creature.

No dog disturbed the household peace, nor any cat. Lizards scrambled about the veranda, orange and dark blue in colour and up to ten inches in length, often fighting each other for the best place by bashing their foe with their tails, as I have described elsewhere. Little geckos with their clinging feet climbed the walls and ran along the ceilings, underneath of course, fascinating to watch. Also kept by my wife, Barbara, were a couple of hens, each with a family of small chicks, each family in a cardboard box, one in the tool shed, one under the house. And that completes the menagerie. The disciplinary arrangements were of course not my concern.

It was time for bed after a busy day. Having done my hospital night round and visited the engine house to reduce the voltage I returned home, and in due course we slipped under our mosquito net. The children were asleep, lulled by the steady diesel engine's quiet explosions, and all was still.

Not quite still however, for the chirrupy sounds of the innumerable crickets and the accompanying croaking of frogs were always present, and made a pleasant sedative music as we slept.

But there was another noise. Suddenly came a distant "cheep, cheep," and lots of frantic "cheeps" and "clucks'" to follow. Our Emergency Ward 10 sprang into action. Donning mosquito boots and light dressing gowns we hurried to the tool shed whence came the sounds of alarm and joined the fray, for an affray there certainly was. The ants had found the chicks in the shed and had launched an attack; the chicks cheeping desperately, the hens clucking distractedly, the ants silent and disciplined, attacking and biting. Rapidly we gathered up the hen and her chicks and retreated up the stairs to the pantry, stamping on ants and brushing off any on our garments. With pairs of dissecting forceps or Spencer Wells artery forceps we picked off numerous ants, squashing them on their way to the waste bin. One chick we painted with kerosene, sadly it was fatal to both ant and chick. Forceps did the trick and at last peace was restored and mother hen and her chicks were safely housed in a box in the pantry.

A cold drink of orange juice, at room temperature for we had no fridge, perhaps a biscuit, and we returned back to bed under the net to relapse into the arms of Morpheus...

But it was not to be. Hardly had our eyes closed when more cheeps commenced, urgent, frantic. Again it was up and into boots and gowns, and with torches back to the theatre of operations, not in the hospital but under our house this time where the other family had been attacked by the black raiders. Again we stamped on ants, collected the chicks and their mum, fled back up the steps to the pantry and began de-ticking with the useful forceps. Not so long this time, practice made for speed. Box on floor, in pantry, chicks under mum's wings. Peace reigned.

Did it? It was difficult to detach our minds from thoughts of the fierce little black raiders, as we wearily moved back to our room. We popped into the bathroom for a wash. "Look, John, there are a few ants coming up inside the wall."

"So there are. Let's have a look at the kids' room."

Inspection showed ants climbing up the outside wall of their bedroom. They were not the same Safari ants of Africa, but nasty little half-inch fellows, very vigorous and very vicious if they were in the mood. Were we the target for tonight? The unknown destination of that disciplined army?

This looked serious, chicks were one thing, children quite another. With a torch we looked over the balcony onto the ground below. Consternation! To our horror we saw, not an inch wide trail of ants in steady marching order, but a vast seething mass of black ants over two feet wide and the whole length of the bungalow, round the bathroom corner, on the ground outside our bedroom, past the steps towards the children's room. There was no discipline here, just a furious mob looking for an entrance whereby to attack us. A fearful sight!

Our job was saving life, but now we had no option. We declared War!

Shouting for the gate watchman to come and help, I pulled on trousers, tucking them into my mosquito boots and prepared for battle, collecting the 3ft sticks used for propping up the shutters, and wrapping a length of cloth around the end of each one. My wife carried on in similar fashion, dipping the cloth-covered ends in a tin of kerosene before handing them to me and the watchman, one by one. The discipline had now changed hands to those of the defenders. The watchman and I lit our torches from a candle and descended the steps, calculated murder in our hearts. Methodically sweeping our blazing torches to and fro across the mob of ants we slowly advanced incinerating thousands of the murderous horde. When the torches went out Barbara supplied more, and with care and diligence we moved along, sweeping our fires to and fro and making as sure as we could by torchlight that our enemies were destroyed. It must have been an hour by the time we felt that victory was ours. Ants that we did not reach departed, whither we knew not, nor cared. The charred corpses could await a brush up by the garden boys in the daylight. I thanked the watchman, who with bare feet and legs had done an excellent job. Hope he didn't suffer too many bites; I expect his skin was tougher than mine!

It took a while before we could retreat from battle to bed, defying the mosquitoes instead of the ants as we climbed under the net. But there was quiet with the engine throbbing, children sleeping, crickets and frogs serenading, the fireflies and mossies dancing around our net, and finally sleep came to lull the excitement and heal the anxiety. Dreams of nasty little black assassins rather disturbed our slumber, and when dawn came we welcomed the glorious light of the returning day with relief and happiness. The disciplines of domesticity and hospital operating theatre now took precedence and occupied fully our hands and our minds, but memories of the night and of the horrid threats of the attacking fiends were not easily dispelled.

It is a Bad Worm

Such would be the opinion of a 'native doctor' when confronted with an ill patient, and in view of the circumstances at the time this opinion would command respect, unless a better diagnosis were available. Intestinal worms were commonplace and found so often in human faeces that the worm was accepted as a normal inhabitant of the human system. So if any abdominal complaint occurred, "it was a worm"' Some worms might be vomited; some might even be produced when coughing (small ones), so this made quite good sense. They could sometimes be found wriggling under the skin, or in the eyes behind the transparent membrane covering the white of the eye. Worms were therefore reckoned to be the cause of much trouble, and in fact so they were, and the native doctor was often right. But not always. The headache of malaria, the violent spasms of tetanus convulsions, the huge abscesses of thigh and leg, the deep pain of osteomyelitis with the resulting dead bone and the outpouring of pus; when these and great numbers of germ originated infections were simply treated with 'native medicines' the results were often fatal. If 'The Coast' as it used to be called, was dubbed the White Man's grave, very much more was it the grave of our dark-skinned brothers and sisters, and that is a point that needs often to be mentioned.

Thankfully, through the introduction by missionary societies and government agencies of modern medical, and surgical techniques, with up-to-date maternity and childcare, great improvements have been made in the lives of our African neighbours. A story or two would illustrate: -

You've heard about the one concerning the non-intussusception where the native doctor was right and I was wrong, so let me get my own back with

1. The man who lost thirteen feet.
2. I got one of 'em back again.

He Lost Thirteen Feet

"Dad," said my youngest, peeping over my shoulder at the title of my story, "people only have two feet, so how could the man lose thirteen?" "Caterpillars have six," said my budding entomologist, two years older, "and six claspers too"- wisdom indeed! "That's because they're going to turn into insects," said Boyo, "how about centipedes with a hundred, or inky-winky spiders?" he added looking at a certain small girlie who at once shook with horror and threatened hysterics. She hated the very mention of the arachnoid's species.

"I can beat you all" from my teenager, "how many legs has a millipede?" But Boyo liked the final word "A boa-constrictor has none," said he.

"Be patient," I said, "and you will find out."

Jacob was a Yoruba farmer, tall, agile and hardworking at raising crops of yam, cassava, maize, plantain, tomato and peppers. He had some persistent tummy discomfort following a most painful episode several years ago when a chronic bout of what is called indigestion over here suddenly turned into a violent abdominal pain. This kept him confined in his mud-walled house on a floor bed, attended by the native doctor of his village in the African bush. This was likely to be due to perforation of a peptic ulcer with subsequent peritonitis. He was very ill indeed.

He suffered grievously and was lucky to survive, recovering at last but unable to work at his farm for many months. His wife and neighbours took over his labours and, helped by the sunshine and plenty of showers of rain, brought his crops to fruition. Eventually Jacob, with the aid of two sticks got his strength back, was able to eat carefully, and could after months of poor health, return to his farm, needing help however with the heavier work of digging and soil care.

There came a time when new ground was needed, for the old soil was no longer productive and there was no means of fertilising it back into production, nor knowledge of such an art. So a new section of ground was marked out, big trees cut down by men well versed in such labour, bushes and branches chopped, bundles of wood carried home for future use, all the family helping with loads of wood on their heads. Roots were dug up, many piled into bonfires and burnt, and ground dug and made ready for planting.

Jacob did not find this exercise, such as he could manage, at all easy, and often suffered pains in his tummy and also vomiting. Colic was frequent and intense. One day he could move about only with difficulty, and it increased the pain. The medicine man attended him and prepared concoctions of leaves for him to drink, but he vomited them back. He passed a dreadful night and following day. Relatives and friends came offering advice and potions, to no avail. All said that it must be a very bad worm.

The village teacher had wide experience. "Take him to the Mission Hospital" he said, "perhaps they can help him." Jacob himself was past making decisions and as usual it was granny, backed up by her friends, who decided. Arrangements made, a space on a lorry was found and at last Jacob was lifted onto its back and made as comfortable as possible. Relatives accompanied him. Payment was made.

He endured a very rough journey along the bush roads, over ruts and potholes, to reach at last the gates of the hospital to the relief of all concerned. Two ward-boys (hospital porters) lifted the patient onto a wheeled stretcher and brought him to the Male Ward. There a bed was rapidly made ready. Sister noticed the small procession passing her office door, and shortly received the message from the Male Ward nurse-in-charge, with details of complaint, temperature, pulse and respiration rates recorded. She took a quick look at Jacob and sent me a message.

Knock, knock on my veranda door post. "Please Doctor, there is a new patient," and junior nurse handed to me Sister's note.

"Thank you nurse, please tell Sister I'm coming" and she returned quickly to Sister's office.

I found Sister at the patient's bedside, and examined him noting the pain in his face, and the fast pulse, and listened to the relatives' story, translated by an efficient young nurse. There was a central, round, painful abdominal lump, movable, as big as a large grapefruit and painful to light pressure, not a hard lump but firm.

I considered, assessing the patient's condition, and ordered morphia by injection and a glucose saline preparation for me to administer intravenously.

"I think we must certainly look-see Sister, though his condition is obviously poor," I said. "Yes Doctor, I have ordered the big stoves to be lit for the sterilizer and nurse is preparing the instruments for a laparotomy."

All was in competent hands. Sister checked nurse's instrument selection; they were immersed in the already hot water and the big primus stoves roared beneath the old sterilizer. The theatre would be properly prepared, and I turned to the patient to place his arm on a padded splint and bandage it in place. Using a little local anaesthetic I cut down onto a vein in the arm, inserted a glass cannula, tied it in place and turned on the sustaining fluid from Allen and Hanbury's intravenous bottle.

Sister had sent a ward boy on a bicycle with a message to my assistant, Hezekiah, who lived in the town, requesting his presence at an emergency operation in an hour's time.

I repaired to my house and opened a textbook of operative surgery, and noted the time, about 11 p.m. My wife prepared a cup of tea and wished me good success, with a little prayer for the patient, and for the surgeon's hands. An hour passed. Nurse knocked on the door post, "Sister says the patient and theatre are ready, Doctor."

I found the patient already in the theatre and Sister who had called her senior off-duty colleague to look after the hospital, had started the anaesthetic, gas, oxygen and ethyl chloride and ether. Hezekiah was scrubbing up and I joined him and explained the situation. The nursing staff had prepared the abdominal skin, painting it with Bonney's Blue, and had covered the same with sterile towels. We adjusted our shadow-less lamp to give optimum lighting (story of that to follow later) and now wearing gowns and gloves we placed towels and sheets in position to expose only the offending area, repainting the skin with the above preparation. The paint was an excellent germ killer and wound infections were rare.

I looked at Sister. She nodded, as also did Hezekiah. Two theatre nurses had been called to prepare the instrument trolleys and table; bowls of warm saline were to hand as was a numbered quantity of gauze packs each with a string attached, and all was ready.

I raised the scalpel and made a suitable incision; Spencer Wells forceps to bleeding points, to be tied off later. I opened the abdomen and inspected the offending lump. It consisted of a quantity of small intestine, its coils matted together by an inflammatory process that must have been of long duration. A careful and very gentle feel all around to identify the parts of the gut entering and leaving this maze of intestines all adherent together. To endeavour to separate the coils would need handling and dissection that would cause fearful surgical shock and the non-survival of the patient. Removal of the whole lump of gut was the sole option, with end-to-end anastomosis of the entering and exiting gut to follow, so, "Clamps please Hezekiah."

Two clamps were therefore applied to both entering and exiting coils; packs with forceps attached to their strings were placed strategically to absorb any spillage of gut contents. Two cuts between the clamps. Dissect and cut the whole mass from the mesentery with forceps to severed arteries and veins and tie them off with care. Using fine catgut suture the two ends together.

I took a look around the interior of the abdomen. Finding nothing else amiss the abdomen was closed with the usual layers of stitchery and clips, bandages completing the job.

"How is he Sister?" I enquired.

"Alright, I think" she replied cautiously, "pulse rather fast of course, but no other adverse signs so far." I looked at the saline bottle and mentioned that it was running low. "Yes, I've another bottle handy" she said. Sister didn't miss a thing.

In due course Jacob was transferred to a stretcher, and cosied up with blankets (it would be cool at night and post-operative care and warmth were essential). He was taken back to bed, closely watched by the relatives waiting outside the Theatre. I told them that we had dealt with his trouble as was needed, and that while he was not out of danger there was good reason to hope.

A nurse was stationed beside Jacob to remain until he regained consciousness; after that a further dose of morphia to be injected. I returned to the Theatre now being cleared up, and asked Sister for a tape measure. "Whatever for?" she said. Then, looking at our hands where Hezekiah and self were separating out intestinal coils in the sink, "Oh I see", she added with a smile. Our specimen was rather obstinate and a good twenty minutes elapsed 'ere the full length of troublesome gut was disentangled. The tape measure did good service, and we were able to announce that in future the patient would have to manage his yam, cassava, tomato, maize and occasional mouthful of goat's meat or antelope, minus thirteen feet of his digestive tract!

On that we said "Goodnight"- Hezekiah cycling home by torchlight. I looked in at Jacob's bedside, and then walked down under the palm trees to my house. Sister checked that all was cleared, gave last instructions and gladly breathed the night air as she too went to a well-deserved rest.

Jacob survived the night well, his condition settling nicely, and was glad to be pain free. His relatives were of course delighted. Normal post-operative care now took place. Gradually he could begin to take fluids, then gradually soup and further nourishment. All went well and he was eventually able to resume his normal diet and function well. Several weeks passed, Jacob getting up and toddling round the ward and verandas, and he was able to be discharged. He walked to town to catch a lorry back to his home village. Off he went on two feet, but left thirteen feet behind!

Good luck and God bless Jacob.

I Got One of 'em Back Again!

Infections common to European countries were not necessarily found in Africa, and of course vice versa. Thus while bronchitis, pneumonia and other germ-orientated infections were common to both there were some diseases peculiar only to one. My years in the poor quarters of Edinburgh provided experience in recognition of the dreadful diphtheria of old days, now thankfully eradicated, one hopes, from our land, thanks to Polio, Diphtheria and Tetanus immunisation during many years past.

In Yoruba land no diphtheria occurred to my knowledge, but at one time there happened to be three cases of a similar type that were brought to our hospital. Each appeared to be an infection of the larynx causing swelling of the vocal chords sufficient to cause breathing difficulty with severe stridor, the patient being in imminent danger of respiratory restriction that could be fatal. Two of the patients were children, one of about two years of age, the other aged four. The third patient was a young woman in her eighth month of pregnancy. All occurred within 48 hours.

Urgent action was imperative, and in each case I performed a tracheotomy (the insertion of a tube into the trachea through which the patient could breathe). Sadly the smaller child, though able now to breathe, could not cope with the infective agent, a germ unspecified, and died a few hours later. The older child and the woman could breathe satisfactorily and survived.

The operation was simple, quick and effective. A local anaesthetic into the skin just below the larynx allowed a quick vertical cut in that area down to the trachea; forceps on cut blood vessels; an incision through the front wall of the trachea below the larynx and a tube, slightly angled and suitably sized for the particular patient, was quickly inserted, the tube being provided with two lugs attached. To these strings were fixed, passed round the back of the neck and tied, so keeping the tube in place. Air was now rushing steadily in and out as the patient breathed. The awful stridor and gasping stopped. The forceps on the small vessels were tied off with 'cat-gut' and a stitch or two of silkworm thread completed the procedure. The pregnant woman was taken to a side ward. A nurse sat beside her with the job of keeping clear the indwelling tube by passing in and out of it, between breaths, a small pledget of gauze held by forceps. Any amounts of phlegm or mucus that might threaten the airway were thus removed. A second year nurse, suitably instructed, coped with this procedure effectively.

The four year old was finding that she could breathe with no difficulty and was placed in her mother's arms to be carried up to the Children's Ward, settled in a cot with mother and nurse in attendance. Here a senior nurse was rather necessary, for the child's confidence needed restoring and the tube kept clear by a nurse of obvious experience. So for hour after hour the tube was so cleansed by the little gauze pledgets confidently applied. The child and woman patient too managed to swallow a dose of M& B. 693, our sole antibacterial agent. They both relaxed, and slept, exhausted.

Looking into the wards later when the lights had come on I found all well, the nursing staff coping nicely. "Time for you to have a break, Sister" - "Yes. I'll have a cuppa when the night staff come on duty" she replied. She would have time for an evening meal and possibly an hour or two of sleep, but I had forgotten the fact that senior nurses were too few to spare a second one for the care of the little kiddie overnight.

When going up to the hospital for my night round, past the faint whisper of the casuarina tree in the night breeze, past the regular thudding and hum of the engine providing light for hospital, homes, and paths bordered by the shadowy palm trees, I mounted the steps to the Children's Ward. On one side of the child's cot sat its mother, soon to relax on the floor in slumber. On the other side sat Sister, forceps and pledgets of gauze in hand, bending in faithful attendance over the little one, gently cleaning the tube, no other nurse being available.

And then, hour after long night hour she remained bending over her little charge, cleaning, clearing, straightening up; then a fresh pledget to her forceps and bending to the delicate task again. Perhaps occasionally the nurse from Maternity could be spared for a short while to give her a break. I never knew, but what I did know was that at morning light she would be at the hospital gate bartering with the local market women to get the best price for meat and vegetables for the day's supply for our patients, Cook assisting with the trade and transactions. Thereafter she would attend 7 a.m. morning prayers with the staff.

A Third World Hospital? You Tell Me!

But that was not quite the end of the saga where we did battle with the supposed bad worm. Our tracheotomies were progressing favourably and relatives were smiling happily, perhaps wondering a little about the future of the tube business, but evidently accepting our nurses' reassurance. Doses of the M & B. were being swallowed and retained; temperatures were improving, and pulse rates dropping to normal.

I felt that my wife and I could safely accept an invitation from the District Officer to have dinner with him. The European compound was a mile or more the other side of Ilesha town, and thither we went leaving our very competent Sister in charge.

The D.O. was a very pleasant chap hardworking in his task of keeping the local chiefs in order, sorting out squabbles and attending to all manner of palavers. The *Pax Romana* of our dear country was a most valuable part of the then Nigerian economic and political climate. We got on well together and his wife found it good to have another European woman with whom to talk. In the middle of a very nice meal the D.O.'s steward went to the outside door. He returned with an envelope, handing it to his master saying "A ward boy from the hospital done bring this Sah". The D.O. looked at it and passed it to me; "It's for you Doctor," he said.

I opened the missive and read Sister's short note. She wrote, "The pregnant tracheotomy has gone into labour. It is her third." My pulse quickened. I rose from the table and "I fear that I must depart" I said, "an emergency threatens". My wife rose also, "I'll come too" she said.

Hurried excuses and apologies, met with understanding, into the car and speeding out of the compound, back to the Ilesha road, engine roaring, lights blazing, slowing for the town and marketplace where trading continued by bush lamp, palm oil lamp, and Tilley light, into Otapete Street and past the Methodist Church, speeding up again, streaking through the hospital gate, whizzing round the Outpatients' Department to a halt, brakes screeching and tyres skidding, outside Sister's office. A quick dash to Maternity, and behold dear efficient Sister Elsie at the door of the ward, a lovely big relaxed smile all over her face, and cuddling a small bundle in her arms.

"She did well Doctor, no panic. She pushed the tube out at one end and the baby at the other. With a piece of string and a pair of forceps I got one of 'em back again."

Well, well, Sister Elsie of the unequalled humour, lovely Irish wit and presence of mind to boot was Nelson Ludlow's own sister. Arriving in 1929 she spent 31 years on the staff and became Matron of the new hospital, exerting a sound Christian influence on nurses and patients alike. Stella Liony and Elsie built up a wonderful record of care and competence in the service of our Lord. No wonder that patients went home cured, healed, and happy.

CHAPTER 14

Pale People Came Too

While visiting Australia in later years I had the chance of a trip along the dry hot road to the Kalgoorlie gold fields. A very large and interesting project indeed with a little train to carry us round the extensive area where the precious metal was extracted from the soil. Huge mounds of earth reminded us of the vast heaps of soil and rubble of our own coalmines. We gathered that a small percentage of gold dust still lay, unclaimed within these mounds, but panning for the same was not for the general public.

In the soil of Africa, also, gold is a much-prized commodity, and a few prospectors worked at the extraction thereof in Nigeria. The gold was obtained by 'place mining', 'hydraulic' giant method or 'dredge mining' all essentially being methods of washing away the lighter soil and rock, leaving the heavier gold behind.

Engines and pumps are needed to bring water or extract it from deep mine levels, and much employment is created to remove rubble and service the machines. I came across a couple of gold mining folk who needed medical help and came to our hospital.

A large Lebanese gentleman came one day complaining of abdominal pain; leaving his gold mining business in the care of an overseer. The examination table creaked under his weight, and I realised that whatever was wrong with his tummy his considerable obesity would prove a problem. The usual questions were asked and temperature, pulse and respiration taken. I did a gentle examination. There really was no doubt, his appendix was inflamed. Appendicitis was uncommon among African patients, probably we thought on account of their mainly vegetable type diet, but this chappie surely had more varied and expensive tastes.

He managed to walk the short distance to the Male Ward, bearing his record card marked 'T.C.I. for op.'. Sister took charge and soon the theatre was being prepared, and pre-operative care of abdominal skin was in progress. Pre-operative injection of morphia and atropine was given.

In due course came the message, "Theatre ready, Doctor" and I joined my assistant and theatre nurse to 'scrub up'. Not under running water, of course, just a basin-full with soap and Dettol, then gown, hat and gloves to follow. The patient occupied the operating table over-spilling the same at both sides. Sister had a lint-covered mask over his nose and mouth, squirting ethyl chloride plentifully onto it to 'put under' a man of such generous proportions, followed by ether anaesthetic. The big four burner kerosene primus stoves roared under the sterilizer 6 or 7 feet behind the patient's head. Nobody even thought of explosions. The windows were very adequate, gauze wired to keep out the insects and a current of air drifted gently through the Theatre. It took the ether fumes away from the flaming stoves!

I took the scalpel. "Alright, Sister?" She nodded. His skin was more amenable to the knife than the tough sunburned integument that covered many of his local labourers, and a large incision was needed on account of his generous layer of fatty tissue. Eventually I reached muscle layers and pushed them aside, resisting their vigorous contractions as their owner persisted in breathing deeply the ether-laden air. Open the peritoneal lining of the abdomen, extend the cut, resist the slippery efforts of intestinal tubing to escape into the outer air, and delve into the interior with two fingers.

"Spread the retractors please Hezekiah" I said, needing more space. He did, and again the slippery gut tried to escape defying my efforts to prevent its emergence. Between us we succeeded and it was possible to locate the swollen, inflamed appendix, rather like a nugget of gold at the bottom of a deep mine! Clamps applied, a cut between them and out came our prized appendix to be popped into a specimen bottle for posterity. A 'purse string suture' was stitched into the gut wall around the appendix stump; the stump pushed inwards, the purse string pulled tight. It only remained to close the wound against the vigorous resistance of wily coils of gut pushing against my restraining hand by muscles contracting vigorously under the old-fashioned 'open ether' anaesthesia.

Triumph at last with the final stitch in place and bandaging to make assurance doubly sure! Our patient recovered well, glad to be free of a nasty emergency, and amused to have his specimen in a bottle. He left us clutching his little bottle, and in grateful appreciation leaving in our care a little gold nugget!

Also in the gold mining industry was a bluff and cheerful Yorkshire man from Hull. John, a short, strong chap, lived a couple of miles away with his African wife and was a valued friend of the hospital staff. He was well versed in the complexities of the diesel engine, operating his mining business with the aid of modern devices, and should our diesel-powered machine give trouble he would willingly spring to our aid and restore our essential lighting facility.

In Outpatients one morning I was busily attending to one of our customers when there came a good Yorkshire voice at the open door behind me, "Marnin', Doctor." I turned my head, "Hello John," I said, "busy just now, I'll be with you shortly." "Aye Doc, ah'll wait." Outpatients was nearly finished and John waited patiently until I could attend to him.

"Well John, what can I do for you? Are you off colour?"

"Nay Doc, ah'm alright. It's me dog. He's got the rabies."

"Oh, has he bitten you?" I enquired. The reply was in the negative, but to the further question whether the dog had licked any skin scratches or abrasions, he was non-committal. I wrote a card for John, 'For anti-rabies vaccine', telling him to see Sister, but then remembering the dog, asked what he had done with the beast. "Oh, I shot him, of course; he's in the kit-car."

The car, a 10cwt. load carrier, was 20 yards away in the hospital compound. I explained to John that I had a couple of minor procedures to deal with, and would soon join him to operate on the dog's brain, requesting my clerk to arrange for some instruments and a specimen jar.

The details of the surgical job on the poor dog are of no special importance, but in due course its brain was deposited in a bottle of alcohol which we could ill spare in war time days.

"Now John, can you take that to the laboratory of the hospital in Lagos and give them this letter." "Aye, Doc, ah'll do that," he said and off he went, on a journey of 185 miles in hot sunshine. The hospital was busy and I forgot about the episode.

About a week later I received a letter, couched in not very polite terms, telling of my serious error in sending this specimen in alcohol, and instructing me to use formaldehyde for future specimens of such nature.

Oh dear! Well one can't win 'em all, and preparation of pathological specimens was not my speciality, and anyway I had plenty to do in the hospital!

Another week passed and on a Friday morning there was John at my back door again.

"Marnin' Doc," said John.

"Hello," I said, "more trouble?"

"Aye Doc, t'other dog's got the rabies, so I shot him too." I did not doubt his diagnosis, and after seeing a few more patients gave my attention to John's problem, and mine! A thought occurred to me; why not let the experts do the job?

"Look John, take the dog away, cut off the head, wrap it very securely, and get it down to the laboratory, and John, use a pair of rubber gloves."

"Aye Doc, ah'll do that." I wrote a letter for him to hand in to the laboratory in Lagos, another long and very hot journey. John carried out the instructions, but it must have taken him some time. Were there polythene bags in the early 40's? A hot journey, and the laboratory was closed on his arrival in Lagos. Not knowing what to do, he left the parcel outside the door, the letter with it. The day was Friday. The door would open on Monday after a very warm weekend…

A week later I received from the laboratory another letter. It was most unpleasant! Oh dear! Oh dear!!

But our hospital was busy with the troubles of humans and I felt sure that the lab. expert had a good incinerator!

*_*_*_*_*_*_*_*_*_*_*_*

"Committee members are arriving Doctor," said Sister, looking through her office window. Alas! The idea of a committee meeting, with members fractious in the torrid heat of mid-day, tearing each others' ideas and propositions to shreds, voices arguing, rising in heated conflict, as often happened in the hot humidity of Africa, did not appeal. I groaned.

"Its alright Doctor, it's the Hospital Liaison Committee."

That was better. A small company of a dozen or so folk from Ilesha town, Yoruba business men, chiefs, managers of small companies, church folk, Salvation Army and a distinguished Muslim Hadji, invited by myself to form a committee for the purpose of advising on hospital policies, and also explaining to the local townsfolk and surrounding villages the plans and ideas that we were developing to help the health of the community. A peaceful, helpful, progressive committee, arranged at first to organise a Hospital Week to raise funds for the work. This they did and were also very useful in the liaison business. We doctors enjoyed sessions with them.

Hospital Liaison Committee

Sister and I were thinking of the patient now leaving the Operating Theatre. It would shortly be my task to write to the committee who had appointed her, an English missionary lady of some 60 odd summers, to the work of a mission church in Ilesha. It was her first time in Africa, first time indeed out of England, and she had found it difficult to face the climate and conditions. She had no appetite for food and would only consume fruit of one sort or another. The appointing committee could not have known this, but no doubt were aware of the difficulties that an elderly lady could face. To my own mind, and with hindsight, tropical Africa was not for her.

Early that morning I had received a message from the aforesaid mission station's pastor, Pastor Elton of the Apostolic Mission requesting medical help. One of the staff had become ill with severe abdominal pain and please would I come. Morning prayers with the nursing staff were over, my breakfast was inside me, instructions to carpenter, garden boys and mechanic could wait, and the big hospital car quickly conveyed me the two miles to the patient's bedside. Pain was evident. The story of recent arrival in Nigeria, the trying climate, the lack of appetite and persistent munching of fruit of all kinds were soon told, spasms of pain interrupting.

I knelt to examine her; sixtyish, white hair, slim of build and with a 3 or 4-inch long sausage-like lump in the right abdomen, tender to touch. I had to confess surprise! An intussusception seemed to be the diagnosis, and if so it must follow as surely as night follows the day that surgical intervention should begin as soon as possible. Not for her the X-rays, imaging scans, laboratory investigations that, along with calls for second opinions may serve to delay effective treatment in our wonderful, advanced, modern world hospitals!

Yes, there was an up-to-date hospital for pale-faced people at the great town of Ibadan, only 75 miles of twisty-turney roadway away, with its potholed surface, liable to fallen tree obstruction in rainy weather and roadside bush fires in the dry. Not an easy ride but of course excellent facilities when you reach such a centre of medical expertise. But for our dear lady time and some degree of comfort were of the essence, and we were glad to be able to offer both, even in our little hospital in the bush.

I explained the urgency to the patient and to her senior pastor colleague and transport by way of the comfy Oldsmobile was promptly arranged. Admission and preparation of the patient for operation was rapid and efficient under Sister's eagle eye, and the two four-burner primus stoves roared away furiously beneath the instrument sterilizer. I managed an hour's session with the waiting outpatients before nurse brought the message that all was ready.

So while we walk to the theatre you wish to refer to the statement that intussusception is a condition affecting babies. Yes, in this country that might be so. In the tropics where eating habits may change, adults who take only fruit and vegetables may cause some irritation of their intestinal system thus making an unusual movement of the gut possible.

While waiting for the theatre I was able to get on with the Outpatients' clinic until eventually nurse came with Sister's note that all was now ready.

"I'm coming, nurse," I said, and on entering the Theatre found the patient on the table, Sister administering ethyl chloride on to the face mask, the old-fashioned type with lint stretched over a metal frame held on the face, to be followed, when the patient was 'under' with the time honoured ether. There followed the usual 'scrubbing up' and masks, hat, gowns and gloves and my competent helper Hezekiah and I were ready for the fray.

Not that there was any fighting to be done. I have always objected to the emotive words of the news media out to create drama and excitement, when battles, struggles, fighting by doctors and surgeons are the ideas put into the minds of their readers and listeners. Not at all: surgery is a matter of undertaking procedures in a calm ordered manner, gently and respectfully treating and manipulating tissues encountered, when needed repair is effected calmly and properly and final closure of a surgical wound is a neat and tidy procedure.

So it was with our missionary patient as with others. The abdomen was opened, revealing our expected 'sausage', diagnosis confirmed. A large moist swab, soaked in warm saline was placed around the swelling, and very gentle squeezing was commenced at the ‘front end’ of the swelling, causing the invaginated intestine to slowly slide out backwards. More swabs, more gentle squeezing until at last the whole of that captive piece of large intestine was freed, and returned to its original place. A quick check all round, maybe remove appendix, close the abdomen, bring muscles together, sutures to the superficial tissues and skin, clips and dressings and the job was done. The patient being a fellow missionary was to be nursed in Sister’s own quarters, bless her!

“Where’s the meeting being held, Sister?”

“I think on your front lawn, Doctor, and I’m sure your wife has got it all in hand.” And so it was. A very helpful committee dealt with various matters ably and not too long afterwards I returned to my Outpatients’ Clinic, patients still waiting, poor souls.

A quick check on our latest inpatient, a quick round with Sister, and it was time for lunch with my wife and children. A bit of an afternoon siesta for an hour; a small Outpatients’ Clinic at 4 p.m. and afterwards I unearthed my typewriter. There was a letter to be written, advising retirement of a lady missionary on medical grounds. I addressed it to her mission committee in London.

Happiness, Sadness, and Success

In the years long ago the hospital ward round conducted by a consultant physician or surgeon with the ward’s senior nursing sister was an institution of immense importance and dignity. Attending the round would be the registrar, senior and junior housemen, a small cluster of male and female students and staff nurse with her junior.

Woe betides a student who had omitted to bring his stethoscope or a nurse whose stiffly starched headgear was set at an unbecoming angle. Discipline and correctness were the order of the day.

In our hospital in the ‘bush’ the daily morning round was also conducted carefully with Sister and a senior nurse accompanying me. On one occasion or even several, a little levity prevailed. As we passed from bed to bed there were restrained giggles from nursing staff and patients’ eyes opened widely as my pet squirrel provided entertainment. He sat on my left shoulder beneath my shirt presenting a squiggly bump that intrigued the beholder. Occasionally he popped out his little head for a view of the bedfast company, and then, turning, displayed his frisky little bush of a tail for admiration.

I had rescued him from the clutches of my cook who had caught him in the garden and hoped to present him suitably cooked and garnished on a platter as an interesting alternative to the goat’s meat that had become my staple diet. He became a most charming little pet, much smaller than the red and grey squirrels of our islands and full of fun. The nursing staff loved him and, with me, found his antics a delightful relaxation after some of the grim scenes in our wards and Theatre.

When leaving to return home on furlough, I presented him to little Ruth Elton, the lovely daughter of the apostolic missionary in Ilesha. She also fell in love with him. No doubt he learnt a variety of different hymns and maybe he attended church services and diverted the minds of the parishioners from the tedium of over-lengthy sermons! At any rate he was lovingly cared for.

To write of success is delightful, but to write of distress is painful. But of course, distress there was, and between the happy occasions of good medical or surgical outcome there came times of sadness.

A man walked into the Male Ward one day, bypassing the Outpatients' Department supporting and half carrying a little chap of 8 years or so, evidently his son. One of the child's forearms was wrapped in copious coverings of leaves and tie-tie. One of the father's hands held a parcel wrapped in a banana leaf. We listened to the story. The father had been tending the farm, preparing new ground. Trees and bushes needed chopping and disposal. A mighty swipe at the branch of a tree went astray, slipping uncontrolled. The child's forearm as he held on to the lower branch was in the way. The banana leaf contained the hand, severed at the wrist.

We did our best, of course. Anaesthesia, removal of damaged tissue and bone fragments, closing of arteries, trimming of radius and ulna and managing a skin covered stump. But alas I was not 'in the business' of joining together traumatically amputated bits and pieces, such artistry needed time and expertise and modern days. The healing was good but the sadness persisted.

--*-*-*-*-*-*-*-*-*-*

Felling of trees in our own country is certainly a task for the professional. Hard hats and much knowledge and great care are always needed. The amateur is rightly discouraged.

In developing countries such knowledge and expertise is often lacking and the amateur must just do his best. In the growth of a tree tremendous power is stored up as its trunk grows vertically defying the fearful force of gravity, spreading out branches whose strength must exceed the huge force of mighty winds. The tree could be said to take power to itself that can only be unloosed by accidental breakage of branch or trunk, lightning power being often the cause, or by planned intervention of mankind.

But in planning his exercise man must realise the forces being released and avoid damage to people or property by making and observing appropriate rules. One of them must be to see that nobody gets in the way of a falling branch.

A kit-car drew up one day to be met by a hospital trolley and stretcher. From the car was carefully lifted the unconscious form of a ten year old. He was wheeled to the Male Ward and placed on a bed in 'recovery' position. Then came the story of a tree chopping expedition, a falling branch, and the little chap's head being in the way.

Examination revealed of course bruising of the scalp but beneath the bruise could be felt alteration of the skull outline that indicated a depressed fracture of skull bones. I looked at Sister, "As soon as we can, please Sister." And she sent an urgent message to theatre and to the ward 'boy'. The stoves were lit and soon roaring beneath the big sterilizer. That stove and sterilizer really were kept busy.

Not long after, "Theatre ready, Doctor" was the message. Sister had all under control. To make a large curved incision, raise a good-sized flap of scalp, clean the area carefully and expose the damaged bone did not take long. Arrange further sterile sheets and prepare for trephining.

No up to the minute (state of the art!) drilling gadget here in the bush, just an old fashioned hand-held job with a circle of bone cutting, steel teeth, stainless of course and just a steady hand to rotate the instrument to and fro. Two holes made through healthy bone and a pair of slim instruments inserted with utmost gentleness. Using them the depressed area of fractured bone was levered into position. There was little bleeding and drainage for the area was now available through the trephine holes. We could stitch up. Sterile dressing, a large pad and a head bandage applied. It was good to see him returned to the ward with a nurse to remain beside him until consciousness returned. When I visited him later he was awake and smiled sleepily.

His father and family rejoiced; and we too were very pleased. Recovery was without further incident, and home-going was a happy occasion.

CHAPTER 15

Exorcism

What Canterbury's Archbishop or the President of the Methodist Conference would have done I've no idea. The thoughts of Albert Schweitzer of Lambarene would have been of value I'm sure, but time was of the essence. What would Bunyan have done with a real lion facing him? Such was my dilemma one morning in the middle of my hospital rounds; thankfully the lion was only imaginary.

I had inspected the dozen folk in the Female Ward where they were progressing well, and the ureteric transplant was doing nicely, to our relief as well as hers. I had walked upstairs to the Children's Ward where twenty or more little treasures were being cared for. Here was a little girl of four years with both legs suspended vertically by a pulley arrangement. One leg had suffered a fractured femur and had a weight exerting some traction; the other was raised to provide some balancing effect for the little poppet and to assist in toilet palaver. She was happy.

Here were children with malaria, kwashiorkor, diarrhoea and chest infections. But here also was a new problem. A small girlie of eight or nine stood beside her bed, shaking uncontrollably, terrified. Nothing would induce her to lie on the bed. I enquired of the senior nurse, and she replied, "She says there is a devil under her bed, Doctor."

That was a new one. My eminent tutor in psychiatry at Edinburgh had not thought to mention the simple matter of exorcism of devils or evil spirits; maybe he regarded such matters as pertaining to the university chaplain. My study of textbooks when at Ilesha dealt very largely with surgical topics. The human spirit was rarely mentioned, and evil ones less so. What to do?

Obviously get rid of the devil, and that demonstrably. A John Wesley sermon, the tub-thumping of John Knox would be inappropriate and useless. Burn him! Send him up in smoke! Suddenly I remembered that I had a little Vesuvius left over from my November 5th party. I told nurse to bring the child to my bungalow in ten minutes.

It had been my custom to manufacture small fireworks, using saltpetre, sulphur and charcoal, when entertaining young friends at home. I had not lost the art. In Ilesha I had made a number of cones filled with my gunpowder. On November 5th I had set them around the swimming bath to illuminate the scene with torrents of golden sparks when darkness set in. A little light diversion after the medical emergencies of the day! Our kids loved it! Was there one left?

I found my small firework and set it on the concrete veranda floor to await my guest. Soon she came, still shaking, still very scared, and holding nurse's hand.

Oh dear! Is this within the biblical teaching? I stayed not to discover. After all the word was that evil spirits had been shot over the cliff in the herd of sheep. So, forgetting archbishops, presidents and even dear Albert of Lambarene, I took a match, lit the touch paper and sat back.

The volcano responded, roaring purposefully; showers of sparks flew up with gusto, smoke was generous. Most dramatic. November 5th migrated to Africa!

The child watched, eyes and mouth wide open, breathing in gasps, shaking with terror, urinating on the floor. She looked as though the devil itself was appearing before her. Gradually the firework show subsided, the sparks and smoke diminished. Only a tiny flame and a small plume of smoke emerged from Vesuvius.

"It's gone," we told the trembling child. "It can never come back, so your bed is now quite safe for you."

She left peacefully, holding the nurse's hand. The nurse took her back to the ward. She climbed into her bed and was instantly asleep.

Isaac shook his head meaningfully, and washed and mopped up the floor. Later I popped up to the ward and checked the child. "She is happy now," said the nurse, and she would explain to the mother how the power of God could heal.

What was wrong with her? Why was she admitted to the hospital do you ask? Good questions, but you must forgive me, - I've forgotten!

It Happens by Night and Day

The hens at night perched on their long 12-foot iroko joist snuggled cosily up to each other. Bambi and baby lay peacefully for the night on their leafy bed. The squirrel and chameleon were long gone. Children were peacefully asleep. The game of Monopoly was lost and won, the night ward round was completed and the voltage reduced. I closed my book telling of contours and snowy heights, and stretched. My wife tidied away her knitting and twinkled her eyes at me.

"What about it?"

"Yes," I replied, "time to roost."

But hark! A patter of feet on laterite and up the wooden steps. A gentle knock. "Please, Doctor"

"Yes nurse."

"Please Doctor there is a new patient."

My wife picked up her knitting, and I followed nurse to the Male Ward to find Sister already there.

A man of some 40 summers lay groaning, hands protectively on his abdomen that looked swollen. Relatives were anxious to tell the story. The patient had suffered sudden dreadful pain causing him to writhe helplessly. He had vomited. He lived in the town and they had brought him at once by car. He was unable to communicate. The abdomen was tight, rigid. The pulse was rapid.

This was no time to make diagnostic guesses - "The Theatre please, Sister".

"Yes Doctor, it will be ready very soon," and the ward 'boy' having lit the stoves cycled off to summon Hezekiah. It was not long before nurse announced that the Theatre was ready and Hezekiah had arrived. I ran down to inform my wife.

Returning to the hospital after suggesting to my wife that she should go to bed, and passing the engine house, I popped in and raised the voltage.

Hezekiah was already scrubbing. "Hello H." I said, "Here we are again." He turned, smiled and shrugged. The big shadow-less lamp blazed with a light intensely focused on the patient's abdomen. He was already mercifully unconscious under the gentle ministrations of Sister's hands that held the anaesthetic mask in place. He was at last peaceful and free from pain.

Hezekiah and I scrubbed, saying little, but of course, wondering what awful internal abnormality we were about to discover.

Capped, gowned and gloved, we completed the group with Sister and two nurses assembled round the patient who lay quietly, breathing regularly. I took the scalpel. "Ready Hezekiah?"

"Yes Doctor."

The incision readily divided skin and fascia and with the muscles pushed aside the peritoneum was visible. The contents behind appeared dark. Dividing this lining to the abdomen we could view the small intestine. The whole gut was dead black, shiny in the brilliant light. There was no pulsation in the mesentery; only the steady rapid beat of the big abdominal aorta behind it could give the impression of life. Clearly the large arteries supplying blood to the small intestine had suffered severe blockage; the superior mesenteric vessel was thrombosed, hopelessly blocked, and there was no procedure possible to improve matters. Sadly we closed him up. Stitches, clips and dressings applied, we sent him back to a side ward with additional morphia. Survival was impossible.

Relatives were waiting outside the Theatre and we tried to explain his condition in terms that they could understand. All we could do was to give freedom from pain, rather hoping he would not wake up. They seemed to comprehend, and did not appear surprised.

Most of us found sleep was rather long delayed that night. In the morning Sister reported that he had found permanent rest.

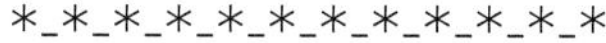

The cock crowed; 'Tappa' the crown bird squawked, standing on his old tree stump in the garden; the morn had returned brightly and it was Sunday. What chance of a quiet day; or what excitements to make it memorable?

A walk in the sunshine for a quarter of a mile to church. The hymns translated into Yoruba, the lessons, prayers and announcements in the same language, and not at all comprehensible to me. My mind could not follow the sermon and wandered. So also did my eyes, to the window. Outside in the nearest house compound a mother was plaiting her daughter's hair. Shiny black hair, healthy and beautiful in the morning sunshine, was expertly arranged in that lovely African fashion in tight plaits across the head. A delightful job carried out every Sunday and watched with pleasure.

Midday dinner was composed of the usual tough goat's meat, yam and greens, followed by banana fool. Then a siesta, but what's that commotion at the hospital gate? A kit-car entered, the usual makeshift ambulance, carrying, uncomfortably on its ridged iron floor two male patients, moaning dreadfully. The Dane gun is the favourite method of shooting game for hunters in Yoruba land, and cheaper than double-barrelled shotguns. It requires gunpowder however and hunters make their own, quite expertly, of sulphur, potassium nitrate, and charcoal, in correct proportions. Did the Chinese send the gunpowder formula to Africa direct? Or were we, the European fraternity to blame? Anyway, the powder must be dry to operate properly. These two chaps thought the heat of a bonfire would do the job quicker than the rays of the sun, and spread their mixture before a blazing fire. But bonfires shoot out sparks. There was a fearful conflagration, dreadful burns and awful pain. How far they had come, how long they had waited for transport we did not discover.

There was morphia, an effective dose; fluids in plenty, veins for intravenous infusion hard to find, merciful anaesthetic given by Sister. Burn treatment of the old-fashioned kind, involving gentian violet and tannic acid. We managed to save only one of them.

He spent a long time with us and became a happy and cheerful member of the Male Ward, growing new skin millimetre by millimetre, and almost enjoying the nurses' caring ministrations.

We were quite sorry to say "Goodbye", and felt glad to be able to save somebody. For a long time the nursing staff looked askance at anyone who mentioned gunpowder.

*_*_*_*_*_*_*_*_*_*_*_*

The months went by and summer and autumn brought the usual crop of accidents, hernias, ordinary and strangulated, difficulties in the Maternity Ward and Labour Theatre, measles and whooping cough, pneumonias and wormy infestations. The malarial mosquito caused havoc as always and gastro-enteritis, the feared enemy in the Children's Ward, continually afflicted the little ones, often with deadly results. But there were many successes to hearten us, and the folks of Ilesha expressed their gratitude in genuine fashion.

The rainy season with cool weather and wet drizzle that caused nurses to don pullovers and doctors to unearth their flannel 'bags', had washed clean our roofs and begun to fill once more our big concrete water tanks. Autumn was also bringing electrical storms, fierce winds, falling trees and torrents of rainwater, of which the latter was most welcome.

Tanks overflowed, flowers flourished, the temperature rose again from 60 degrees Fahrenheit into the 80-degree levels. We made ready for the four or five months of the dry season.

November arrived. Good gracious! What about the 5th? Africa had no tradition of Guy Fawkes attacking Parliament and the rockets and wonderful fireworks of home were unknown. How to celebrate?

That naughty word 'gunpowder' returned to haunt me. Surely, lacking ju-ju tradition and 'native medicine', surely I could use primitive chemistry to enliven the famous occasion. Hunters were not the only expert amateurs, so why not have a go....

I found the old chemistry book and looked up proportions of saltpetre, sulphur and charcoal. They were plentiful in the United Africa Company store, and I spent spare time in gunpowder manufacture, without the benefit of bonfires! A collection of cardboard cones followed duly packed with explosive, not too tightly, touch paper made by soaking it in a strong solution of potassium nitrate, dried in the sun if you please, and pieces tucked into the cone tops. Arranged them in a good number on the dry edge of the swimming bath and awaited darkness.

The daylight faded swiftly and sky blackened except for the silvery light of the moon and stars. It was time for matches. Children cosily wrapped to combat mosquitoes, gathered round the shallow end of the bath, a few nurses on their way back from day duty peered inquisitively as in duty bound. I struck a match and lit the touch papers. A little glow sank into the mouths of the cones. Suddenly volcanic fires burst forth mounting with gentle fury. Matches, touch papers, volcanoes, all the fun of the fair blazed, reflected in and around the still water of the swimming bath, hissing, spurting, with volleys of sparks all illuminating little faces entranced and joyful. When the last volcanic outburst had ended, ginger drinks and biscuits in our bungalow completed the fun and bedtime was welcomed by all.

CHAPTER 16

Light and a Weekend Break

While Africa sizzles in the sunshine protection from excessive heat is a necessity for personnel engaged in careful, thoughtful and intricate work. Such protection often shades the working area, reducing the brightness of the light essential for such work. Dark corners within a building often occur despite blazing sunshine outside, and in a hospital good lighting at night is as essential as is the bright light of day.

Candles, palm oil lamps, hurricane lamps, Tilley lamps pressurised with incandescent mantles were the original lights to combat dark corners and make night work possible. However electricity was most desirable, and a scheme to light the old hospital by means of a large set of lead-acid batteries was brought to fruition and gave good service for years. It was superseded by a pair of twin diesel engined generators running at 110 volts and 15 amps each. Wards were lit, theatres, kitchen, laundry, engine house, pathways and staff houses all rejoiced in illumination for all twelve hours of darkness. The Operating Theatre was given two lights, one at each end of the operating table, but leaving a middle area where the surgeon's hands themselves could cast a shadow, and some difficulty was thereby experienced.

The telephone for the hospital was in my house. A call one day found me there and at the other end of the line came the voice of Bill Mann, our vigorous accountant in Lagos. "The army here are selling off equipment, and some of it is medical. Can you spare time to come and look it over?"

It seemed an opportunity too good to miss. Soon afterwards the hospital seemed, unnaturally, fairly quiet, and I felt able to leave it and my family behind and go. There were times when duty called elsewhere and would provide relief from the 'common round' and a refreshment of spirit. This was often much needed in the heat, humidity, and hurly-burly of a hospital in the tropics.

Thus it was that one weekend found me driving our big Oldsmobile (the used car wisely bought by my predecessor, Dr. Hunter) mile after hot mile via bush, village, town, and big cocoa plantations, palm and banana groves to the coastal capital of Nigeria, until I reached the sea with its wide expanse of blue water in the harbour and lagoon, and its most welcome on-shore breeze.

A large double fronted house stood well back from the road that ran alongside the marina of the harbour at Lagos. A narrow band of trees separated the road from the water's edge. On a path beside the harbour walked an African woman traditionally dressed in Yoruba costume, carrying, expertly balanced on her head, a basket of supplies and edibles, and striding purposefully along on sure feet without the benefit of shoes to encumber her progress. Beyond lay the sun-drenched wavelets and, at her mooring, a fair sized passenger ship with canoes and small boats scurrying along, driven by oars or outboard engines, to provide attendance of one sort or another for the big vessel.

I found the scene peaceful and charming, immediately restful after the fast long hot drive. The eyes found relief from stress as I lifted them to look far beyond the ocean-going ship towards the bar at the harbour entrance.

The car in the compound before the house was in the shade of the trees, and two ladies loading bags into it were grateful for the protection. I gave them a casual wave, aware that they were about to travel up-country on the hot dusty road by which I had just come to town. "How's the road?" they said. "Hot" I replied, and they groaned. Energy for mid-day conversation was in short supply.

A man clad in a white shirt and shorts emerged from the house and spoke to the ladies briefly. He spotted me and said "Hello John, you've arrived then?" "It was a long haul," I replied, "so I hope you'll have something worthwhile to show me." Bill was our financial expert ordering supplies for mission schools, wise in business matters, and it was he who had told me of the ex-army sale of medical items, advising me to make the 185 mile run to Lagos to have a 'look-see'.

We all had lunch together in the big house, and after a short siesta the ladies, teachers at an up-country girls' grammar school, completed preparations and set off by car for this 100 mile trip through the Nigerian bush, through the cocoa plantations, under the palm trees, past the villages with their wayside stalls of fruit and bales of Lancashire cloth.

Bill advised a quick run to the Army Store Department, and on return promised a refreshing sail in his dinghy. Through the township sped Bill in his ageing motorcar with myself hanging on for dear life. Cycles and pedestrians fled sideways, mothers clutched their children, men muttered imprecations, dogs and fowls leapt and flew to safety, shopkeepers and stallholders cursed, and one seized an old and obviously blind man, drawing him out of the path of the mad Englishman!

We found the store; sorted through old stethoscopes, forceps, enamel bowls and medical bric-a-brac and finally spotted with joy a large shadow-less lamp. That, thought I, would transform the Operating Theatre of our bush hospital. It would give a brilliant light precisely where needed, with no hand shadow to delay or make procedures difficult and awkward.

The storekeeper offered it at £5 and we paid up willingly. "Cheap at the price" I remarked to Bill. "Couldn't be better," he replied, "let's go for that sail." Back through the main street, hardly recovered from our recent passage, back to lock Bill's office, and off to the Yacht Club along the marina to find the sailing dinghy all made ready for putting into the water.

Our previous sail with Bill had shown me his expertise at boat handling, so I had no qualms. We pushed off, hopped in and we were water-borne. Bill paid his club fees by selling his catch, mostly of jack with occasional barracuda, the latter rather inclined to snap at any toes or feet, and so great care was needed when lifting one into the boat. Bill hauled up the sail, handling the centre-board, rudder and sheets with practised hands while I put a couple of rods, lines and lures into position for fishing, fixed one rod firmly and held the other. The bright painted wooden lures would attract fish and being loaded with hooks a catch was fairly certain. The on-shore wind still blew well and Bill's *Bunty* flew happily along at 6 or 7 knots, heeling over and cutting through the small waves easily. Outside the harbour we were at the bar and there was surf with breakers but the fishing was excellent. Five or six passes to and fro and an equal number of jack of 8 or 9 lb. weight were enough for my inexperience, and Bill headed back for the Yacht Club on a now rapidly falling breeze as evening grew on apace, darkness drawing closer. We reached the slipway, hauled the boat up, sorted out sail and rods, avoided the hooks, strung up the fish, covered the boat and made fast.

Into Bill's car and we careered home to his bungalow six miles out of town, again scattering humans and animals in the streets. Sail or drive, all go!

Into Bill's compound with a screech of brakes, slamming of doors, a shout to his cook-steward to deal with the fish, and a quick march to the front door, where waited his patient wife and a bridge partner. "Just time for a rubber before chop" said Bill. The rubber, like the drive, was fast and furious, and the 'post-mortem' tended to be acrimonious at times.

The camp bed wasn't my favourite for nightly repose, but I slept happy with the thought, not of marketable jack and barracuda, port and starboard, sheets and sails, but of future possibilities of operating with the aid of a brilliant light that could be accurately directed towards the surgical scene with no offending shadow.

Next morning I loaded the new treasure into the hospital car and returned to Ilesha to show the Sisters our prize possession.

For days afterwards my spare time was occupied with a screwdriver, spanner, pliers, forceps, cleaning materials and a modicum of elbow grease, cleaning and polishing the many mirrors of the lamp and testing the lighting until all seemed perfect. It only needed to be suspended over the operating table in the theatre. But before this tricky procedure it required suitable wires and counterbalancing weights. There were no weights with the lamp that was found to weigh 33 lb.

Three weights each of 11 lb. attached to wires running over pulley wheels fixed to the ceiling joists and fixed to the lamp at equidistant points would provide good suspension. The lamp could then be adjusted as required, so giving a brilliant shadow-less light on any operating area.

The weights were to operate by sliding up and down within a wooden cylinder some 3 inches in diameter, fixed above the lamp to the ceiling, its lower end being closed to prevent any dust from falling onto the operating area. How to create such weights each of 11 lb? We needed a supply of lead, and some elementary knowledge of chemistry and mathematics.

Rejoicings! The old lead batteries, formally used for lighting, had been stored beneath my house. In my office I discovered a chemistry book left by one of my predecessors. Now it was up to my brain, a little rusty in such matters, my knowledge of simple maths and the expertise of our very capable driver-mechanic Mr

Laniyan. Trained by gold mining people, he possessed a wide and quite expert knowledge of engineering problems.

The chemistry book provided the specific gravity of lead. Paper and pen were to hand, and I put my ageing mathematics to work to determine the size of the weights that were to slide past each other, silently I hoped, within the 3-inch cylinder. I'm not telling you how I did it. Work it out for yourself! In due course I gave the final drawings to our mechanic who produced, from a kerosene tin, three moulds of the correct size and shape. He melted 33 lb. of lead from the old batteries, (I did not find out how that was done), poured it into the three moulds, and inserted a length of wire into each before they cooled.

So there, dear reader, is a delicate little problem for you. If you can calculate for me the diameter and length of the moulds so that each lead weight should be capable of sliding up and down smoothly in the cylinder, each one weighing 11 lb. to support the lovely shadow-less lamp hanging over our heads while we sorted out somebody's innards, then please do so. The choice is yours! (The risk is ours! - oh, and please tell me how to do it, I must confess that I've forgotten!)

The day came when, the morning's Outpatient duties finished, the minor operations coped with, ward rounds with Sister accomplished, orders given to carpenter, garden boys and driver there was time to think about installing the lamp in the Theatre. With cylinder, weights, a supply of wire, forceps and pliers, screws and screwdriver, pulley wheels and a torch and not forgetting a ladder, I commenced the attack; fixed the cylinder, fastened the pulley wheels, hung the lamp in place, tested it for adjustment, felt satisfied. Then to climb into the roof of the Theatre, an airless, appallingly hot dark hole, the awful heat radiating down from the corrugated galvanised iron roof. There to check the screwings and fixings and finally to find an electrical supply wire and arrange the lamp's wiring appropriately; wire to a switch, switch to the Theatre wall, and we were ready. Message for junior nurse, "Please ask driver to start the engine." - "Yes Doctor."

Soon was heard the familiar diesel thudding and the usual lights appeared. A dramatic moment, "Everybody ready?" I pressed the lamp switch. A brilliant light flooded the centre of the operating table. A nurse moved her hands over a pretend patient. There was no shadow. Joy was unconfined! We celebrated in Sister's office with orange juice, while some of the nursing staff did a little dance and applauded.

A week or so later I began to shiver uncontrollably as a dose of malaria rewarded my exertions, but never mind - we had light! It remained to pay for it with....

MALARIA – Lets put it in capital letters! Water supply has been an important topic, what about little mosquitoes to whom it is life itself? Every little pool and empty tin, every pot, plant pot, un-inspected water tank, and even the little collections of water between the leaf and stem of a plant may provide housing for mossies and their indwelling parasites. Evening brings out the wee insects; don't let 'em bite you. When they do they inject a little saliva to prevent your blood from clotting while they suck it up. In the saliva are dangerous beasties, the malarial parasites. About ten days later comes the shivers, rigors in fact, rise of temperature, pile on every blanket and take your tablets!

Of course we all took anti-malarial pills regularly, in those days it would be quinine or mepacrine, and later paludrine, and if we started to have headaches we doubled the dose. For an attack of malaria proper it was very essential to take the drug in proper dosage as ordered by the doctor, and preferably by one who really knows about malaria. This disease is no joke!

Why did I get it this time? Well, it may happen that after vigorous exercise or after a sudden change of climate from hot to cold or vice versa, the little brutes already in the human system may become very active. My exertions in the roof of the operating theatre had been energetic and very over heated.

Anyway shadow-less light on the sleeping patient's tummy was an excellent investment and well worth a dose of fever!

Diesels, Steam and Great Balls of Wool

The work at Ilesha involved a wide range of new experiences, not only medical, and often entertaining. Happy and sad ones, charming and grim, a daily feast of wonderful interest, often taxing one's competence to the limit, often providing opportunities for new ventures and formulation of ideas.

Each day brought problems of interest, minor and major. The hospital carpenter asking for instruction; the driver mechanic needing advice re machine maintenance; requests from Sister for better lighting; calculating the electrical load of lights and power against the wattage available in the engine room; nurses shrieking for help when a snake invaded their common room, at least 8 inches long, and more terrified than they; orders for supplies, drugs, instruments, engine oil and petrol, all in the days work before morning outpatients could begin. A great boon was that Sister, bless her, dealt with care and economical bargaining for the supply of all the hospital food requirements, and carefully counted sheets and bedding items delivered to the laundry man, and with equal care the tally of clean items returned after his soapy water frolic.

To receive the morning post from our driver after his cycle ride to the town's post office could be a light relief sometimes.

One day it was indeed an excitement, and with rapture I sought Sister and read to her a letter from 'the powers that be'. We were told that money was available from the Nigerian

Government for mission stations to equip themselves with capital projects such as electrical installations, water supply schemes and other things of high cost outside our own financial abilities.

Joyful possibilities came to mind. The idea that, instead of two powerful four-burner paraffin pressure stoves underneath our Operating Theatre sterilizer, these could be scrapped, and, instead, by a turn of the tap or touch of a switch, would instantly be available the power needful for an emergency operation by night or regular theatre operating sessions by day.

Enquiries soon brought us further help. We learnt of the name of an English engineer of high repute who would be interested to advise us. Contact was made, he was willing to look-see and shortly he travelled to the hospital complete with his knitting needles, a large ball of wool and a scarf in the making! A competent engineer indeed! We found that his knitting skills (he travelled by train usually knitting to pass the time, and persuaded fellow passengers to hold his skein of wool) were equalled in good measure by his ability as an engineer. He assessed our needs and, in short advised an installation of steam sterilising equipment for use by day and electric sterilising by night, involving new engines and generators of twice the present power. In Biblical terms 'a pillar of smoke by day and fire by night'! We were quite thrilled and agreed and were happy to find that he would order all the necessary gadgetry from home.

We informed the financing authority who agreed to make the money available. What a thrill to receive a letter from the local town council inviting me to collect the cash! Even greater was the excitement of taking the hospital car to the Town Hall in the Ilesha market area, and return with a suitcase packed full of three thousand pound notes! I had never seen or handled so much money, as much as it cost to run our mission hospital for one year! Fifty years later I can still remember the numerical code for operating the heavy little safe locked in the office in my bungalow. I discovered later that the office lock could easily be opened with the aid of a knife from the kitchen next door!

Too excited by this thrilling event to keep it quiet I went to share the news with the Sisters, whose faces lit with happiness and whose voices countered with their own news..."There is an emergency in the theatre Doctor and I've ordered the lighting of the big four-burner paraffin stoves!" and indeed looking towards the small room where this procedure was initiated I could see the smoke pouring from the window where the boys had pumped up the stove pressure and created the hot rings of flame to heat the sterilizer. While waiting we indulged in a few happy fantasies. No more smoke, no paraffin flames or burnt fingers (we forgot about high-pressure steam burns!), better lights, even bedside lights, electric gadgets, not fires of course in tropical temperatures of 80 degrees F; steam sterilised theatre gowns, sheets and gloves (and even powder for donning same, instead of gloves boiled and soapy solution to ease them onto one's hands - nasty slippery experience!)

We were brought down to earth by a door knock from the Male Ward nurse. "It is time for the patient's injection, Sister, shall I give it now?" Ah well, sufficient unto the day would be the fun thereof!

Some weeks later the day arrived, ushered in by a phone call from our Lagos accountant who gladly assured us that a lorry or two were being loaded up with our new equipment.

The eyes of all the hospital staff excitedly watched the big lorry carrying two huge wooden cases easing its way on to the grassy area opposite the engine house. Our twin set of 1½k.v.a. diesels and generators had served us well for years, replacing an old battery system whose remains still lay beneath my bungalow that was raised on 6-foot iron stanchions and provided space for a locked storage area for timber and any heavy equipment. That electric plant could still fetch a good price.

Now to unbolt the old diesels. You had to ease them with care out of their erstwhile home and arrange the rebuilding of their concrete bases and built-in bolts, paying special attention to the levelling of the concrete surfaces. Our African builders, carpenters and mechanics were very expert in such matters and the details could be safely left to them.

A phone call to John Mellanby, our engineer in Ibadan, brought him the 75 mile train journey complete with knitting needles, balls and skeins of wool, and an army colonel in the carriage, who disgustedly held the skeins as required - not his cup of tea or glass of sherry! A large suitable steel tripod with lifting gear was arranged around the lorry and ropes around the cases hooked to the load.

A firm pull on the rope and to the admiring gaze of the hospital staff, ward boys, garden boys, the cook, our driver, and not a few patients and relatives, the big cases were raised up one by one, the lorry driven away, and the cases lowered to the ground. Mr Danson, expert carpenter of Ilesha was very efficient in such matters and such details could be safely left to him along with Samuel, our hospital wielder of saws and hammers. They happily set to and opened the wooden cases, revealing the new gleaming steelwork, well oiled and cared for, to our delighted vision. These engines were, of course, bigger than their predecessors, and to manoeuvre them through the door of the engine house with a few centimetres to spare, the upstanding brickwork of the veranda roof being opposite the door, this was indeed a feat of much good Yoruba ingenuity! Mr Danson arranged the business superbly, overseen by John Mellanby, engineer in charge.

Lister diesels arrive

Engines and generators were positioned, bolts screwed down, belts adjusted, engine oil poured into sumps, diesel into supply tank, pipes connected. The big new switchboard installed and wired up, and the winding handle was offered to our mechanic. Delightedly he turned the heavy flywheel and having attained a useful speed thrust aside the valve lifter. Compression was immediate, and the diesel fired with its typical powerful thudding, increasing to full revolutions. The voltage crept up quickly on the switchboard. The main switch made contact, and the new light blazed forth. Hand clapping and merriment broke forth too. We were in business!

Three thousand watts of power rising to six thousand if needed when the second engine was required for extra power - this would be quite adequate for our needs in the wards, houses, pathways, main Theatre and Maternity and Outpatients' Theatre. We rejoiced.

Soon came the next phone call from Bill Mann, our expert Lagos accountant "Your steam boilers, sterilizers and all gadgetry, pipes and so forth have left Lagos for Ilesha, expect them tomorrow."

Two 7-foot steam boilers were awaited expectantly. I prepared a supply of ropes for gradually lowering these cast iron, precious commodities to the hard sun-baked earth outside the Female Ward, with instructions to the staff to notify me immediately of their arrival. It was the afternoon on a baking hot day, and the ground as hard as iron. A junior nurse toddled down to my house. Knock, knock, "The lorry has come Doctor." I leapt to my feet from my chair borne siesta, and hastened down the steps and up the path to supervise the most careful off-loading that I could devise. Too late! The lorry drivers had given the boilers a hefty push or two, and they had crashed to the ground, iron against iron; my careful preparation was in vain. My fears rose to screaming pitch, but no use expostulating, the job was done.

And thankfully the boilers were not cracked and no damage had occurred. Now it was up to John M...

Soon he had them erected, and a useful protective shelter constructed, open at the sides, framework of iroko wood, and two cylindrical chimneys protruding through the galvanised roof. For insulation? What better than 2 or 3 inches of good Ilesha clay, watered, and with brown tow liberally mixed in and well trodden by willing feet, the mixture slapped on with grins and much gusto. Bind it from top to bottom with 6 inch bandages, slap on a nice wet layer of Plaster of Paris, and, when dry, a good dose of aluminium paint to complete the mixture and defeat Nigeria's humidity.

Fill the boilers as required with water and apply heat. We began with used engine oil dripped on to a hot plate with another pipe dripping a little water, resulting in very hot flames. But the oil supply could not be maintained and we reverted to wood from the bush, cheap and plentiful.

The steam gauges rose to 15 lb per square inch. There were no leaks. John M. had done a fine job yet again!

On the new sterilizer instrument for linen and gowns and gloves were just two knobs. We twiddled them, Sister's eyes gleamed as the water bubbled, and the big gown and sheet sterilizer indicated that it was operative also.

Our Hospital Liaison Committee was informed of the successful outcome of this project, and through them was issued an invitation to the Owa, the King of Ilesha and Ijeshaland, to come with his chiefs and officials with due ceremony to switch on the lights at the big switchboard, and turn on the steam taps for the sterilizer. On an arranged date the Owa was driven to the Hospital with his retinue and invited to enter the engine house where our big new diesels were thudding away merrily, but there was no protective covering over the large flywheel and generator belts. We carefully shielded the Owa's lovely robes from harm.

Taking the big switches in his hand he pushed them into closed position and light flooded the scene to the joy and wonder of them all.

Then to the Operating Theatre where further explanation was made and the insulated pipes were demonstrated as they descended the wall after entry from the boilers outside. Their connections to the sterilizers was shown; it was of course a very new concept to them all, and lots of questions were asked and answered. The Owa was invited to turn on the taps. He did so and they all gathered around the instrument sterilizer, and waited…

Nothing...

Wait a little...

"Ah! Ah! – Look - see!"

A few bubbles appeared; they multiplied noisily and soon the whole mass of water was bubbling furiously. The Owa smiled and waved a hand appreciatively. His retinue exclaimed, laughed, clapped and clapped and maybe danced a step or two in applauding the wonders of modern science!

Our engineer, knitter of scarves, provider of light and heat, had done a splendid job. Hospital staff were thrilled and grateful, and their patients would reap the benefit.

Now you know why my title has a Spanner!

Steam for sterilising

CHAPTER 17

Wha' Da Ya Dooo There?

The village or small town of Cavtat is on the Croatian coast a few miles south of the old city of Dubrovnik,a charming situation beside the clear water of the Adriatic, its sea front being a long stout wall having water constantly washing its face, and multicoloured fish to delight the eyes swimming within arms' reach. There is a spacious walk along the sea wall with an extensive flat palm-shaded area behind reaching to the shops, ever busy cafes and restaurants, provided with tables and forms, serviced by eager willing waiters, hands busy with food and coffee.

Walking here one day beside the calm water and blue sky my wife and I gloried in the peaceful ambience, in the sun and shade, indulging in coffee, watching the gentle movements of the fish, their scales glinting in the sun, reflecting many colours.

Round a corner of the village behind us a large coach full of passengers turned slowly and stopped. After a while the folk began to emerge, carefully descending the steps and by their accents informing us clearly that the USA was their home. They walked uncertainly, some staggering as if walking was not their favourite form of progression.

One charming elderly lady used a stout stick, and looked about her evidently not impressed by the quiet place. We engaged her in conversation, and learned of her huge, busy, hometown in the hectic life of the great country beyond the Atlantic. She enquired about our quiet holiday and how long we were staying in this one place. We told her that we hoped to stay for two weeks.

"Two weeks?" – in a tone of disbelief, "Two weeks?" – "Well, wha' da ya dooo?"

We smiled at the old charmer, sympathised with her arthritis, led her to a coffee table and told her to go slowly. So this chapter will take up her delightful tourist query and explain something of 'what we did' some 35 degrees south of here, beyond the mighty Sahara, in the tropical bush region of Nigeria.

There is only one place to begin - Sister's Office. The Sister's Office was the nub and centre of the hospital's work. To it came all reports and information regarding ward and theatre work and the condition and treatment of every inpatient. Here was assessed the needs of each patient by Sister to whom each nurse in charge of a ward submitted her written summary of each patient's progress before the nurse left the ward after her duty stint. From here, after Sister's round of the hospital with the Doctor, were issued to the nurse coming on duty the appropriate instructions for the care of the patients in her charge; Sister's Sanctum, where her authority reigned supreme.

Fifteen yards along the corridor two stretcher-trolleys stood on either side of double doors leading to the Operating Theatre. This could be called the Doctor's Sanctum, and to it were brought many of the sick or injured folk who needed surgical care for their troubles.

A good-sized, 20-foot by 20-foot room, very well lit by windows covered with mosquito wire gauze on two sides. The third side consisted largely of a big opening into the 20-foot by 6-foot sterilising room, similarly lit. A big glass instrument cabinet housed a very adequate supply of the surgical tools of the trade; two wash basins were fed by pipes and taps for 'scrubbing up,' and an effective gas and oxygen anaesthetic machine replaced the old-fashioned 'rag and bottle' and chloroform of former days. The operating table was central with an up and down facility, also the tilting of head and foot ends as required. Above it two hundred watt lights were present at the ends of the table, and a large shadow-less lamp hung suspended over its centre. The operator felt well provided for.

Steam at 15lb per square inch came as a later addition and proved invaluable in rapidly heating the sterilizers, providing sterile gowns, sheets, caps, masks, gloves and instruments as required for theatre work.

An anaesthetic was used as a matter of course in the Theatre where the human body was treated with appropriate respect. Ethyl chloride and ether, nitrous oxide and oxygen for general anaesthetics, given by our trained clerks or by sister, all well experienced. Often for the operations 'below the belt', a spinal anaesthetic was given by the operator. All proved very successful. To give a spinal, the patient, somewhat doped by a suitable dose of morphine, lay on his side, knees and head brought gently towards each other by a nurse or sister, thus opening the spinal bones a little for the needle to pass between them into the spinal canal. A syringe full of anaesthetising fluid was attached to the needle and the plunger gently pushed to deliver a measured amount of anaesthetic into the canal. The needle was withdrawn and the table tilted to persuade the anaesthetic, which was heavier than spinal fluid, to reach the desired nerve trunks; a few minutes to take effect, and the table levelled again. Towels and sheets were arranged and surgery could begin.

What kinds of operations were done? What complicated procedures beloved of our wonderful large and modern hospitals could possibly be carried out in a little 'bush' hospital isolated in Nigeria's southwest hinterland? Such questions may well spring to a doubting mind.

Truly the little portable X-ray machine, housed in a tiny dark room with its developing tanks, had limitations, but it would gladly reveal the complexities of a broken bone simple or comminuted, or a metal object swallowed by a small child, or needle inserted by a nurse and broken by a violent muscular reaction. Our laboratory was primitive certainly, but its simple chemistry could give quite useful answers regarding blood and urine questions. The wily malarial parasite would sometimes be found in a thin or thick film by a microscope where it hid itself away in the liver of the patient hoping to produce another violent rigor in a future malarial attack. At the time of which I write, namely in the forties of the 20th century and even in the early fifties, there was no blood transfusion service, true, but despite this drawback very useful and life-saving things could be done.

Why no blood transfusion service? I am, of course, referring to conditions in a very small hospital in what was at the time a very primitive country, medically speaking. The development of these services was yet to be arranged.

What do you do there? Perhaps an example?

Tabitha was a woman of some thirty years. A small hamlet near the village of Effon 20 miles distant provided home and shelter for her and her farmer husband in a solid mud-walled house, with stout iroko door and shuttered windows of the same good timber, inedible to the destructive white ants. Her happy offspring of six, four and two years, playful and obedient, amused themselves with neighbouring children while she pounded yam or cassava, adding palm oil and red pepper as desired, or kept the children happy with banana, orange or sugar cane.

Helping her husband a few miles away at his farm, she would carry a head load of produce back home, her two year old encased on her back with stout native cloth wound tightly round her body above her breasts, the child sleeping snugly while its mother strode vigorously homewards on bare feet. The middle child might remain with a helpful neighbour, the elder, at six years would be a load carrier, bearing a handy bundle of wood from the farm clearing to supply the cooking fire at home. This also was carried on the child's head.

It happened one day that while journeying homewards, she began to feel a vague discomfort in her lower body on the left side. She was aware that, with her child now two years old, having then returned to her husband's bed, she was a fortnight passed her monthly event. Being now a mother of three the probability of a further pregnancy did not alarm her, and indeed she felt glad, and was quite aware that a pregnancy could bring different feelings.

Having reached home she was glad to lie down, and relieved when her mother offered to cook the evening meal. The discomfort continued, punctuated with little sharp pains and then temporary relief for a while. The elderly granny was still alive and sharp of wit, and soon joined a discussion regarding the best kind of medicine to give for such a complaint. A local medicine man, decorated with signs of his trade, maybe two bones and a few feathers, was approached for his advice and provided a compound of leaves which, when taken, should cure the trouble. It failed. The woman passed a wretched night. The pain was worse. The husband conferred with neighbours, and other, older mothers joined in a vigorous and noisy discussion. The village schoolteacher, being supposedly knowledgeable, was asked for advice. After hearing the story and thinking for a long while, he at last gravely advised that the patient should be taken to the mission hospital, some twenty miles distant. The cost of a lorry journey and thoughts of hospital fees came to their minds, but offers of help and loans from friends and relatives soon solved the dilemma, and the decision was taken.

An emergency stretcher was now quickly made, a length of stout cloth tied at each end to a strong bamboo pole of about three inches in diameter. The patient, placed aboard, was carried by two strong men to the bigger village through which a lorry would pass that day. At about mid-day it came; carriage fees were paid, and patient, husband, mother and granny (don't forget granny) were hoisted aboard to join all the other folk, their packages, chickens, goats, etc., not a comfortable journey! Out of date springs, road potholes and hard laterite road, the pain must have been almost unbearable.

At last the hospital; met by a nurse and two ward orderlies with a more comfortable stretcher, our patient was soon transferred to a proper bed; the Sister on duty informed and pulse, temperature and respiration recorded.

Sister was in the Maternity Ward of ten beds with a couple of junior nurses, instructing them in the mysteries of bed-bathing a patient. She left them to it and quickly joined the senior nurse in the Female Ward, after greeting the patient's relatives outside.

"What is the trouble nurse?"

"Pain in the left lower abdomen, Sister, since yesterday morning and becoming worse."

"What is her name please?"

"Tabitha."

Sister sat beside the patient, noting the fearful expression, and took her hand, feeling the pulse at the wrist. "Tabitha will you tell me where it hurts you please." The nurse translated this into Yoruba tongue. Laying a hand gently on the lower abdomen, Sister noticed the slight tumidity, and the immediate muscular protective reaction.

She proceeded no further but with pencil and paper wrote a short message instructing the junior ward nurse to deliver it to me in my house a hundred yards away. A knock at my open office door, and "Please Doctor…"

I walked briskly in the afternoon heat, under the tall casuarina tree, a gentle breeze humming through its myriad fine needle-like leaves, past the engine house, Sister's laundry store, hospital kitchen and the lovely low hedge of plumbago feeding the humming bird moths with sweetness from its blue and white flowers, brilliant in the sunshine.

I entered the ward and Sister showed me the patient and reported her findings. Briefly, taking the patient's hand I smiled to reassure her saying "Welcome mother" – "Ekabo iya" in her own language, and quietly examined her to confirm Sister's conclusions. "Sister, I shall need to perform an internal examination."

"Of course, Doctor, nurse has everything prepared."

A sterile glove, lubricant, and a very gentle feel inside. Fluctuation was present, and to one side of the uterus a definite and quite tender lump. The patient winced as I touched it and the examination ceased quickly. I had noted the tumid abdomen and the presence of fluid.

"Well Sister, are we of one mind? An ectopic gestation with rupture and bleeding. Do you agree?"

"Yes Doctor. The Theatre is being prepared."

This was a case where the pregnancy, occurring in the Fallopian tube, had, instead of proceeding into the uterus, stayed within the little tube and developed, stretching it painfully, and finally bursting with an outpouring of blood from vessels that were enlarging to feed the growing pregnancy. Here was danger, serious enough to threaten life itself unless operative interference could be mounted.

The nurses carefully prepared the patient, and Tabitha was given morphine to sedate her and ease pain, and atropine to dry her respiratory tubes, so helping the anaesthetic procedure, which would be given by Sister's colleague. Activity in the Theatre was ordered and rapid under Sister's supervision. The steam sterilising facility made for very rapid preparation. Before long, 35 minutes perhaps, all was ready, my assistant and I were scrubbed, gowned, capped, masked and gloved. Sister was ready with her anaesthetic, and the patient carefully wheeled in on the theatre trolley and gently lifted on to the table.

Sheets arranged, and anaesthetic proceeded smoothly. Sister indicated that the patient was nicely under, and I could carry on. "Plenty of big swabs, Sister?"-"Plenty" she replied, I had no need to ask. At that time we had no suction apparatus to remove blood from the peritoneal cavity, only swabs.

I looked at my assistant, Hezekiah. He nodded, ready with artery forceps to catch bleeding vessels.

I lifted the scalpel. A central abdominal incision big enough for fingers and instruments to reach the damage was essential. No keyhole surgery here.

Speed was essential, but so was gentle care. Maybe the bleeding had eased. Don't start it by rough handling. Artery forceps to the bleeding points; tie them off later. Cut through deep fascia over the muscles; push muscles aside. A cut through the deeper fascia behind muscles and a nick through the peritoneum behind that, lining the abdominal wall. Open the cut to allow two fingers in, to protect the intestines, enlarge incision up and down to the full length of the skin incision. Blood! A lot.

Swab, swab, swab, but gently. My assistant to use the retractors to open the wound wide! Swab again, removing each swab, blood soaked, until away down deep was seen the swollen tube, with more blood behind and below in the Pouch of Douglas, the space between uterus in front and bowel behind. Continue swabbing with care, trying not to move the tube suddenly. Now to catch the tube with a padded pair of long forceps and ease it up a little so as to place a tie in position and isolate it from the uterus, and at the same time catching and tying up the bleeding artery.

Alas, as the tube moved slightly so did the blood clot temporarily closing the damaged artery, a good-sized branch of the big uterine vessel. Blood spurted furiously in time with the patient's heart rate of 120 per minute. In no time the Pouch of Douglas had refilled and the artery vanished, still pumping.

Emergencies need emergency measures. The senior sister had entered the theatre. "Sister," I shouted "come and put your fist on this abdominal aorta," the very large blood vessel at the back of the abdomen which supplies the whole lower body with blood. In seconds she had grabbed a sterile glove from the instrument trolley, shoved in her right hand and pushed it into the abdominal cavity. Pushing aside intestines, she felt for the pulsating aorta. And pressed and pressed. I swabbed, Sister pressed. More blood soaked swabs, nurse opened more tins of swabs (sterilised) and before long the blood level dropped enough to reveal the artery, no longer bleeding. A quick forceps on to it, and another to make doubly sure; a sound tie with chromic No. 2 catgut, a careful cut, and the tube removal was safely accomplished.

"Alright Sister" I said, and she slowly removed her hand while I continued to swab with care. All bleeding had stopped. We could relax, a little. A thorough inspection of the area, carefully clearing up with warm moist swabs and we were ready to close up. A check on swab numbers, suitable layers of stitches with correct type of 'catgut', muscles replaced, skin wound closed with stitches and clips. It was time to check up on the patient's condition.

"How are things, Sister?" I said. "Well," she replied, "she's survived, but breathing is rapid, (anaesthetic had ceased and oxygen was now being supplied) and pulse is fast and not strong." I saw and felt and agreed.

"Blood is what she needs," I said; and we regarded each other sadly. We had no blood bank; no arrangements for taking blood and storing it. Not even any means of assessing patient's blood group. The need of Tabitha was plain to see. The operation had been successful, but could she survive?

Suddenly came a thought. "Sister," I said, "We have five strong garden 'boys', what do you think?…" "Its worth a try" she replied. A ward 'boy' rounded up the young men, who assembled in the corridor outside the Operating Theatre, where our patient awaited recovery from the anaesthetic. I explained the urgency. "The patient needs human blood to save her life. Perhaps the blood of one of you would be suitable. I have often given blood as a student. It is painless, and you feel quite well afterwards." There followed a short discussion. No questions. Much head shaking, and "I think no can do" came the reply from them all. They melted away.

We sighed. Hezekiah, my able assistant and interpreter spoke. "Doctor there is an old lady here," he smiled indulgently, "She wishes to say something." It was Tabitha's grandmother, some 60 years old I thought, looking older but quite vigorous and healthy. She spoke her piece, offering her blood for her precious granddaughter, perhaps thinking that her remaining life would be short anyway, and willing to make the sacrifice.

We hesitated not a jot. Sending Hezekiah to the lab for a microscope and glass slide I prepared with a small syringe to collect a few drops of blood from one of the very visible veins on her arm, and with another syringe a few drops from the patient. The microscope was placed on a windowsill in the Theatre, two drops from each syringe placed on the slide and gently mixed together with a small needle.

Slide on the microscope, my eye to the eyepiece, the mirror to shine light up through the blood mix. Waiting. Breath-holding. Two minutes, three, four, five. Joy! Relief! The huge numbers of tiny blood cells, pink in the light, were still happily mixed, each one discrete, no clumping together. Wonderful! A suitable donor found, as far as we could tell, without all the modern means of investigation.

Decision. We must try it. "Sister, a receiving vessel and a giving set please." "Hezekiah, tell the good granny we can use her blood, and pop her flat on a stretcher and trolley and bring her in."

Time was of the essence. Granny was brought near her unconscious granddaughter and one arm splinted for stability. A firm hand placed on the upper arm, engorging the veins. A long wide-bore needle pushed into a big vein at the elbow, a good flow of blood, dark red, into a suitable sterile vessel and a little patience until a pint was safely collected; out with the needle, a firm pad and bandage to the arm and a hot sweet drink for the donor.

Tabitha's arm quickly bandaged on to a padded splint, the giving set with bottle, tubing and needle now to hand, the blood transferred to bottle, air bubbles in tube eliminated, and the needle pushed, not without difficulty into a thin, collapsed vein. A little clamp on the tube adjusted to provide a steady, rapid drip of blood drops visible in the glass connection. An hour later the procedure was over, her pulse was strengthening and slowing and breathing was easier. The patient's eyes opened to find granny holding her hand and a return to the ward followed, the relatives outside the theatre expressing relief. Two sat beside Tabitha as she relapsed soon into peaceful slumber, the nurses checking her pulse frequently, with Sister carefully overseeing their work and the patient's condition.

Everything progressed well. From fluids only at first, a little food was allowed and tolerated. Normal diet followed. The drainage tube revealed no sign of internal leakage and was soon removed. Stitches and clips came out and before long our patient could try her legs and toddle happily past the closed doors of the Theatre and down the corridor for exercise. Family delighted, children dancing! Two more weeks passed, making a total stay of one month.

It was with joy that we wished her "God speed" as she walked down to the market place to find a lorry for a happy home going.

What can a third world hospital do?

Are you answered yet?

Who are you?

Ants and a Lovely Football

As a youngster wielding a high-pressure hosepipe to help a friend's father in Lincolnshire to clear up the interior of his chicken house, I became temporarily seized by the idea of returning on retirement to Somerset to a chicken farm. In preparation therefore I thought, in tropical Ilesha, that to keep hens would be a useful sideline to medical skills and bought a dozen Rhode Islands from the Moor Plantation of Ibadan.

They would need a compound of course with wire netting. No problem. And also a hen house. Being enthusiastic I began to plane a 12-foot plank, 12 inches wide and 1 inch thick, of solid iroko timber. Have you ever tried? It's a difficult grain, and hard heavy wood. After completing one side and two edges I begged the help of the hospital carpenter, who laboriously finished the job: 12-feet long, 4-feet wide, 4-feet high, one long perch, and marvellous to relate, 12 nesting boxes, 12 inches square, more or less!

I've already mentioned that the hens taught me tricks about being matey and only using two or three of the nesting boxes for laying their much-prized eggs. I learnt, if a little late!

I taught them a wee lesson too. The poles supporting the wire surround to their compound were stuck of course into the ground. "Money for jam," said huge numbers of white ants, as they attacked the built in provender. "Grub for my fowls," said I pulling up stick after stick and offering their lower ends, loaded with luscious white ants to the eager hens, a useful source of extra protein for them. Well-fed fowls, bigger and better eggs!

White ants were a pestilence, prepared to eat all except iroko wood and metal. At risk was the Senior Doctor's house that was built of pinewood and brought out from England. When my colleague and his wife were on furlough I was deputed to care for their bungalow. On one occasion I found that white ants had climbed up a series of wooden boxes in the store beneath the house, and, finding that these were touching the house floor, they rapidly progressed upwards to discover very edible roof rafters, and gorged themselves happily. How to end the invasion? I was not at all sure but finding a good supply of sulphur in my hospital store, and being aware of its poisonous fumes when burning into sulphur dioxide, I put a tablespoon or so into a series of saucers, placed them about the house, set them alight, and departed hastily. So did the ants, those surviving, and the roof also survived.

As stated elsewhere, other ants of the same species found my precious carpentry tools in my bungalow store and took revenge for their comrades by devouring the soft wood handles of the chisels, saws, planes and screwdrivers. Some you win, some you lose! Among the latter I was pained to discover that in the garden one morning, having been left there overnight by my daughter to whom I had given him, was the demolished corpse of my childhood's very precious teddy bear! Alas!

Of black ants and their ferocity you may read elsewhere in this narrative, we respected them but were wary of their presence, as they crossed the compound in long straight lines like Roman soldiers. We left them alone.

The little sweet cakes made by our cook and served on our iroko side tables we gobbled up at tea time, after tapping them first to inform the tiny sugar loving ants of our intentions. They hopped off like paratroopers and left our sweetmeats to their owners. Live and let live!

Our hospital was the only institution in Ilesha to have at that time, all-night electric lights in the buildings and above the main pathways. At certain seasons swarms of flying ants would emerge from holes in the ground and perform a nuptial dance in the air flying around the lights in huge numbers.

This occurred at night of course. The ants would descend, becoming thick on the ground, shedding their wings, and townsfolk would enter the compound to collect them in handfuls, carrying them off triumphantly to be fried and eaten as a most acceptable protein addition to their morning breakfast. If I was called to the hospital at night I would sometimes view this happy cull of the flying ants with much interest.

However ants were not the chief reason for our presence in Ilesha. Even more interesting were the people whose humanity was troubled by illness or sometimes just bodily abnormalities that they regarded with fear or disfavour.

One such in the latter category was a Yoruba woman of middle age who had endured a large abdominal lump for very many years, probably from infancy I judged, and had at last been persuaded by her husband, family or friends, to see if a cure could be effected. No doubt local medicine men had been consulted, and perhaps a big worm or some evil spirit had been suggested as the cause of her annoying possession. No doubt some nasty medicine had been given, swallowed or red pepper unguent massaged into it, to no effect certainly.

It was with some trepidation that she presented herself on a hot afternoon in our O.P. consulting room, and hesitantly announced her desire for help. Examination revealed to my astonishment, an umbilical hernia that approached the size of a small football, not all that small either! She was assured that we would try to help her and Hezekiah, clerk and operating assistant, gave her the little record card bearing the letters T.C.I. (to come in) and directed her to the Female Ward, while I watched her going off happily and wondered when and how to effect that help. Sister and nurses welcomed the patient, admitted and made her comfortable and admired, goggle eyed, the offending object. Perhaps a junior nurse shifted out of sight behind a door to indulge in a little giggle.

Next day there entered into the compound another woman, driven in an elegant car, a lady, whose appearance surely matched the elegance of her vehicle. An English lady, slim of ankle and trim of figure, pleasant of feature with brown eyes and carefully waved hair to match, with charming smile and the mien of one accustomed to command, graciously, her fellow workers.

One might well suppose her to perform a leading role in the Shakespeare theatre as Portia delivering justice to Shylock, but we discovered that such was far from the case. The theatre was certainly her chief habitat, but it was a theatre where she would stand beside a table whereon lay the silent form of one who was connected by mask and tubing to a machine bearing bottles of anaesthetic and cylinders of gas and oxygen. Around her would stand Theatre Sister and capped and gowned nurses and operating assistants with trolleys bearing surgical instruments gleaming in bright light. Her eyes, over her facemask, would be watching for the nod of the anaesthetist, and one slim gloved hand would be raised holding a scalpel….

She was indeed a surgeon of considerable repute, touring Nigeria and visiting hospitals, mission and government, and other medical institutions, bush dispensaries and so forth, and had now arrived, by prior arrangement to have a critical look at our little hospital in the bush. My wife welcomed her warmly, making her comfortable with the inevitable cup of tea and scones baked by herself in the cook's wood-fired oven. Our guest was introduced to our pet antelope, Bambi, who was accustomed to leap out of the chicken enclosure and mount the steps to join the party. She admired also our chameleon perched in frozen attitude upon a branch of a houseplant, its two eyes rolling in fascinating manner in different directions.

From the talk of natural wonders conversation moved towards medical matters and included a request from her to have a look at our hospital. I agreed of course and shortly we proceeded up the path to Sister's office. Sister likewise made her welcome, and led the way along the wide covered corridor to the Male Ward. Conversation here suddenly quietened. Nurses quickly straightened uniforms and stood still. Patients looked surprised at the unusual sight of a European woman; did they suspect that doctor had taken another wife? Her name? Memory fails, sadly. But to me in my obvious admiration of so charming a visitor she will always be Lady Portia F.R.C.S.

We passed along the beds, one man with a fractured leg, a femur perhaps, suspended on a Thomas' Splint from a wooden Balkan beam. Another with a tube draining a liver abscess, several post operative hernia patients, others fighting malaria, pneumonia, typhoid fever or a large abscess of the thigh draining its contents away. Some smiled and gave her a Yoruba greeting to which she responded with a smile and the Yoruba "Adupe O" (Thank you).

Across to the Maternity Ward where some of the mothers were ensconced, with treasure cots at the foot of their beds. Several of the 'treasures' were sleeping peacefully and others were being breast fed by their obviously happy mothers. One mother did not look happy, and one cot was sadly empty. Our guest smiled at them all and gently touched the hand of the sad woman.

Along the corridor to the Children's Ward upstairs. Here we found mothers lying on the floor beside cots of very ill children, some malarial, some dysenteric, some with chest infections and a few playing a game together. Our guest enquired how we managed to treat those very malnourished and obviously Kwashiorkor subjects, and understood our difficulties. Kwashiorkor was indeed a dreadful trouble occurring in so many small children due to dietary deficiency when their mothers stopped breast-feeding. As already stated a lack of protein was the result. All we could offer was milk in the form of powered Klim and water. Often they were too far-gone to manage digestion and absorption of it, and just deteriorated before our eyes.

The Female Ward lay below the Children's Ward, and patients and nurses were happy to see our lady visitor. Nurse introduced her to several folk and they touched hands, smiling. We approached our lady with the football, and I wondered how this would be viewed, and perhaps our surgeon would like to take on the job!

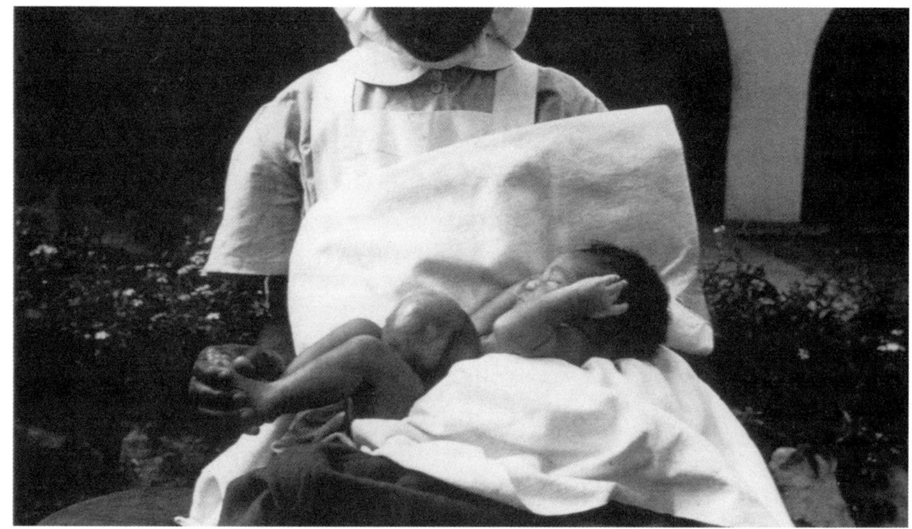

A football with a baby
(Umbilical hernia)

"Good gracious," she said, "What have you got here?" Nurse pulled back the cover to reveal our latest prize pathological specimen. Our visitor's eyes opened wide and "What a beauty!" was her delighted reaction.

She examined the monstrous object, and clapped her hands.

"Oh! I'd love to have a go at that!" she said.

"Well, tomorrow is operating day" I replied, "be my guest."

"I'm awfully sorry doctor, but I can't possibly. I have another appointment at X hospital."

She mentioned a town 170 miles away. It wasn't possible of course.

"Perhaps you could give me a few ideas about the needful operation?"

"Yes, I'd be glad to do that."

After supper we went into serious discourse, and very useful ideas indeed were passed on to me.

Our guest left soon after breakfast - lovely grapefruit straight from the tree, guinea-corn cereal with Klim milk, toast and English marmalade. I turned my steps to the Operating Theatre, and between operations told Sister about the ideas for dealing with our patient with the football. We fixed a date and asked nurse to tell the patient. Such joy! What excitement when the relatives came to visit and heard the glad news of a hopeful cure! Whenever not needed in the hospital I opened the pages of my operative surgery textbook to seek for detailed advice on the nitty- gritty of hernia surgical procedure. I discovered, as suspected, that the eminent writer did not discuss footballs. Not his cup of tea!

The patient was prepared the day prior to the operation. The skin of abdomen and the hernia were scrubbed, washed and dried. The skin painted with Bonney's Blue and sterile towels to cover the area were bandaged in position. This was all repeated the next morning. An injection was given; the patient placed onto stretcher and brought to the Theatre. A prayer was said by a nurse in Yoruba asking for wisdom and guidance, and all was ready. A spinal anaesthetic was administered to the patient, already drowsy from injections. Sterile towels were applied around the 'football'. Sister gave the 'all clear'.

Scalpel and artery forceps in plenty lay ready to hand. Needles curved, round-bodied and cutting type lay beside glass ampoules of 'catgut' of different thickness. One ampoule had the words 'Kangaroo tendon' inscribed on the glass. It seemed quite appropriate for the job of holding tissues together to close so large a hole. I had found it lying forgotten in an old wooden cupboard in the theatre adjunct.

An incision was needed on each side of the hernia, a rather large area on the anatomy of so small a lady. The intestinal content of her hernial sac was persuaded to retreat within the abdominal cavity, the large hernial sac was removed - chopping with garden shears would have been appropriate - and the business of repair could begin.

At this stage the advice of our visitor surgeon was found most useful, and acted upon gladly. Soon the peritoneal edges of the wound could be sewn together with fine catgut. Then the deep fascia and fascia not so deep - strong layers of tissue enclosing the front muscles of the abdomen - were brought together in suitable apposition using the ampoule of 'Kangaroo tendon'. Hopefully this arrangement would ensure no breakdown of the wound when stresses and tensions occurred. Several strong black sutures and a long row of skin clips completed the job, with a pleasantly tidy result. Dressings and a good abdominal binder to give extra support, and the wheeled stretcher returned her to the ward. Waiting relatives were overjoyed to see her, murmuring excitedly. Joy was in the patient's face when, having emerged from her drowsy state to full consciousness, her two hands, seeking information found, for the first time for years, a nice flat tummy! Others in the ward joined in handclapping and little songs were sung!

All went well and a fortnight later Comfort, for that was her name, was toddling up and down the main hospital corridor, a lovely big grin on her face, patting her new abdomen, and showing her long scar to an admiring audience of other folks' relatives visiting the wards.

Soon afterwards, healed and happy, Comfort toddled down the long dusty road to Ilesha market place to catch a lorry to her village and her home.

Nice to record a happy outcome –

Next Patient Please!

CHAPTER 18

Tetanus et Alia

The door of our lecture theatre opened to quiet strains of the favourite 'Alexander's Rag Time Band' accompanied by gentle foot taps, hand slaps, humming, whistling from the student mob as the owner of that famous name entered quietly. He smiled as he looked appreciatively round the hundred odd merry young faces and approached his lectern. He waved his hand in graceful acknowledgement of the customary tribute. As the song died away he placed his notes on the desk before him, inclined his head politely to the women students nearby and announced the subject of his morning lecture. Always a popular tutor, a much respected teacher of medical subjects, the student crowd held him in high regard, and rightly so.

Years passed and the students of that year separated to whatever the future held for them in those years of war and peace. In Ilesha, Nigeria, I was sitting with my wife in an afternoon siesta out of the blazing sun, our children playing quietly on the wide veranda of our bungalow. The sound of a car's approach alerted us and we waited as it rounded the house corner and stopped at the bottom of the steps leading to the veranda. The steps' hand rails were covered with the lovely flowers of Morning Glory, mixed with masses of tiny pink flowers making a charming and welcoming sight to the visitor.

From the car, ascending the steps, hand outstretched in greeting who should enter our mission station hide-out in the depths of tropical Nigeria but the self same tutor of bygone student years!

What a surprise! And what a welcome we gave him! Yes, he could stay for a night or two on his round of many places in several countries of Africa, where he was researching less frequent tropical diseases and would be glad to have a look around our hospital in the 'bush'.

Over a cup of tea and a piece of sponge cake, carefully tapping the cake to remind the sugar loving tiny ants to jump off before being eaten alive, he indicated that he was particularly interested in cases of tetanus and the treatment and survival of its victims. I told him that we had such a patient in one of our isolation rooms, but whether our rather primitive record system could help in revealing information and statistics regarding patients over previous years I was unable to say. I sent a message to James Balogun, our head clerk, (we only had two!) asking if such information was possible. His years of service at the hospital were invaluable in such matters.

We went to look at Amos, quietly, thankfully asleep under heavy sedation, well isolated. Amos was a farmer, and like many such in the tropics he was obliged from time to time to clear his land for growing his crops when his present soil had become less fertile. It was hard work involving the cutting down of trees, mostly small, but occasionally larger trees, when help from friends would be needed or even from professional fellers of good timber. But mostly they were trees and bushes less than twenty feet in height whose branches were chopped, bundled up and carried home for firewood by family and friends.

Of course, at times when thus occupied small accidents would occur. Abrasions, lacerations from falling branches, small penetrating injuries from sharp broken ends would need bandaging, sometimes with native medicine applications. Amos did quite well suffering only minor tears and scratches. He cleaned his new paths of land, digging out roots of small trees and bushes and making bonfires.

The time for planting came and he planted maize, guinea-corn, yam, cassava and tomatoes and so on, his wife and children helping, as they were able.

Resting one evening he became aware that his neck moved slowly and stiffly. This continued for a few days and arm and leg muscles were stiff and slow too. He thought it was the result of all the vigorous farming work, until one morning he had a sudden involuntary clamping of jaw muscles with violent and painful neck muscle contraction. This relaxed after a little while but when someone touched him or spoke loudly there was an immediate and violent response with the arching of the back and immensely strong contraction of the muscles of limbs and abdomen and chest. Breathing was difficult. Face muscles were drawn into a nasty grin, the typical rictus of tetanus infection.

What agony he endured during the transport by lorry or kit-car to our hospital could hardly be described. At some time 6 or 8 weeks previously he must have had a deepish penetration of his leg or foot perhaps by a sharp woody splinter, possibly a bit dirty from contact with the soil or animal faeces. The spores of the tetanus germ were carried in. The small wound healed, the spores developed into adult bacteria, enough to produce the dangerous toxins that would cause these awful spasms. No sign of injury was found. We possessed no supplies of anti-tetanus serum. Medically, all we could do was to provide, by injection, powerful painkillers and heavy sedatives with appropriate nursing care. This we did and eventually the patient slept. We watched him silently; glad to be protected from so awful a disease by the tetanus injections before we set sail for Africa.

After inspecting the hospital facilities we ambled back to the bungalow where my wife and her cook had a meal waiting for us. There was much talk of things medical, things African and reminiscences of Auld Reekie. The night was peaceful, crickets singing, fireflies flitting, and engine thudding reliably. No emergencies.

Next morning our visitor felt that he should get going on his itinerary, but not before James, our faithful clerk, came with good news. He had found records of tetanus cases treated over the years, wonderful! The results revealed that half of the sufferers had survived to return home, far better than might be expected. "You've made my day," said our old tutor as he stepped aboard his transport and waved goodbye.

A message from him some weeks later told us that our results were at least as good as those of the big hospitals with their anti-tetanus serum. That made our day!

What fun injections are! As I write the intense furore of the MMR jab is waging to the great joy of the media, and causing my mind to slip back in time. First to the day when in the waiting hall at Bristol Royal Infirmary my children shrieked frantically in anticipation of their fearful torture, a tiny needle prick to save their lives from the Yellow Fever of the tropics. I'm sure the roof rose up a little and made a gentle dust to fall and settle on the sterile instruments! Then to the day in Ilesha when we learnt that H.M.G. would provide free Yellow Fever inoculation for the town's citizens. There were shrieks of joy as the Ilesha populace besieged our gates and crowded our Outpatients' Department.

Did some athletic types climb over the wall? Opening ampoules, rubbing skin with methylated spirit, jabbing in the needles, all was received with delight by the town's folk, who of course had no idea of the nature of the treatment. But free injections! Manna from heaven! They pushed, pulled, climbed to reach that wonderful needle! In despair we called for the local police. They came flourishing batons and creating even more chaos. We told them to go away! We were quite thankful when the supply of vaccine was exhausted and some degree of normality was restored.

Yellow Fever is caused by viruses carried by the mosquito, injected into human tissue when it pushes its needle like proboscis into the skin to collect a dose of blood for its dinner! Symptoms develop in less than a week varying from a headache and fever to far more serious symptoms including jaundice, kidney failure, coma and death. Vast numbers of people could be affected, both African and European, and many were the graves dug to accommodate the fatalities. Yet just a needle prick every ten years would protect.

At Ilesha we saw none of it. I felt fortunate to have been vaccinated in 1942 with no side effects, and often wished that such a useful protection were available against the highly prevalent malaria. A report in the British Medical Journal on February 2002 records that several persons vaccinated against Yellow Fever were known to have died within two weeks following an illness, which included symptoms suggestive of the disease. As the vaccine has been used to my knowledge for 60 years very safely and advantageously maybe a different virus caused the illness. Without doubt the risks of Yellow Fever are vastly greater than the risks of the vaccine.

The same might be said of smallpox, now a thing of the past, thanks to the vaccination campaign of the World Health Organisation, who declared in 1997 that the disease had been eradicated. No longer will it happen, as I well remember, that a man admitted to the ward in the Wesley Guild Hospital with high fever, headaches and extremely ill, should be given urgent anti-malarial treatment and next morning found to be covered with the dreadful rash of smallpox. A nurse came running to me bearing the fearful news on a note from the hand of Sister. The emergency of the steps taken to obtain smallpox vaccine in quantity can be imagined. A journey to Lagos hospital was imperative. We were successful and every patient and all staff were vaccinated. A small hospital under the care of the local council received the afflicted patient, but of his subsequent fate we had no information.

The malarial parasite presents a different story. The life of this little chap involves humanity and the female mosquito of the genus *Anopheles*. Growing in the mosquito and being injected in its saliva into the human tissue when the lady mossy needs a dose of good rich blood, it happily develops, multiplies and in 10 days or so produces a malarial attack in its host: fever, shivering, headaches and body ache. Treatment with anti-malarial drugs can be a rapid and effective cure although the wily little parasite can develop resistance to one drug after another, and is not always easily done away with. There are three forms of the parasite and one, the malignant type, can be extremely dangerous. Very many people especially children in tropical climes lose their lives every year to the unpleasant 'bug'. Three million such annually would not be an over-statement. Going abroad? Take your anti-malarial pill precisely as instructed. Malaria is not a joke. Your life is precious.

Think you know better? Think the anti-mosquito sprays in a big Boeing or other aircraft will kill mossies lurking therein after a stop in a malarial area? You hope so certainly, but can you be certain? If not, could their next victim be you? Be advised; take that pill (note – see Chapter 11).

One day when we went to commence a ward round with Sister in our hospital I was approached by a very smart young Yoruba man, well dressed, well spoken, who asked if, as a Public Health Inspector he might have a look at our hospital and compound. Permission was granted of course and a ward porter was appointed to show him round. Half an hour later he returned saying, "Yes, Doctor, all very nice indeed. But did you know that you are growing mosquito larvae in the water tank behind the Infant Welfare building?" Astonishment! Horror! I was unaware of the existence of such a tank, and went with him urgently to inspect. A 44-gallon drum fed by piping from the roof gutters and full of rain water was happily providing sanctuary for huge numbers of larvae all poking their spiracles through the water surface to collect their needed supply of air! On our approach and at a tap on the drum they dived for cover! A pipe through the wall supplied the nurses with water for bathing the babies. On my enquiry, "Oh yes, Doctor," they said, "we often have a few mosquito larvae coming through the tap."

Well you can't win them all, but this time when the Inspector suggested, "a few drops of oil Doctor?" I felt we had put an enemy to flight and was grateful. Oil on water of course increases the surface tension and defeats the spiracles in their search for air. My bungalow was near that tank, (the other side of our tennis court), and the prevailing breeze would waft the insects straight to me! So it was oil on the water, and the bottom of the 44-gallon tank was shortly covered with the corpses of mosquito larvae!

No wonder I knew about malaria… Take that pill!

CHAPTER 19

Running, Driving, Scalpel and Spanners Up Front

Normally attention to one's duties at the hospital was taken at an ordinary walking pace. There was time to notice details that needed attention: water pipes that required adjustment, roof guttering alterations, and engine oil and fuel stocks to be replenished; that quite persistent red pepper plant which stoutly resisted the gardener's efforts (decidedly half-hearted) to remove it; a couple of red peppers which I had plucked absentmindedly en route to the operating theatre one morning, proved intensely irritating when, gloved and gowned I suffered their itchy and burning effects in my trouser pocket. Alas when I was warm and perspiring in the midst of a tricky operation not even Sister could be of service! Of course one could not hurry the operation, though the desire was certainly present!

But sometimes there was need for haste. I know of no more urgent demand for speed than when, as I unhurriedly descended my house steps, a nurse, running wildly from the hospital met me with the breathless message, "The Sister wants the doctor in Maternity". No "Please, Doctor", no note, no decorum. Action this minute! My steps would change to a rapid run; hat dropping and stethoscope flapping round my neck. If Sister wanted help, urgent attention could be vital to a mother or child or both.

Sometimes a breech presentation, sometimes a reluctant placenta, sometimes a pre-natal or post-natal haemorrhage, perhaps a foetal heart badly out of order and Caesarean Section indicated rapidly, or maybe just a helpful forceps delivery. The rest of the hospital could wait; Maternity took priority.

Eighty-five miles east of Ilesha, towards the Niger River, at Ikole we had established a 12 bed maternity hospital as a valuable addition to the existing dispensary and had appointed Sister Louie Trott and one of our trained nurses to cope with the undoubted demand, and help the already present trained nurse from Ilesha. Both proudly wore the badge of the Wesley Guild on their neat uniforms. Every month a doctor from Ilesha visited by car, calling at other dispensaries en route and attending to patients gathered by the nurse in charge of each. Mothers brought children with faces disfigured by yaws for intravenous injections into tiny veins; folk with leg ulcers, sores, wounds, chest infections, worms of all kinds, hernias to be directed to hospital; folk with many varied troubles attended.

Sister Trott gets light at Ikole

A monthly trip was due. On a gloriously sunny morning the hospital car, serviced by our mechanic and loaded to capacity with boxes of medicine bottles and medical paraphernalia for the hospital at Ikole, stood ready for action. Our clerk, Hezekiah, ever smart and efficient (later to become manager of the hospital at Ilesha) would accompany me for the journey. Along the laterite road, quite well serviced by the P.W.D. we made good progress through shaded woodland regions, and running from there into bright sunny areas. Often huge swarms of butterflies sunning themselves on the warm earth road would rise and dissipate before the approaching car, and occasionally a snake, disturbed from its warm slumber would slither rapidly to safety. Up hill, down dale around many corners tree-shaded, over little bridges, being careful to locate the front wheels on the double planks awaiting them, else disaster could easily occur, we sped from village to village to their dispensaries, welcomed by nurses and patients as we progressed through the day's heat. At each village with a dispensary we dealt with the little crowd of folk collected by the resident nurse for doctor's attention.

A night's rest 60 miles along the way with our missionary friend, Jonah, where he ran a training school for young teacher students, and on to meet our Sister Louie after a dispensary stop at Ijero, 15 miles towards Ikole where we found our efficient nursing colleague in spirited form as ever.

There was dispensary work with the waiting patients, a minor operation on a hand infection, and a good meal and exchange of stories and information.

Time to leave and return before nightfall. Waving goodbye I noted in the car mirror a more than usually vigorous wave, frantic in fact, from Sister. I stopped. Running, she laid a hand on the car door. "I think you'd better come back, John," she said "it could be a Caesarean". I returned. It was. And on the table in the labour room Sister gave the patient an anaesthetic. Hezekiah most efficiently assisted, and soon the baby was delivered safely. All was well, and we waved goodbye again. Great fun in the Third World!

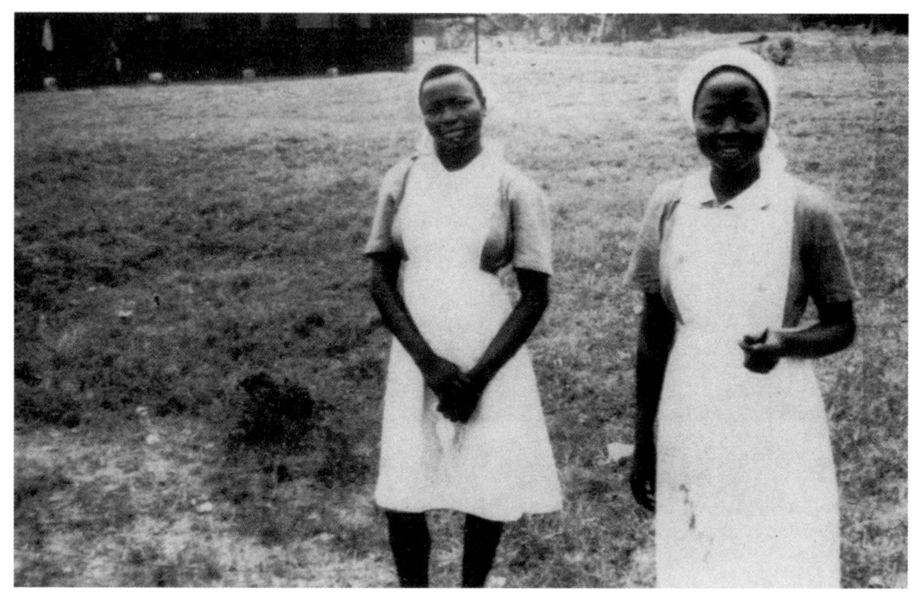

Ilesha Midwives at Ikole

Returning we passed the villages where cooking fires were sending up quiet plumes of smoke, pleasantly perfumed. Night fell with moon and stars brilliant and challenging our headlights as they picked out the road. The open windows allowed the incessant chirruping of crickets to massage our eardrums for many miles until the oil lamps of Ilesha market stalls told of our approach to the waiting Wesley Guild Hospital. There were greetings from the night watchman at the gate, and welcomes from the staff. No waiting emergencies, and after a meal and later a night round of the hospital, the duty nurses kindly wished me a "Happy night's rest".

Of course, I must not disappoint my more mechanically minded readers, who might find tales of endless medical matters not entirely to their taste. Elsewhere I described my fortunate encounter with our Ifaki blacksmith, vigorous of arm but entirely bereft of lower limbs due to polio when a child of four years. Elsewhere I mentioned a gold miner friend and French engineer who came to our rescue when our diesel failed, and our Muslim electrician who taught me the business of wet drooping palm leaves and short circuiting palaver! But occasionally my own expertise, or lack of it in mechanical matters, was called into question.

Again it was at Ikole, and Sister Trott who after providing an excellent dinner accompanied by a delightful story and information swapping, just happened to mention as I was letting in my clutch to depart that the brakes on her car "didn't seem to work very well"!

I stepped on mine, said, "Oh dear!" and searched our boot for a bag of tools. Why do ladies always retail their woes at the eleventh hour, or later? Success rewarded my search. Spanners, and screwdriver, car jack and stout gloves were to hand. At least I knew the secret of removing a wheel and proceeded to jack up Sister's little car, the make and vintage of which I forget. The instruction manual was helpful. I identified the brake drum and took it off, unscrewed a couple of screws perhaps? Then there were things called 'shoes' in the diagram, held by powerful springs that I at last removed, praying that I'd be able to get them back on again. There was a cylinder with bits of rubber and oil too; it looked tatty and in need of a clean. So I did something about that as well. All four wheels were involved; did I do them all? Memory fails. But when all the bits were together again I found in the handbook something about pumping the brake pedal and expelling air until oil emerged, is that right? And something about a master cylinder? All very complicated. The human body I found much more simple! Testing the car afterwards proved satisfactory. To my astonishment the brakes worked nicely. The spanner job was equal to the scalpel!

It was a late return to base, but village fires were busily smoking, crickets and frogs singing and croaking as we cheerfully sped through the cooler air of night. They made music to relieve and soothe the mind and body. The sisters had been a little concerned at our late return, and my night round of the hospital was late indeed, but things in all wards were well controlled and again the nurses' nightly wish of "May you have a happy night's rest, Doctor," was most welcome.

As I reduced the voltage on the engine switchboard I thought of Sister's brakes at Ikole and hoped that they would behave as she sped over hill and vale to relieve the troubles and distress in her Ikole parish. All credit to Louie Trott in her lonely outpost.

Keeping Down the Grass and Goat Trouble

A 'cutting-grass' was an implement, which did what its name implied. It cut grass. A strip of then iron, one inch by twenty, with a wooden handle bound on at one end, its edge sharpened by rubbing on a stone, wielded by a vigorous arm, controlled the lush grass between hospital buildings and staff houses most effectively. With such tools our garden boys created a neat and pleasant grassy compound.

Outside the hospital quarters, two roads bounding the compound, merged into one, which led to the town of Ilesha. Houses, solid mud-walled jobs with stout iroko doors and corrugated iron roofs lined the roads and the occupants doubtless observed and noted our gardening procedures. These folk kept chickens, a goat or two, and often a dog to eat up offal and rubbish. These were mainly fed on food scraps and corn but goats were very fond of grass. The owners, wise folk, awake at cockcrow, often quietly urged their goats into the hospital compound, so helping the garden boys to keep the grassy areas tidy with less labour. But the goats did not confine their diet to the plentiful grass. By no means! Flowerbeds attracted them, especially those planted with roses that delighted the hearts of doctor's wives and Sisters. Prickles were no trouble to goats when they could munch roses!

Now my wife loved her rose bed and cultivated it with joy and care. The observant eyes of a well-qualified nurse and midwife, for so she was, did not fail to spot the raiders of her lost flowers. She laid in wait successfully and ambushed two of the culprits, and, with strings around their necks, led them to the hospital mortuary, fortunately unoccupied at the time, and therein she incarcerated those criminals!

A message was circulated outside the hospital gates to the effect that upon payment of a fine, sixpence for each goat, their owners could collect these monsters. There was no immediate response.

Peace resumed, for a time, and later darkness fell. That night there emanated from the mortuary sounds as of souls in torment. Dante's Inferno had nothing on this; moaning, shrieking, weird wailing rising and falling, breaking out in a crescendo, shattered the peace of the compound. The noises came and went horribly, unceasingly. That night's sleep was woefully disturbed until morning light eased the howling!

After breakfast our steward announced that two ladies from outside the gate wished to speak with my wife. They were so sorry for the goat's depredations, they hoped we were well, they appreciated the hospital's good work, but their goats were part of their livelihood. They knelt down; it was very dramatic, "We have no money, you are our Father and Mother, please will you return our animals to us…" They humbly begged and entreated; if humble entreaty could not make my wife relent the thought of another night of infernal horror most certainly did. The goats were duly released to the care of their two owners and with happy smiles and protestations of gratitude they led away the offending creatures; doubtless not heeding the warnings given regarding repetition of their naughtiness - whose?

We strongly suspected that the ladies were market women who made a good income from selling to the Sisters every morning food supplies for the hospital kitchen. We had made our point, but it was they who had won the battle!

CHAPTER 20

Trekking, by Wheels

The Doctor's monthly trek (by car) to Ifaki and Ikole gave us some moments of interest and experience of not too hazardous a nature. On my first expedition thither our senior Sister, Stella Liony, was anxious to visit Rev E.J. Jones (Jonah) at Ifaki, 60 miles distant, where he ran a teacher training school as well as being in charge of church and village out stations. We coped well with the usual dispensary work en route, giving injections for yaws and the old M&B 693 for gonorrhoea, *et alia*, and in the evening after a pleasant tea party with Jonah, Stella wished to visit the Church Missionary Society Hospital at Ado-Ekiti, some 25 miles distant. Off we went, the light fading rapidly. This was my first experience of wooden bridges over small streams some six feet below. There was no warning, no sides to the bridges, simply stout iroko planks laid across a well-built trestle, and a pair of planks, parallel, laid lengthwise over them. The whole structure was level with the road, and lucky was the driver, coming unknowingly up to them, who succeeded in getting his front wheels plum in the centre of the planks. When wet, the headlights indicated the danger only when we were rather too close for comfort.

The hospital was rather small with a Sister in charge, but no doctor. The ladies enjoyed a good yarn together. A few years later when visiting Ikole there was brought an unfortunate man with a strangulated inguinal hernia whom I drove to this hospital having given him a dose of morphia. He had suffered for five days, but one had to try, and the sister prepared the Ado operating theatre. Anaesthetic - yes, but no intravenous fluid was available. For light only two Tilley lamps, which attracted flies from the bush through open, unglazed, un-proofed windows. Not an easy one was this hernia, and despite successful operation the patient, to nobody's surprise, succumbed during the night. Hernias going bad on their owner in the far bush were often a death sentence. Sometimes relief of pain was all that could be given and for him that must have been an unexpected bonus after his five days of despair.

*_*_*_*_*_*_*_*_*_*_*_*

A return from Ikole was somewhat dependent on the weather, and on one occasion my clerk and I, when only fifteen miles from home came across a large tree lying straight across the road, its trunk over two feet thick. A big lorry laden with timber joists 12 feet long and 3 by 4 inches wide was in front of us facing the tree. What to do? On the other side of the tree two lorries were waiting, drivers content to wait until the Public Works Department brought equipment to saw the tree into logs and clear the road, the normal custom. However I had a hospital waiting my return.

I found a driver who was also an owner and said, "Why not use your timber to make a ramp on each side of the tree? Then we can drive over it." I added that if any of the joists were damaged the hospital would buy them; we could always use good iroko or mahogany. He agreed and in due course two good ramps were created. He revved his engine, climbed the ramp, scattered some joists, and crossed over the top and down the other side. Applause! Clever driver!

We repaired the ramp and I persuaded the long low Oldsmobile to try its luck. Up we went and front wheels surmounted ramp and tree. But alas, I had forgotten that its clearance was far less than the lorry's. We were stuck, and were lucky indeed to be able to reverse down the pile, helped by plenty of good manpower. To go any further upward and forward was impossible. Sympathetic noises from the helpful lorry drivers! I had no option but to turn back, and, like the Wise Men avoiding Herod, I returned another way. Some miles back a road led off to the village of Esa-oke, the same being fourteen miles from Ilesha. We took it and found en route a ten-mile switchback of short, steep little hills needing power and brakes to negotiate successfully. Along this road a loud crack was heard beneath the car. Investigation revealed an intensely hot, nearly red-hot brake drum - alas! However we arrived at the hospital safely and found that Sister had been able to deal with Outpatients and the wards most competently, as usual. It took some time to acquire a new brake drum. Strange how often we were afflicted with loud noises underneath our vehicles!

Transport in Africa could be hazardous; thank goodness for friendly native folk. On another occasion Hezekiah and I suffered an engine failure on our way home in the evening. There was only one thing for it – a night in the car, with a couple of biscuits! Cramped and uncomfortable! Mosquitoes - blood sucking little brutes!

Next morning we waited, and after some hours a lorry came by and stopped. The driver kindly made room for me, while Hezekiah remained with the Oldsmobile. Again I was late for Outpatients. Again we needed the expertise of Momodu, our excellent mechanic to rescue Hezekiah and the car. All good fun! It must be said that our up-country treks were wont to disturb hospital outpatient clinics considerably, but for the distant village folk they were a boon.

More distant expeditions were seldom possible but on one Ikole trip my wife and the two girls came also. A visit to Louie Trott at Ikole was a real attraction after spending a night at Ifaki in Jonah's house. Louie was delighted and offered to care for the girls if Barbara and I wanted to visit the River Niger only some 50 miles further on. A good offer, too good to miss, and off we went.

The road was a good laterite job, with few hills and the country largely open. Coming across a pleasant stream some 4 feet in width we were thrilled to be able to indulge in a bathe. None to disturb us, and only a distant monkey who had not sufficient interest in a pair of white skinned humans to investigate! Cooled and rested we drove on to see the mighty Niger. The town of Lokoja stood by the river's edge, perhaps Mungo Park had made contact with it, hope he got past safely!

Near the river which flowed past in a huge flood of water, very wide and featureless, we found a well of water some 5 feet wide and perhaps 10 feet deep, with a foot or two of water at the bottom. It was home to somebody's crocodile. We had no desire for closer acquaintance and hastily retreated, to return, now warm and weary, to Louie and the children and a night's rest.

Journeys for medical conferences were a rarity indeed, but an occasion did arise once. Travelling east to the Niger again we were aiming for the Church Missionary Society Hospital at Onitsha on its east bank. Our accountant, Bill Mann from Lagos drove expertly part of the way, and I drove the rest, passing via Benin, where we rested over night. I found myself driving next day to the great river and on to a ferry to cross the half-mile width of water, which had come a huge distance from Sierra Leone, joined by other rivers en route. Applause greeted me from a collection of young Ibo lads on the other side as I reversed, fortunately on to dry land. I suspect that they were joyfully anticipating a European ducking himself and vehicle in the Niger's muddy waters. "Oh ho! Expert driver" was the cry. Looking at the wet alternative I was glad of being clever enough to back on to the dry solid land of eastern Nigeria.

Our day's conference at Onitsha was most enjoyable. It gave us a chance to meet the medical staff - a delightful lady doctor, and staff from Ituk Mbang hospital and Uzuakoli leper colony, with nursing sisters from each. Seldom could any of us afford the time away from our hospitals for so long and so far. The return journey was a long one. Arriving at Benin where we had booked a night's rest in the Guest House, we found it already occupied by folk who refused to give up their accommodation - pirates all! We would not argue and at 8 p.m. opted to continue to Ilesha, a further 180 miles. Bill drove expertly again. Somewhere on the road we spotted a sign 'Elephants crossing'; Bill ignored it. In the early hours we were glad to find beds at our own hospital and in our own home, a tiring adventure.

A Welcome Break

At the end of a tour of eighteen months or longer a break in home climate was essential after the hot, humid, exhausting conditions of the tropics. In the days of shipping journeys, the sea air and Biscay experience could be quite stimulating. However when followed by bus and train journeys in the UK to unknown town and country churches to talk about 'the work', overtired personnel could well find the so called 'furlough' very stressful. But what of a 'break' when on the 'coast'? A short absence from hospital routine and emergencies of day and night could only be beneficial. It was the middle of a two-year stint, and my colleague, Dr Jack Souster was available to do duty in my absence. Hurrah!

A day came when we packed up children and luggage and set off for the coast with James, our cook-steward, leaving our colleague in charge. A manager of the local branch of the United Africa Company had kindly arranged for us to borrow the U.A.C. holiday house at Tarkwa Bay. This was as a 'Thank you' for treatment of his troubles on the veranda of our house, the eight-foot width veranda gladly accommodating a bed. A night in Lagos, a little shopping at Kingsway stores, and we were ready for a canoe trip over the bright waters of the harbour to the long coconut planted island that faced the Bight of Benin. Our particular bay however was still within the protected harbour area. The trip went well, we paid the canoe man and moved our supplies into the capacious house, while the children rapidly donned bathing suits and rushed into the quiet, warm water of the bay. Only tiny wavelets and ripples disturbed its surface, while the sun's heat performed magic on the water, 80°F quite spoiled us. Soft golden sand, unmarked save for a host of little crabs who, spotting our ambling approach afar off, dug furiously, disappearing into the sand before we could reach them to say, "Hello".

It was an idyllic time, sea bathing, swimming, sun bathing, walking under the coconut palms, resting and reading, even trying to use a fishing net lent by a local fisherman. I only caught a hole in the net, and paid him five bob for the privilege.

On our first night James was lighting the Tilley lamps. A mistake, and petrol poured over his hand and forearm, catching alight immediately. Find a cloth, douse the flame quickly, but how to treat the burn was something of a dilemma. We were not prepared: no tannic acid, no treated gauze and no bicarbonate of soda. But my wife remembered that baking powder contained soda bicarbonate. So the arm and hand, duly cooled and wetted with fresh water was powdered very liberally with the cooking preparation, covered with a tea cloth and wrapped up. I think we gave him two aspirins. We spent the evening thinking of how to arrange a canoe for a trip to the mainland and the hospital. Morning came. James proudly displayed his damaged arm. The skin was perfect.

Our holiday was joyful. We drove back to Ilesha fit and well, and ready for work.

Fun With Wheels, Fractures, Ramadan, and Animals

My old headmaster, when told of my desire to switch from Classics to medicine efficiently changed my curriculum. Some years later he suggested that I talk to the school about the fun of being a medical missionary. That opportunity never arose, probably because of his retirement after all the excellent work he had done for all his pupils, educating them in mind and thought in so many ways. However the fun in my life remained and does so to this day: fun with diesels, generators and a Javelin; fun with antelopes, goats and a sad, sad donkey; fun with hens, squirrels and the flying species that bite.

What about a diesel or two? Having acquired our new generating plant it was up to us, the medics, to maintain its good health. Stocks of fuel in 44-gallon drums sat in good order on the covered veranda outside the engine house. But lubricating oil needed attention and at the appointed time I instructed our mechanic-driver Kekere to change the engine oil. He did so and cleaned up afterwards nicely.

That same evening after the lights came on with engine happily thudding away, my wife and I went to a dinner engagement with the District Officer, always a very pleasant change of scene. Conversation was of England and a cooler environment, moving as usual to Africa, chieftain palaver, house servants and cooks. The D.O.'s cook was a real treasure and the cooking was excellent. During the meal, as on another occasion, a message arrived per bicycle from Sister. (Why did Sister again choose to interrupt our dinner with the District Officer and his wife?) 'Dear Doctor' she wrote, 'the lights have gone out and the engine has stopped.' Maybe Sister's missives were becoming a habit but this sounded rather an awkward problem. Sister would rapidly organise Tilley lamps and hurricane lanterns, but the matter of getting the new engine restarted could require more expertise than a mere medic wielding a spanner could provide. Our local mechanics who liked to see a spark at the points were not acquainted with diesels, "Ah, ah! No spark at all, sah, 'ow 'e go?" Its operation was left alone by them, to the engine's benefit, as previously mentioned! As no medical emergency was involved we would finish our dinner, chat briefly and depart in a fairly leisurely manner.

I reported to Sister who had all the hospital affairs in good control; my wife returned to our bungalow and checked on the children whose baby-sitter, our steward, could now return home. I took myself a little apprehensively to the engine house. I stood in the doorway, appalled. There was oil, nearly black oil, everywhere. Engine and belts, floor and walls all drenched and spotted with it. Even the ceiling was not spared. Treading gingerly I unearthed the rubber gloves from a cupboard, picked up the big handle and tried to turn the flywheel, the big heavy two-foot diameter job, to no avail. I pressed harder - nothing. I invoked Shakespeare - "Budge," said I, "Budge not," said the flywheel - "Budge," said I - "Budge not," said the flywheel. "Budge." - "Budge not." I tried a Biblical quotation - "Go," said the Lord, - "Not go", said Moses, - "Go" - "Not go". I gave up. The engine was thoroughly immobile. I looked at our nice new engine helplessly and my eyes sought the oil-filling hole. There it was, wide open. But I noted that whereas the hole in the old engine was on a level portion of the engine body this one was on a slant. Each was closed by means of a thumbscrew. Evidently when changing the oil Kekere had not tightened the thumbscrew very tightly, and with the engine vibration the lid had worked loose. It was better not to envisage the horrid pulsing of black liquid oil that would ensue! I gave up and went home to dream of - I know not what.

Speaking to the District Officer next day he told me of the presence of a French engineer in town. “A good chap and excellent engineer if you can detach him from his bottle of whatever!” I heard him gladly and sent a message to the rest house hoping to catch monsieur. Monsieur was ‘at home’ and came, with a bottle!

Monsieur cottoned on very quickly. “I’ll be glad to help,” he said and brought an ample kit of tools from his car. “Have you got any spares?” he enquired. We were lucky. Our friendly engineer, when ordering the twin diesels from Lister’s included a comprehensive set of spares, pistons, rings and bearings and I was able to show them to monsieur who expressed his pleasure.

Quickly he dismantled the engine, carefully filed the roughened crankshaft, fitted bearings, piston and rings and pronounced it all as nearly new. Cleaning of belts and flywheels, generator wheel and belts, the bits and pieces, and all the walls floors and ceiling, - don’t mention it! Then all was ready for a trial run. All was satisfactory and our light was restored ready for the next emergency. Monsieur said it was his pleasure entirely and accepted another bottle. What fun!

*_*_*_*_*_*_*_*_*_*_*_*

Thinking of things mechanical the mind turns inevitably to transport. A further two years at Ilesha and I should, for family reasons, need to settle at home as a G.P. A car would be essential, and if taken overseas for two years much tax and duty would be avoided. I settled for a Jowett Javelin, a newcomer, a highly regarded flat four engine – a car ‘in advance of its time’ was the blurb. Having checked the tightness of every nut visible I took it with me for my last tour of duty. It seemed excellent, and I was happy to take the family both on local journeys and up country to Ikole when servicing the dispensaries.

One day in the dry season, my colleague remaining in charge of the hospital, I set forth with my wife in the Javelin to visit Shagamu, where we were invited to see the famed Mission Station of the Methodist Missionary Society. The road to Ibadan was dry, somewhat corrugated, but fairly maintained; a tarmac road for some miles, then east on an extremely rough corrugated road towards Shagamu. A badly rutted road with innumerable transverse ridges, busily used by lorry traffic loaded with humans or timber, very uncomfortable and bumpy. After some 12 miles came a sudden loud crack from beneath the car and the nearside dropped suddenly, nearly, but not quite, on to the wheels. Not a job for my customary spanner. Obviously some part of the suspension had given way, but what it was I could not determine.

The car could move, and very cautiously we returned to the main road (tarmac) and drove several miles to Abeokuta. A phone call to Lagos, the Jowett agent, and the instruction, "Bring the car to Lagos". We proceeded south, very slowly in the afternoon heat, glad to find shelter and welcome at the house of Bill and Dorothy Mann, our accountant and wise adviser in Lagos. He and I took the car to the Steiner's garage. Diagnosis – collapse of welding attaching the torsion bar to the car frame. Treatment – Good Welding!

We enjoyed the shopping expedition next day at Kingsway Stores and a late afternoon sail in *Bunty*, Bill's yacht, with a fish caught for supper and of course, the inevitable rubber of bridge with Steiner. The following day we collected the car, "Good as new, Doctor," and were relieved to hear that Jowett's would pay the bill. They'd had trouble in their welding department. The ride home was quick and trouble free, apart from a furious thunderstorm on approaching Ilesha, quite a terrifying business in a little car amid tall trees. But no trees fell, though the rain obscured the windscreen and progress was reduced to a crawl for a few milcs. It was good to be home, safe and sound, to find all well looked after and our children glad to see us.

Ramadan - Emergency!

Speaking of lorries, these were the chief means of transport in those days. Some six or seven backless forms placed transversely in the rear, occupied by people, their luggage, goats, sheep, dogs, fowls and children. The driver, if a Muslim, often displayed a notice above his cabin indicating that Allah would give protection. One hoped that the driver would also care for the needs of his brakes, tyres, petrol and water! And that he would drive with due care… It was Saturday, and during the ward round I had found 23 folk ready for discharge. By midday they had paid their bills and gone home. Those unable to meet their bills were, of course, excused.

All was peaceful. I took two steps down the concrete pathway outside the Theatre towards my house, and stopped. A lorry, nay two lorries, had come round the corner of the Outpatients' block and halted outside the Female Ward. They were packed with casualties, some walking, some needing stretchers and trolleys. There were groans and cries, there was blood and distorted limbs.

It was the beginning of Ramadan. Public Works Department workers on roads for miles around had boarded a lorry bound for Ilesha and home and feasting. The driver who had had previous accidents had been warned to take more care, but he still drove with too much abandon. Did he carry an 'Allah will care' notice or did he ensure that his brakes were efficient? I never knew. My job, and the hospital's, was to apply the required medical care as best we could.

The driver had tried to take a bend in the road over fast, and the lorry had tipped over, - an open backed lorry, and all the passengers had fallen out on heads, shoulders, hands, legs and knees.

I had discharged 23 patients that morning. The number needing admission amounted to 29. A multitude of injuries faced us and they needed to be quickly assessed for degrees of severity. An unconscious man with a depressed fracture of skull obviously came first, after which were deep cuts and lacerations with fine gravel in their depths, fractures of long bones, jaw, ribs and shoulder damage with widespread abrasions of same, face and scalp troubles, knees and elbows. The big sterilizer was set to work, an extra table set up in the Theatre, injections given and all due preparations made while doctors and sisters had a quick lunch. A message, "Can you help?" was taken by car to Ife, 20 miles away to the Seventh Day Adventist doctor. He was out but came later, and most welcome he was. Dr Souster was at home on furlough at that time.

My wife cleaned and stitched at one table while James, our laboratory expert, administered ether. I took the other, Sister ably operating the anaesthetic machine. For the depressed skull fracture - our trephine instrument was not the electrically powered drill but the very old fashioned thing like a circular saw with teeth, operated by hand with a wrist twisting it to and fro! But it worked. Washing grit out of wounds, drawing rough edges together, chopping away useless bits, 'debridement' first, sutures afterwards; splints and Plaster of Paris with just a firm bandage to the fractured jaw - no wire or screws in our armamentarium.

We completed our task at 1.00 a.m. and bade our helpful Seventh Day Adventist colleague a big "Thank you" and a "Good night." Beds were back in the centre of the ward and on the verandas. Our fractured skull patient failed to recover, but the rest survived happily. Of the driver, no record of his health was taken, and of his future we had no information. Hopefully he would one day learn that –

'The Lord helps those who help themselves!'

*_*_*_*_*_*_*_*_*_*_*_*

Our success with healing of bones was, of course, mostly a matter of ensuring that the fractured ends were persuaded into reasonable apposition with each other. After that, and with a reasonable period of immobility, the normal repair system could occur with quantities of new bone laid down in and around the fracture region.

Perhaps we should not have been surprised when a local farmer, knowing of these bony triumphs decided to seek help for an old friend of his. The friend was a gentle chap with four legs, to wit his beast of burden, a donkey. Somehow this poor beast had sustained a fractured foreleg, not a simple fracture but compound. The poor creature had managed to make its way to the hospital on three legs, the fourth hanging free, with the broken end of bone protruding through the skin. A brave patient, in what pain we could only guess. Alas it was beyond our capacity to deal with it and we could only recommend that the disappointed man should seek a hunter with a gun. We felt very sorry about that. There was no fun in that episode.

*_*_*_*_*_*_*_*_*_*_*_*

Peter, my garden 'boy' was a cheerful lad, willing and competent, and when my wife requested him to bring the baby antelope for a feed he set forth willingly to do so. Two or three years previously a hunter had been on his rounds and had shot and killed a duiker, a small species of antelope about 18 inches in height, with tiny horns, a very peaceful animal. It was a female and had a small baby, only a few days old. The hunter was sorry about that and brought the tiny animal to my wife hoping she would care for it and give him a 'dash'. He was right, she cared and paid!

So Bambi became part of the family, fed by pipette (an old fountain pen rubber) from a bottle of Klim milk. She became a charming pet for our children, growing well, and full grown in about two or three years. She was lodged in the chicken run in a wire enclosure, and was very happy. She often went with us for walks around the compound.

When history repeated itself with a similar request from a hunter - (the same one?) our family became extended again. The baby was kept in a cardboard box, grass lined, for a few weeks, like its predecessor, and then introduced to Bambi. The older animal accepted the baby and mothered it happily, and of course, my wife continued the feeding as usual, collecting it from the chicken run, Bambi co-operating.

Than, one day she was busy cooking on her oil stove on the veranda, so, "Peter, will you go and bring baby for her feed please." Peter laid down his 'cutting grass' implement and went in to the chicken run carefully closing the gate behind him. Shortly our ears were assailed by shrieks and yells, and our eyes beheld a never-to-be-repeated vision of Peter streaking around the run as fast as he could go with Bambi madly chasing him and butting his heels and ankles with her little horns. At length in desperation he threw himself against the six-foot wire fence that gave way sufficiently to allow his escape. Poor old Peter! Having sobered a little from my laughter I sent him up to the hospital for treatment of a few small wounds and abrasions. My wife collected the baby.

Peter returned later, hobbling most realistically, moaning and suggesting that compensation would be desirable.

Well, why not! What fun!

Companions

Pets, of course are well recognised and valued here in the UK as entertaining and diverting creatures, attractive in their natural beauty and innocence. Of great value to our children for their gentleness, they make excellent companions to the older folk.

In the Tropics the choice of pet is limited. The local canine is a scavenger, so not very desirable. Horse riding is impractical, so unless one opts for the chameleon or a grass snake the remaining choice must be a cat. We had Bambi and her baby, of course.

I did form an attachment to a chameleon, as I have mentioned elsewhere. He stood firmly clasping the branch of a houseplant, and remained immobile. He appeared to eat nothing at all, but if an insect settled on the wall within reach of his very long tongue it was interesting to note how quickly it disappeared. The tongue was housed in a coil within 'Chamy's' mouth. A lightening quick flick of the same would collect the insect for dinner, the movement so fast as not to register on our retinas. 'Chamy' was our children's name for him, and they were fascinated by his wonderful eyes. Sited on either side of his face these big watchful orbs protruding and mesmerising could roll around in different directions, a remarkable sight. He stayed with us for some weeks but suddenly disappeared. The houseboys believed he was a devil and we felt that being afraid of him they might have organised his departure. Cooked chameleon? No thank you!

So we acquired a small cat; a very wild cat indeed. No nice, furry, soft, comfort-loving pussy this. Petting and patting, stroking and cuddling were out. This feline hated us, tolerating us only because it was fed. Our approach to it was met with hisses and striking claws. Our steward, James, however, was quite fond of the little horror, so we offered it to him and he gladly accepted. But first to catch the beast. Our approach, quiet and careful at first became a chase, wild and yet more wild; under tables, over chairs, under the bookcase, round and across the furniture in the sitting room and bedroom, bathroom and veranda. At length a little guile. A half-spherical basket plonked over him while spitting fiercely in the corner did the trick. Perhaps a small dose of anaesthetic too so that James could convey him peaceably to his home? I opened a chloroform bottle and pouring a dose onto cotton wool inserted it below the basket edge. But a vet I was not – I did not know the right dose; I had failed to allow for the rapidity of breathing and furious heart rate after a vigorous chase. The cat's consciousness had certainly been lost, nor did it return alas! James kindly removed the corpse – roast pussy for supper?

Petless we remained until one day a Prince of a local royal house in town presented us with a Crown Bird. Very kind indeed. 'Birdie' was quite handsome standing some 30 inches tall, his head in regal pose and surmounted by golden feathers that splayed out to form a charming 'crown'. The children called him 'Tappa' – why, I've no idea. He stalked about on his long legs round the lawn and graciously allowed us to offer food to him. He did not fly, he had no song, but at dawn and dusk he greeted the changing light with six loud raucous squawks, reminiscent of the six pips of the B.B.C. at news time. When we left Ilesha in 1952 we left him and Bambi and the baby antelope to the care of our successors, and were sad to bid them farewell. Meanwhile, of course, Bambi added to our happy adventures.

CHAPTER 21

Trouble with Antelopes, Hens, Snakes and Typhoid

Bambi the duiker was a charming and friendly creature, and when released from the chicken enclosure in which she chose to stay, would accompany my family on their afternoon walks around the compound, nibbling bits of vegetation, and teasing the children, playing games of 'can't catch me', running and jumping high with twists and turns in the air which intrigued and delighted them. She showed no disposition to stray and returned behind her six-foot fencing to join the fowls quite happily. That did not mean that she was confined there, not at all. The six-foot fence could be jumped at will.

On a warm Sunday afternoon I had been reading a book, my favourite cooling account of Smythe among the snowy heights of the Himalayas. There came a knock and a ward 'boy' entered. "Please Doctor, Bambi get out of compound and fall down well," he reported. It was not uncommon for her to escape and toddle down to the town when one of us would use the car to rescue her, but this was different. She had jumped the wire, wandered up to the hospital and finding an area of broken compound wall had passed through, crossed over the road to investigate the collection of houses over the way. Someone had tried to dig a well but had stopped on reaching a depth of ten feet or so. A hunter carrying a Dane gun spied the antelope. He tried to catch her, and in escaping she had fallen into the hole that was quite dry. The hunter loaded his gun and prepared to shoot his dinner.

But villagers nearby came to her defence and told him vehemently, "It is Dokita's antelope, you must not shoot her." And a vigorous argument broke out until my arrival decided the matter. Bambi took an aversion to her deep prison and jumped.

She leapt up vertically, to my amazement, to within a foot of the well top; and leapt repeatedly, quite an astonishing performance. The crowd now assembled around the well, expressed admiration. At my request the ward 'boy' brought a ladder from the carpenter's quarters and we carefully lowered one end into the well, Bambi still leaping. I descended with care and, the little lady consenting, picked her up and cuddling her closely climbed up and out to return through the crowd into the hospital compound. Back down towards the chicken run carefully holding my prize. But on espying the cage Bambi had only one desire. She struggled and kicked, tore a hole in my shirt and jumped from my arms to streak for home with a lovely leap over the wire into safety. Freedom was too adventurous altogether.

*_*_*_*_*_*_*_*_*_*_*_*

The dozen Rhode Island Reds were interesting too. Laying eggs, clucking as hens will, using at least two of the dozen square foot nesting boxes so thoughtfully (and needlessly) provided by their lord and master, they perched nightly on their 12-foot perch, appeared again at dawn, fluffed out feathers, exercised, ate their mash and food scraps, dust bathed and snoozed in the sun and shade. Come evening they made ready to toddle up their access slope into the commodious twelve foot hen house. The eggs were a useful by-product.

Every two or three months the house required moving to provide fresh ground for them, with the wire also suitably re-arranged. Peter, my garden 'boy', called his fellow gardeners to provide the necessary muscle; for the twelve foot iroko hen house was heavy. A journey of 20 or 30 feet would do nicely, and this was carried out. No objection from the choocks! The day advanced and bedtime came along. I was telling my children a bedtime story when Peter sent a message for me to attend the hen house. I went. Gathered in a companionable cluster the hens were waiting at the spot where they were accustomed to ascend the boarding ladder into the night quarters – but no ladder, no house! We were obliged to pick up each one and carry is to its newly sited ladder twenty or thirty feet away. Well! One lives and learns! Lots of lessons in life!

--*-*-*-*-*-*-*-*-*-*

I emerged from the Operating Theatre on Thursday morning after two ordinary hernias, hoping for a cup of tea and a piece of Sister's creamy sponge cake. Bayo, her cook, was an expert. Seated in her office enjoying a cup of English tea was an English police officer, pleasantly spoken in tidy tropical uniform. He was on a short holiday. "Good morning, Doctor," said he, "I wonder if you could tell me whether the two big snakes in my kit-car are poisonous or harmless." I felt slightly apprehensive and enquired further. It seemed that he had been wandering in the bush country some miles away and had found these two snakes curled up in a little stream, cosily entwined. He had, unthinkingly, used his double-barrelled shotgun hoping to find out later whether they were dangerous. It was standard practice.

I went with him to inspect. Two lovely creatures, some seven feet in length, pale yellow and black markings, as thick as my forearm. How to answer his query was a problem. I had only small knowledge of West African snakes. A little inspiration came to my mind. Didn't snakes eat frogs? A request to the gardener for a live frog soon brought results in the shape of a three-inch frog, unaware of his possible fate.

At the kit-car I picked up a snake's head and, with care, opened its jaw. Two fangs appeared protruding from the upper jaw. Careful pressure caused the needle sharp fangs to penetrate the frog's dorsal skin. Finger pressure now on the area in the mouth where I supposed the poison sacs, if any, were lying. The frog was released, none the worse, into the grassy area outside the Theatre. The officer of the law observed him with interest. I entered the Theatre, my sponge cake within me, to deal with a case of retroverted gravid uterus. The womb when pregnant should point forwards, not backwards. The matter was dealt with. Half an hour later I joined the policeman. Froggie sat quietly in the grass. A gentle poke and he gave a mighty leap to remove itself from those awful humans. Police and Doctor shook hands and agreed. The snakes were harmless, or so we thought. The frog was cheerfully hopping. So the snakes were not of the poisonous variety. Really? Let's think please, Mr Policeman. They certainly had two fangs at the front upper jaw. Why? Were these to inject poison into an enemy or victim? Their startling colours of yellow and black strongly suggested danger, unlike the silly red colour that we use at traffic lights. (Why red anyway? Ladybirds and butterflies, beautiful and harmless use red, wasps and tigers sport black and yellow stripes.) Maybe my fingers had not found the poison sacs, which I have since learnt are at the back of the mouth on each side. Maybe in their death throes the snakes had bitten repeatedly their partner's flesh or their own, thereby exhausting their poison supply. Lucky frog! There are many species of poisonous snakes in Nigeria, and they are better left in peace. I do not remember any single case of snakebite reaching the hospital alive.

The black mamba is a highly venomous variety of snake in equatorial Africa, and if disturbed can become quite aggressive. Since it is reported to be capable of moving at 11 kilometres per hour it is a fearful foe indeed. Its poison is quite deadly. On our trips to Ikole every month we sometimes encountered a chief whose brain had been severely damaged by the poison of a snakebite. Had this been a mamba he was lucky to have survived at all, if luck is the correct term for an existence that could only resemble a living death.

*_*_*_*_*_*_*_*_*_*_*_*

Laparotomy is really quite an impressive sounding word. When, standing beside a patient's bed the surgeon quietly mentions the word to Sister, a whole array of well organised routines swing into action. Ward 'boys' to light stoves; theatre sister to supervise staff and instruments; trolleys, sterilizers, anaesthetic trolley, gowns, caps, gloves, the whole paraphernalia for arranging a safe operating procedure on a poorly patient. There came a day when our Outpatients' Clinic came up with a farmer who had suffered his abdominal symptoms for long enough; had also swallowed the usual leafy concoctions of his medicine man without benefit and finally decided to try our more advanced methods. Investigation was certainly needed. But deep X-ray, scans, gastro-scopes, sigmoid scopes and so forth were for future days; the available alternative method was 'look see'.

So the mysterious word is given and Sister makes the appropriate arrangements. Before long Theatre staff are ready. A spinal anaesthetic seemed to be the method of choice and the long spinal needle was put to good use. The patient was peaceful. I raised the scalpel and drew a straight line down his mid-abdomen. Only a surface scratch appeared. The patient had the toughened skin of hard farming work and hot sunshine. I tried again and a few small blood vessels oozed slowly. I mopped the shallow wound and took firm hold of my scalpel preparing for a savage onslaught. I looked across at Sister and opened my mouth to protest. She beat me to it. "It's a poor workman who blames his own tools," she said! With wrath subdued, and a little patience, the abdominal cavity was opened. A careful investigation all round revealed normal intestinal coils. One abnormality presented in the form of a three and a half inch roundworm in the region of the descending colon. Dear me! Where did he come from? Answer came there none, despite a further search for a hole in the gut. I removed him and, still mystified, sewed up our farmer's tummy and applied the usual clips and bandages.

Talking to relatives later there emerged the story of a typical typhoid illness lasting about three weeks and of a nasty abdominal pain subsided now from its acute beginning. He had taken a first good meal after the fever left him, and then had come the pain. Evidently he had had a perforation of a typhoid ulcer, the worm escaping through the hole, and healing of the hole had followed. Lucky farmer! His tummy healed too.

What about the scalpel? Supplies were restricted in wartime of course, and our clerks sharpened used scalpel blades on a stone outside the Theatre - lucky us!

Eleven a.m. and Eleven p.m.

"Please Doctor"

"Yes, Nurse?"

"Sister says bed eighteen has pulled his catheter out."

"Alright Nurse. Tell Sister I'm coming."

This chapter you can skip if you prefer, but as it was, and probably still is, very much an important part of the African scene, written it must be...

Joshua was a normal adult Yoruba male, of average physique and intelligence. He worked as a farmer and mobile trader. He has acquired three wives and several children. He had also acquired gonorrhoea. For years he suffered discomfort. He also suffered the effects of 'native medicine' and the fees charged by the medicine man. The sacrifice of chickens to deities gave no relief.

At last, after discussions with other men about symptoms, medicines and all kinds of hopeful remedies, he heard about the magic M and B, and how people were cured thereby. How much he spent or borrowed to obtain a supply of this wonder drug one can only speculate. What dose he took and for how long he could not say, and of such matters no record would be made.

Some improvement, at any rate was effected, and he felt a little happier but as time went on he began to find increasing difficulty in passing his urine. He had heard about such things affecting other men and was troubled, resorting again to the expertise of his local medicine man. He obtained no relief. Inevitably at last came the day when he was unable to urinate. Discomfort ensued, and increased greatly.

"Drink more water," he was advised.

"Try some palm wine," said a neighbour.

And his abdomen swelled. The pain was awful. Consternation in his family; consultation with a local chief and a schoolteacher –

"You must go to the hospital," was their advice.

Friends offered to lend him money for transport and the small hospital fees. Agreement was reached.

A bumpy ride in the back of a lorry for the 15 miles to the Wesley Guild Hospital was desperately painful, but at last the drive ended and a hospital ward 'boy' with a wheel chair conveyed him to a vacant bed in the Male Ward. Nurse sent her junior to inform Sister who came and looked. She immediately wrote a short note to me and ordered instruments to be sterilised.

How went the Roman general's report – 'Veni. Vidi. Vici?' Well, to come was a matter of some yards and a couple of minutes. To see, listen to answers to short questions and to make a diagnosis was easy and quick. But to conquer? Short term that was easy too. A rubber catheter failed to pass through the urethral obstruction. A metal one similarly could not be passed – both under local Novocain anaesthetic of course.

So it was a Theatre job, with quick preparation. General anaesthetic and trocar and cannula introduced through the lower abdominal wall to drain the poor chap's bladder. Draining should be gradual, not too rapid for fear of haemorrhage. Finally pushing in a self-retaining type of catheter and fixing it with a stitch or two and Elastoplast to the abdominal wall. After connecting it to a tube, which led to a bottle, attached to his bed. Joshua, when he woke up, was happier but looked askance at his tubing. His relatives were glad and very trusting. Sister and I considered the future and more permanent arrangements, and made plans accordingly.

And so to the crux of this matter, namely to deal with the urethral (urinary tube) obstruction that was causing his distress. The plan was to get rid of the scar tissue from the old infection, tissue that had firmly closed the urethra in one area. Hopefully, then could commence the re-growth of the tube's lining and eventually allow normal passage of urine and sexual fluids. A much happier man should result.

Again the preparation of the patient, of the Theatre, of anaesthetic. Again the sterilised equipment. Again the Theatre staff. Again the scalpel and forceps.

I inserted the rubber catheter until halted by the scarring. Incised the urethra at that point and I extended the incision in order to reach and dissect away the unhealthy tissue. Then easing the self-retaining catheter along the urethral tube and into the bladder, and close the wound. Then closed with great care the hole made in the bladder by the trocar, and the small abdominal wound overlying it.

The patient was sent back to the ward, and later a full explanation given to him with dire warnings about leaving alone his tube and dressings! Non-interference essential! An effective sedative given and for a few days and nights all was well. And then? Nurse knocked at my door with Sister's message – oh dear! That was where we came in!

The mind boggled! In the words of a six-year-old Yorkshire kiddie, friend of my children in later years, when called to the front of his class to explain a minor indiscretion to his teacher, "What shall we do now?" The teacher coped as always, with some humour no doubt. The surgeon, myself, less pleased at 11p.m. coped too, but you may be spared the details! My bed stayed empty for quite some time!

Joshua, chastened, and healed after a very long stay, returned to his village a happier man. Did they throw a party for him and beat the drums? History did not record!

The remainder of the saga of Joshua is not recorded either. But, as was written by John Donne, "No man is an island entire of itself." The repercussions of Joshua's activities may indeed have been widespread, for had he not three wives! Perhaps other contacts existed also...

So was it possible that all might be infected? Yes, indeed. Was it likely that all would present themselves for treatment? Alas, no. Infections could be unrecognised. Sadly symptoms could equally well be severe… There could be urethritis, vaginitis, uterine infection and salpingitis affecting one or both of the Fallopian tubes. If the latter then sterility would very likely ensue, and there would be another woman unable to bear a child, perhaps having already lost her first-born. There could be low pelvic inflammation. This could cause an abscess. If it burst general peritonitis could follow, with a fatal result. In the 'far' bush of a big country such events were all too possible and doubtless did occur quite often.

Hence a need for a vast increase in medical services to the extended villages and small 'bush' settlements as well as to the big towns and cities of Nigeria. The work of the Wesley Guild Hospital and other Christian hospitals has spread far and wide. Long may the workers in these services have the courage, energy and wisdom to develop them and to continue to serve the people of that great country.

CHAPTER 22

Royalty

The people of Ilesha-land, which consisted largely of Ilesha, Ile-Ife and surrounding villages, rejoiced in a King or Owa, as was his Yoruba designation. He was an elderly, dignified old gentleman. His position among the Ilesha people was of much distinction and he ruled over them as a benign despot, doing much to accord with their desires, often perhaps, in return for a suitable fee. His subjects and many chiefs deferred to him most befittingly and held him in high regard.

The Owa and Dr Souster inspect the new site

He lived in the palace of Ilesha located behind the big Council Hall. It was a building whose design and structure was of an era prior to that of which I write and much in need of an updating exercise. The ancient building was of mud-block type, layers of thick rectangular blocks laid, quite expertly, one upon another and surfaced inside and out with a coating of sand-cement mixture, being surmounted with a roof. The old-fashioned thatching had been replaced with the ubiquitous corrugated, galvanised iron sheets, unhappily rusting in many places. The building was innocent of external application of the sparkling Weathershield with which we protected our hospital walls from the ferocious Nigerian weather of blazing sunshine and furious rainstorms. Interior walls were also unadorned, the whole presenting at that time rather a dull, drab effect, not to be compared with the painted walls of the queen's rooms in the palace of Knossos in Crete, still in lovely colour after thousands of years. It was a thrill to meet those painted dolphins, years later.

In his official robes the Owa presented an impressive appearance. The robes were heavy, long and nearly down to his ankles, coloured tastefully and decorated with long lines of small coloured beads. His matching pork-pie hat was also covered with circles of beads. In his hand he held a ceremonial fan of coloured feathers, which were bound together in a generous handle, again covered in a welter of coloured beads. In all, he presented a very regal figure.

It was no wonder that as I have elsewhere indicated, when the time came for our newly installed, more powerful electricity engines and steam sterilising boilers to be officially put into operation, it was to the office of the Owa that we made application for his kingly hand to switch on the power and turn on the steam knobs. Assent was readily granted.

After the ceremony in the engine house and Operating Theatre, the Owa responded to my wife's invitation to partake of a cup of tea. Graciously accepting, he and two of his retinue walked slowly down to the bungalow and up the steps to be welcomed by Barbara, the children well out of sight. Seated comfortably the Owa ate some of the little sweet cakes and sipped what was for him an unusual beverage. Alcoholic drinks were taboo in this missionary household. Conversation was somewhat stilted, being altogether conducted through an interpreter, and it was not long before the Owa indicated that he would like to visit the littlest room. So down the front steps, holding up his robes, along the path in front of the bungalow, passing two stalwart young Yorubas in gaudy uniform, round the corner to our toilet - a rather clever affair. It consisted of a deep borehole about a foot wide, covered by an upturned bottomless bucket with useful seat over. And all the time while the Owa toddled slowly along the path, and during his sojourn within the toilet, and all the weary way back again, the two young gaudily clad stalwarts stood beneath the palm trees. Having raised trumpets to their lips they, all the time, musically serenaded their august master with penetrating blasts on their instruments that reverberated through the bungalow, reached to the hospitals wards to excite the inmates, and no doubt caused our nurses and employees quietly to dance little jigs with happy smiles of joy. The visit of the royal personage was long remembered. We all loved it!

And High Society

The Rt. Hon. Isaac Foot QC. for years MP for Plymouth, was quite the most delightful guest to stay at our bungalow in the Wesley Guild Hospital.

Having come to Nigeria to visit his son, Hugh, the then Governor of the Country, he had enjoyed a very happy stay at the Governor's Residence, overlooking the marina and waters of Lagos harbour.

He had expressed a wish to visit the Methodist hospital in Ilesha and travelled via Ibadan, stopping briefly at the Wesley College for divinity students. Isaac had been disappointed when the church at Tinubu Square, Lagos failed to do justice to his favourite hymn; he was a staunch Methodist, and found that the college students were also ignorant of it. However at Ilesha the nurses had been well trained by my predecessor, Dr Crosby and the hospital sisters. They sang for him with great vigour the verses 'It passeth knowledge that dear love of Thine, my Saviour, Jesus!' and Isaac was very pleased indeed.

The Rt. Hon. Isaac Foot enjoys Ilesha

He stayed with us for a week, learning all about the hospital, its origin, growth and aspirations. As a Methodist he was interested to learn of its beginning as a project of the Wesley Guild of that church, and noted how it was beginning to form a significant part of a medical service in Nigeria. Having talked to the staff, been photographed with the nurses, and having inspected all our 'modern' innovations, he expressed a desire to meet that eminent figure, the Owa of Ilesha.

I talked with the District Officer who acted most efficiently as a go-between, and a meeting was soon arranged. It was to be held in the Council Hall. This, I believed to be the choice of Ilesha's chiefs when offered by government authorities either a water supply or a place of 'palaver' – guess which! After all water fell from the skies, quite often in generous quantity...

So to the Hall we progressed one morning and the meeting began, with the Owa wearing his impressive robes and seated on his throne with Isaac Foot on one side and the D.O. on the other. I myself, and several of Owa's sons and chiefs were also in attendance.

The usual greetings and expressions of regard, hopes for mutual good health opened the proceedings. Then followed Isaac's kindly question regarding the age of the august personage. He, Isaac, confessed to 78 years at that time. Now birthdays, as to dates, were seldom recorded in our region in Nigeria during the late 19th century, but no matter, the Owa could remember back to the days of the inter-tribal wars; so first blood to Owa. War between tribes had raged for centuries of course.

"Well," said Isaac, "I now have seven grandchildren, (or was it eight?) how many has the Owa?" Was there some slight alteration in the Owa's facial expression? He hesitated, and one of his sons prostrated himself before his father, gently bumping his head on the ground, and begged him, the Owa, to declare to the illustrious visitor how many grandchildren he, the Owa possessed!! A direct answer was evaded most diplomatically, and Isaac did not press the point. After all the Owa was said to have quite a large number of wives! A time for friendly chat (by interpreter) and some verbal sparring went on happily, and the meeting was pronounced a success. I felt sure that Isaac was most content.

A suggestion that he might like to visit Ilesha market and try his luck and persuasive charm with the market women was well received, and off he went to hold palaver in the market! On his return after a lengthy session he seemed well pleased with his bargains, and no doubt the market traders were congratulating each other over their financial deals! So both sides won - very satisfactory.

It was with regret that at the end of his week's stay we were obliged to bid farewell to a very charming gentleman, who returned to the political battles of the semi-civilised islands of Britain.

--*-*-*-*-*-*-*-*-*-*

However, after saying "Goodbye" to our dear figure from Plymouth we were still involved with our problems in the tropics. The dry season came upon us, baking hot by day, dropping to a temperature of 60°F by night! Our nurses were chilly so they put on pullovers in which to huddle themselves on such occasions, poor things! We residents of colder climes were much happier and gladly went back to grey flannels and woolly dresses!

It seemed to happen that local folk, overheated during the sunny hours, sometimes chose to remain outside at night for coolness. Whether this change of temperature was enough to reduce their resistance to infection was arguable, but certainly it was that cases of pneumonia were common during the dry season. There were often such patients in our wards.

However the nasty little pneumococcus (the pneumonia germ) and all his unpleasant associates are no respecters of persons, and one morning there came a message from the Owa's office, - *'Dear doctor, the Owa is ill, please can you come and see him?'* This could be serious. The Owa was aged, and might be in considerable trouble.

On visiting the palace I found him in bed, propped up and very hot, breathing with difficulty. Auscultation of his lungs confirmed the suspicion - pneumonia. This was in the early days of penicillin when the drug was administered by injection, and he duly received an intra-muscular dose of 100,000 units. No doubt his wives (nurses) encouraged the penicillin to act by adding the usual native medicine concoctions. Morning and evening he received further injections, from my colleague Jack Souster in the morning and from myself giving the evening dose.

One evening his pulse had become erratic, and of rather poor volume I thought. His temperature was still high, the breathing still quick and laboured. I spoke to the two sons in attendance and told them that his condition appeared worse and that prognosis was poor. They nodded gravely, and doubtless informed his wives. Perhaps more doses of native medicine? Poor old chap! I gave him an extra dose of penicillin.

Next morning came our usual prayers with nurses at 7 a.m. and breakfast on the veranda. In the middle of the grapefruit, from our own tree, the rush of motorcar wheels was heard and with a screech of tyres the D.O. halted at the bottom of our steps. He flung himself out of the door, slammed it, stamped up the steps, pushing aside the Morning Glory, and opened his mouth; he had evidently been to the palace. "Whatever have you done to the old boy? It's absolutely marvellous. He's getting better." - With astonishment and joy!

Latterly my colleague attended the old gentleman to inject the morning dose of penicillin, and he returned to confirm the D.O.'s statement. Success was the order of the day, perhaps largely due to the Owa's natural strength and recuperative powers.

He must have resisted many noxious germs in the course of his long life. Would a mix of whisky and native medicine have some responsibility? Following the news there would be many emotions stirring in the hearts of relatives, chieftains, friends and the not so friendly – 'Uneasy lies the head that wears the crown!'

Gradually the Owa recovered and lived for years after his rather virulent infection.

Strike

The morning Outpatient consultations were going on busily as usual. There were the complaints, the questions and answers, all to be interpreted. The examination and, hopefully, diagnosis followed with treatment prescribed, and exit the patient to the dispensary or to the ward for admission as appropriate.

Watching one patient making her way from the open back door of my room, over the grass towards the Female Ward, I noticed a small procession of hospital workers walking towards the gate of the Hospital. There were the garden 'boys', the ward 'boys', laundry 'boys', cook, mechanic, carpenter and Jeremiah the rather lugubrious sanitary man (he had a rotten job and never looked happy). They were all muttering angrily, gesticulating vigorously, and looking very glum and serious as they proceeded out of the main gate.

I saw another close procession; nurses in uniform, books and personal impedimenta on their heads, walking with straight backs and grim faces down the compound away from the wards towards the Nurses Home.

I was dumbfounded. Turning to Hezekiah I said, "Whatever is happening Hezekiah?"

"I think they all go on strike, Doctor," he replied.

He obviously knew what had happened and related the story to me. It seemed that on checking the clothes store of sheets, bed linen and so forth, Sister had found that a number of items were missing. She and the laundry man invariably checked the numbers of sheets and so forth before going to be washed and on return. All items were faithfully checked and recorded. Sister was extremely efficient in this regard for such pieces of cloth were most desirable in Africa and much treasured. Discreet inquiries had taken place among the staff and had yielded no results and no confessions. Someone had obviously taken these precious items and Sister had no option but to assume that a burglary had occurred, and the police were informed.

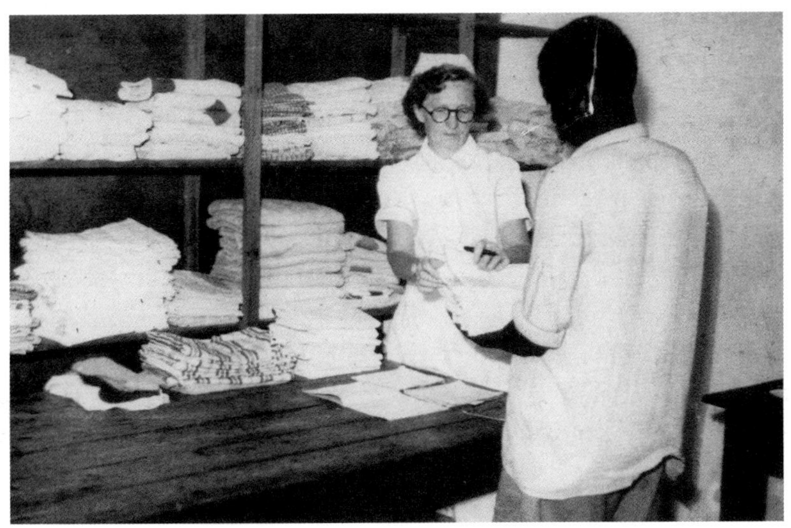

Sister Ludlow inspects the laundry

The police arrived. Oh dear! There was no careful enquiry, no tactful approach. Heavy handed, without care or diplomacy, they marched straight to the Nurses Home, demanded the keys to all nurses' storage boxes, and ransacked every box without any consideration whatever.

The nurses were furious. They called a strike. The rest of the staff, gardeners, ward attendants, laundry men, cook, carpenter, Doctor's and Sister' cooks and house 'boys' downed tools in sympathy and walked out. Only our two clerks, who bless 'em, worked as if they too were missionary staff, our dispenser, X-ray attendant and the engineer were left.

Doctors and Sisters gathered in discussion. It was agreed that 'the show must go on.' Outpatients would continue. Sister would see to the dressings, the dispenser to medicines.

Emergencies would be coped with. Sisters would see to wound dressings in the wards and give out medicines. For feeding and cooking, relatives would be called to help in the kitchen and wards. Children's mothers could stay beside the cots.

For the laundry, Sister Liony took on this mammoth task, asking help from relatives. Sanitation buckets had to be conveyed to the latrine pit, cleaned and replaced. I felt sure that relatives would have dealt with this unpleasant job. At my house there was no problem, the deep 30-foot borehole was a very efficient unit and required no attention, save to the seat. On one occasion I noticed my medical colleague, Jack Souster carrying his latrine bucket from his house to the pit and giving it the needful attention. Afterwards he went immediately to the Hospital to perform a Caesarean Section!

Any deaths in hospital were coped with by relatives. Food for the staff was undertaken by doctors and wives and the Sisters, boiling water and filtering of same also. And so for an extremely busy week we coped and then the staff returned. What about the missing articles? Nobody knew. It was enough that the nurses were back. Did the police apologise? Well, what do you think?

But there was a price to be paid. Sister Stella Liony, faithful, hard working, never giving up, became ill. Tired and with resistance at a low ebb she caught a severe lobar pneumonia and was desperately ill. Cared for day and night under her mosquito net, given hefty injections of penicillin, she managed to hold her own and gradually, very gradually began to mend. I discovered a bottle of brandy in the Theatre cupboard, disguised it with honey and fruit juice, and administered the same with a free hand. A life long tee-totaller, she enjoyed it and asked for more!

Eventually Stella recovered, but was very weak. When strong enough to stand the journey she was conveyed to the Mission House in Lagos, and in due course by ship to England to be nursed back to health. She was never strong enough to return to Nigeria.

Her death, three years later was celebrated with a Thanksgiving Service commemorating her 25 years of selfless service to her African people, on the lawn outside the sister's house - the lawn that she had planned and organised with the lovely array of flowerbeds that surrounded it. The canna lilies, the roses and dahlias, her pride and joy, blossomed beautifully and, when The New Hospital was built, the building at the end of the road and facing the new gateway was, and remains, a new and most significant building:

The Stella Liony Memorial Chapel

CHAPTER 23

Maternity

The work for a teacher's class of eight year olds one day was listed as 'An Essay'. She thought how to present the idea, and decided, telling the children "I want you to write a story for me. It doesn't need to be a long one. Write it at home before you go to bed," and the children listened, minds stimulated and ideas revolving.

Next morning stories were handed in and the teacher selected one at random and read it out. She had given the title for the stories, 'What my mother and father do for me'. So here is the chosen one:

"My mother does a lot for me. She tidies my hair and brushes my shoes; she gives me breakfast and a biscuit for playtime. She gives me dinner and tea and supper, and bathes me and teaches me to say my prayers when I go to bed," and then followed, "my father does not do so much for me. He goes to the bank and gets the money."

The teacher smiled. How delightful to have parental love presented, seen through a child's eyes. What an accolade for motherhood from an eight-year-old boy! His father somewhat distant. Mother is all.

So is motherhood, with minimal fatherly help, of course, the very basis of all life? Ordained by God from the days of Eve? Wise men, philosophers, clerics, psychologists and mothers themselves have written, spoken, preached and prayed for the state of human motherhood, and that of the rest of the animal kingdom has not been neglected. There are mothers everywhere. Praise be!

"I would love to have a baby," has been I suppose the dominant, if unspoken, thought of the normal woman of every age from time immemorial. Even among our modern women and girls whose emotions nowadays are stirred by visions of wealth and the supposed joys made possible thereby, the idea of a live cuddly infant must often be of paramount importance in their minds. To the women of Nigeria, by far the majority of who have never even thought of the wonders that money could bring into their lives, the desire for a child has always been the primary consideration.

To produce that child, to feed it at her breast, to carry it comfortably on her back carefully wrapped and snuggled up to her warm body in sleep, this is the supreme joy that the young Nigerian woman hopes to achieve soon after attaining marriageable age. To be unable to do so would be a tragedy immeasurable.

While a first pregnancy in early womanhood was usually soon achieved after marriage, it was only too often followed by childbirth both difficult and abnormally prolonged. This was usually due to the medicine men's ignorant advice and handling of a woman in labour, not helped by the injudicious use of 'native' medicines. Even if the birth of the baby was accomplished successfully the subsequent treatment of mother and child could well result in sepsis that would prove fatal to the mother or child or both.

In the early days of the Wesley Guild Hospital the Senior Sister, Stella Liony, reported with sorrow that a child's birth in 50% of cases would be accompanied by a single or double tragedy. The popular idea that the African woman could subside on the road verge, pop out a baby, pick it up and carry on is almost entirely a myth, although doubtless it can happen sometimes. Modern maternity care has certainly reached Africa, but it's an enormous continent with areas still un-reached and awful difficulties can and do arise.

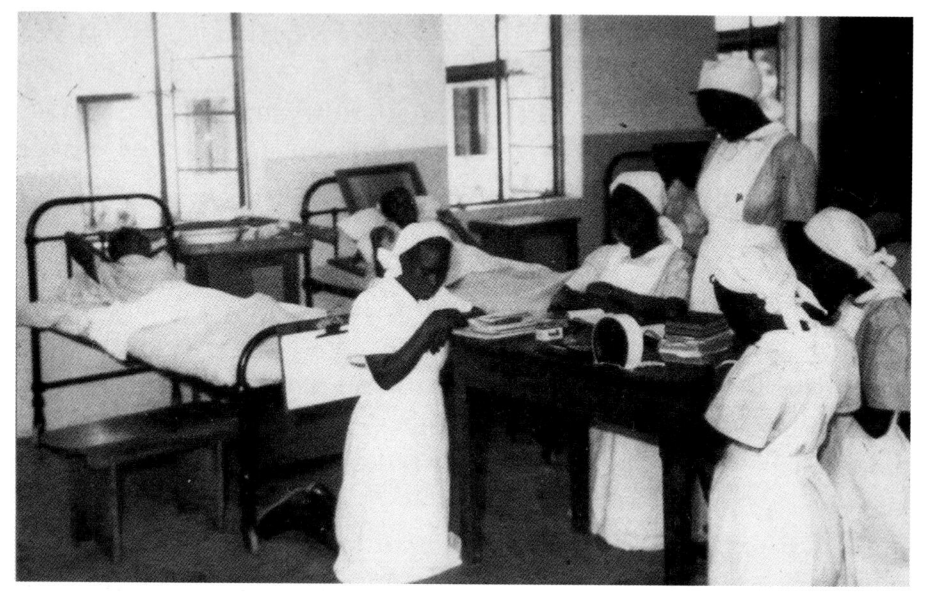

Prayer before work

There was, for example, a small woman, gaily smiling in her late pregnancy, whose hips and pelvis were so deformed that Caesarean section was obligatory. The only way of approaching the abdomen for this purpose was for her legs, flexed to the utmost at the hips, to be bent upwards towards her shoulders! Anyway we obtained a fine little boy and the staff all rejoiced with the mother in her pleasure!

Retained placenta could be awkward at times with unpleasant adhesion to the inner uterine wall (placenta accreta) but with the aid of anaesthetic and suitable means of persuasion could always be induced to meet the light of day...

Our patients were not large people, and their babies would weigh between 5 and 6 lb, seldom over 6 lb. Forceps extraction under general anaesthetic was sometimes needed. Two well-attended antenatal clinics were held each week, one by Sister and one by the doctor. Mine was on a Friday afternoon when up to 80 or even 90 women would wait, mostly outside the waiting room, (not big enough), and often drying their collected supplies of mushrooms or edible fungi spread on wide cloths in the hot sun. These sessions were most valuable and enabled abnormalities to be discovered and righted to the patient's benefit.

But antenatal clinics or not, the unusual can always happen. For example the following occasion arose one day: a small family group were approaching Ilesha, walking from their farm several miles distant.

The mother leading the way. Heavily pregnant, she was burdened also with a basket of farm produce carried on her head. Young children accompanied her, some carrying produce similarly, or bundles of firewood, all expertly balanced as head loads. She knows that the baby is due very soon; it is high time to get home.

Suddenly the pains of labour begin. She must put down her loaded basket and try to carry on despite the contractions. It is too much for her; she must stop and sit down. The children are sent on to their home, the husband supervising their journey. Some time later as she lies alone in the dust of the roadside, a baby is born. There is no one to help and very soon indeed the contractions re-start and a second baby is born, to the mother's horror. The old belief of the evil of twins and that they will cause the mother's death is uppermost in her mind. She does not try to help them, she is too exhausted anyway, and in fear, awful fear of what may happen to her.

A few walkers approach, view the woman sitting naked, her back against a low mud wall; they see the dead babies and rush away, fearful even to know of such evil. She is almost fainting. A local pastor on his bicycle comes towards her and seeing her plight, jumps off and tries to help. He has no midwifery skills so pulling some of her clothes over her he says, "I'll get help for you."

He mounts his bicycle and rides fast to the town of Ilesha, two miles away and to the Wesley Guild Hospital. The story is quickly told and relayed to me at the Outpatients' Department. A nurse and my clerk, Hezekiah, join me in the hospital car, and we rush to find our patient. She is there, as described by the pastor, rested a little, the twins lying in the dust before her. They are not breathing, there are no heartbeats; the umbilical cords are still attached and after-births not delivered. I clamp the cords and cut, bundling the twins into a cloth for nurse to care for. We lift the woman into the car and return rapidly to the hospital, and to the expert care of Sister in Maternity.

I prescribe, and Sister and nurses soon make her comfortable with a drink and a little food. She needs recovery time before attempting removal of the placenta, and I return to the folk waiting in Outpatients.

Half an hour later a nurse came with a note from Sister. "The new maternity patient has successfully produced the placenta and also a third baby, alive!"- Surprise! Surprise!

I saw the last patient and went along to the ward. What a welcome change! What a lovely smile on the mother's face as she sleepily cuddled her baby! It was good indeed to see joy and well being emerge from a situation fraught with sorrow and danger. She progressed well to everyone's satisfaction.

There was really little regret over the twins. Quite apart from the element of fear always present in such an eventuality, the woman would have been quite unable to cope with three babies. All was well. Some you don't win, some you do!

The chief post-natal trouble for a woman, after a long and difficult labour in the bush when the mother was told to push from the start, and her attendant also laid hands on her and pushed too, was a very damaging finale to what should usually be a triumphant exercise. The bony skull of the baby was needlessly pressed for a long time against the rear wall of the bladder, and of course the pubic bone resisting its pressure. The baby would often be still born. Only later would appear the appalling situation where undue pressure had caused a breakdown of the rear wall of the bladder and front wall of the vagina resulting in a penetrating hole. A frightful, continuous leak of urine both night and day would then be the miserable condition, the very much-dreaded vesico-vaginal fistula.

A life of horror would follow. Gone would be marital relations; gone the chance of future pregnancy; gone the hope of a live baby. Just despair!

What help? Native medicine men? Rubbish! As for native medicines, equally rubbish and maybe poisonous, which is where the services of the hospital in the bush are so greatly invaluable. In despair husband brings his wife and the sad story is recounted. Examination is simple and rapid. Then the glad news, it can be put right! Bring her in on Monday; the operation will be on Thursday.

And that evening I take down my textbook of operative gynaecology and read exhaustively! An eminent medical authority pronounced, and I believed, that no such fistula was impossible to repair. It would be nice, of course, if there was still some suitable tissue to stitch together but sometimes there wasn't. Perhaps he had failed, in his long gynaecological experience, to meet some of the tragedies of Africa.

However mostly it was a matter of an anaesthetic, spinal or general, and delicate technique. Lydia, one such lady, had a spinal, doped happily with Sister holding her hand. For the doctor the accomplishment of the intricate procedure was back aching at the time but a great pleasure to complete.

Layer by layer the procedure went ahead. The hole in the bladder wall was identified, tidied up and its edges stitched together. Supporting tissues and muscle behind brought into position and fixed with a few absorbable sutures. The vaginal hole and wall treated similarly, all with great care. Meanwhile a catheter kept the constant trickle of urine away from the repaired area as far as possible. The patient was returned to the ward, laid face downwards to keep the wound 'dry' and remained so for a week or ten days. Then, catheter removed, would she be dry? A big drink of water, and a wait… an hour…two hours… three… DRY! Rejoice all! Lydia went home, happy at last.

It was good to succeed with a life restored. The joy of being normal again can only be imagined!

Of course being very modern people you may think naturally enough that the cure for such a regrettable trouble may be found in that much quoted and bandied about term 'Caesarean Section'. Whether it was Julius Caesar or one of his ancestors who was thus introduced to the Roman world of that time is of little import, and we are unlikely to find out, and it doesn't matter; one just hopes that the mother was suitably anaesthetised, or maybe just deceased!

What does matter is that such an operation should only be undertaken in circumstances where the health of the mother and child is the prime consideration, not the convenience of the attendant medical or nursing staff who would rather not miss their quota of sleep!

"Why worry?" You may say, "It's a very safe procedure nowadays." Well, maybe, but in the forties and in the African bush there were other matters to think about carefully. In those days the 'Classical operation' was in vogue, not the 'lower segment' operation that is now the norm. You'd like to know more? Let me try to enlighten you.

The womb or uterus is, at the end of pregnancy, described as having upper and lower parts: the upper part consisting of an immensely strong muscular bag which, when labour commences, contracts and pushes the baby into the pelvis and finally out to the world. The 'lower' segment relaxes so that this can happen; such is a simple description. So the old 'Classical' operation proceeds as follows:

The operator makes his incision, with patient suitably anaesthetised; straight up and down the front wall of the abdomen, going round the navel (umbilicus to me); such is the 'cut' for the 'Classical' operation.

Rapidity is necessary and, cutting quickly through the strong tissue (fasciae) that hold muscles together, and protect the peritoneal lining of the abdomen; the front wall of the uterus is immediately accessible. Quickly warm moist packs are tucked around it, with long strings and forceps attached to prevent packs being left behind in error. A swift cut through the wall of muscle, forget the blood spurting from arteries, and insert a gloved hand. Quickly find a foot inside, identified by its heel if you can't see it, and yank! Out comes the leg, grasp another foot and continue to pull, gently and carefully but quickly, until the body and finally the head are delivered, upside down. Any mucus or blood in baby's mouth will be expelled as it breathes, a loud cry rewarding the operator. Lay baby in the sterilised piece of sheeting held by Sister and attend to the mother. The uterus should have contracted strongly expelling the afterbirth that is separated from its wall by the powerful contraction. Muscular gripping also tightens very strongly on the bleeding vessels, closing them, and the sanguinary situation is under control of the patient's own automatic functions. To ensure the strong contraction on the blood vessels an injection of ergometrine would be made direct into the uterine muscle; nurse has it all ready. Blood loss is now extremely slight.

A quick but thorough inspection of the inside of the abdomen. Stitch up the uterine wall in three layers; one for the inside lining, one for the muscle and one for the outer coat. Remove packs, and swab away all blood. Nurse counts the packs to ensure that as many came out as originally went in. Finally suture abdominal wall; the strong fasciae, two layers of it behind and in front of the abdominal muscles. Apply clips to the skin, then dressings and a binder to give comfort and support.

Blood loss from the vagina should be minimal. Healing of all tissues is rapid. Baby is bathed and lovely and mother is smiling and happy.

But what of the future? Aye, there's the rub! (Hamlet by Shakespeare) How about future pregnancies? Where does the patient live? Maybe miles away in the bush; is the uterus likely to be strong enough to undertake future contractions of its powerful muscle safely or might that power cause the irretrievably scarred area to rupture, with disastrous results? For the scar where the uterine muscle was stitched together is never as strong as the muscle itself.

You may ask, "Is the muscular contraction really all that powerful?" Well, you may not have had the chance of trying to remove a reluctant afterbirth, firmly adherent to the inner wall of the uterus. With the patient anaesthetised the surgeon inserts his gloved hand to detach this naughty placenta. The uterus detects the intruder and responds with vigour, closing on the hand with tremendous power. The fingers can do nothing. They try to survive the pressure and must wait till the muscle relaxes. Then try again, and again. Believe me? If not, get a strong chap with a large hand to grasp your whole hand and squeeze it hard! Painful? Now you know! That is the power of the uterine muscle. So the obstetrician has a lot to think about 'ere he decides on a 'Caesar'. The woman must come to hospital for the next confinement, a will that 'must' be obeyed?

But don't be alarmed if you are committed to a 'Caesar' for yourself. That operation is out of date, and the lower segment operation is better by far. In those days in the bush we had to think carefully and the 'Caesar' was not lightly undertaken.

So let me introduce you to Abiola in the next chapter. She knew nothing of how the celebrated Julius Caesar or his forebear entered the world, but she did want a baby!

CHAPTER 24

Abiola

Two parents brought up their only child in a small village very near to the great and ancient town of Ibadan in southwest Nigeria. They called her Abiola. Her father and mother were among the early converts to the Christian faith and attended the small village church, doubtless introducing their little girl to their beliefs.

The father was probably of farming stock, while the mother would carry a head load of produce into the big town for trading at a market stall. No doubt Abiola would have started work helping her dad to clear ground for planting crops and carrying loads of wood on her head to the family home. She would be sure to help her mother by pounding the yams in a wooden bowl in preparation for the evening meal. Perhaps she would go to lessons in the village school if there was a Mission School in her village.

The years passed and Abiola became the wife of a Yoruba man, set up house and produced a baby in the normal course of events. A good wife and mother, she managed her home well, and after some years had a longing for another baby, but none came. Her husband was often away working for months at a time.

Time went on. One day she felt a small swelling in her lower abdomen and at first she was very hopeful. However when she counted moons she realised that it could not be a pregnancy, and wondered. Months passed. The swelling was not painful but certainly was becoming larger and felt like a big lump.

Abiola thought a lot and was troubled. She talked to friends about it, but did not believe in their ideas about a big worm or about the wrath of some minor deity. Her faith denied such folly and she turned instead to the wife of her church pastor. This woman was wise and told her of the possibility of hospital treatment.

"It would need an operation," said the pastor's wife, "they put you to sleep, of course, so you don't feel anything. There is a big hospital, quite near in Ibadan. Why not go and ask?" The pastor was told of the matter and spoke to her, saying "There is another hospital, Abiola. It belongs to our church. There, they offer prayer in the Operating Theatre for God's help before putting you to sleep. But it is in Ilesha, about 75 miles away."

Abiola thought hard; she talked to parents and friends, and finally made up her mind, having gladly accepted help offered by her relatives.

There came a fine, hot, sunny day when dressed in her nicest Yoruba costume and, carrying a small package of clothes and some food, she found a seat on a backless form in the rear of a lorry packed with other passengers and their goods. The lorry set off for Ilesha, a long bumpy ride through villages, on 'bush' laterite roads, between great trees with their huge supporting buttresses. For Abiola it was tiring and very uncomfortable as she endured the journey with a biggish lump in her tummy of uncertain origin and doubtful prognosis. But her faith was strong and her mind quite certain. She was glad after hours of travel to reach Ilesha town and to find accommodation for the night, but first to find the hospital.

At the Wesley Guild Hospital the day was advancing. A siesta and a cup of tea had relieved some of the stress of a very busy morning in Outpatients and Theatre, and I returned to the afternoon Outpatients' Clinic at 4 p.m. Most folk had been attended to in the morning so this was for the latecomers. Several people and children were ushered in with relatives, parents and husbands, and some with an extra interpreter of the patient's own tribe or tongue. Occasionally two interpreters might be needed as well as our own clerk, Hezekiah, to convey the symptoms of a patient to my ears. It could be quite difficult to get to the nitty-gritty of a complaint, but with the aid of much expressive body language of hands, eyes, head movements and body and limb twisting and turning we would manage to get down to 'brass tacks'! Bless 'em all!

To convey instructions re treatment was no easier! There had to follow diagnosis after examination, and most illnesses resolved themselves into malaria, diarrhoea, bronchitis, hernias, gynaecological troubles, leg ulcers, guinea worms or the inevitable intestinal worms, not forgetting the children's troubles of measles and whooping cough that could be extremely hazardous. Injections (very popular and much desired), tablets, medicine bottles, baths for ulcers, the operating list for hernias and ward admission for sick children coped with the crowd of sufferers.

At last, after her long journey and lengthy session in the waiting room, the consulting room door opened to admit Abiola. Nicely attired, of good carriage, she was a well-spoken Yoruba woman of some 25 years. She explained simply and clearly. She had noticed a lump in the mid lower abdomen gradually getting bigger.

"It is not a pregnancy, Doctor, and I would like you to take it away."

She looked at me straight in the eye, truthful, confident - no fool this lady!

Examination revealed a healthy woman, with a lump, as she described it. It was the size of a grapefruit, fairly firm, freely mobile, not adherent to other structures, almost certainly an ovarian tumour, probably cystic and most likely benign.

"Yes, we can help, you" I said. "It will need an operation of course."

"Beni," she replied - the Yoruba 'yes'.

Explanations followed; a few drops of blood taken for malarial parasite examination, and treatment given to get rid of probable round worms. She was given a day to return for preparation for operation by admission to the Female Ward, and she departed to find herself accommodation. She found lodgings in town, and a few days later Abiola returned, was admitted and prepared for the operation.

All went well as was anticipated with a smooth anaesthetic and normal opening of the abdomen. The lump was indeed a tumour of the ovary, cystic and benign. Removal presented no difficulty, and, after a quick check round the abdominal interior, normal suturing followed to repair the incised wound. Recovery was normal too and quite rapid, and healing was quick and firm.

Abiola was a most pleasant patient and the nurses liked her. When the time came for her discharge they felt quite sorry to see her go, wished her well with much Yoruba "Goodbye" expressions and waved to her as she made her way to the gate of the Wesley Guild Hospital. She bravely walked the half-mile to town to catch a lorry for Ibadan.

So was that the end of the story? Did she have any more children? Well, we had to accept that in our hospital work we could only ease folk's troubles, hopefully cure them and send people back to the business of living. Seldom did we hear of their future progress and thus it was with Abiola.

But Abiola left behind a vital message for the hospital staff. When filling in details on her record card, Hezekiah had, of course, asked for her address. She told him the name of her village - "But that is 75 miles away just outside Ibadan. They have an excellent hospital there with wonderful equipment and lots of highly qualified doctors, surgeons and nurses. You could have gone there quite easily, so why," Hezekiah asked, "did you come all the way here?"

And this was where the reply from a simple woman from a small village of a 'third world' town in equatorial Africa reminded the educated professionals in medicine and nursing of their dedicated Christian calling. She gave us pause to think deeply.

Abiola had barely hesitated, remembering the words of her pastor. She had looked at us directly and with assurance, replying simply, clearly and positively – **" Because you pray first."**

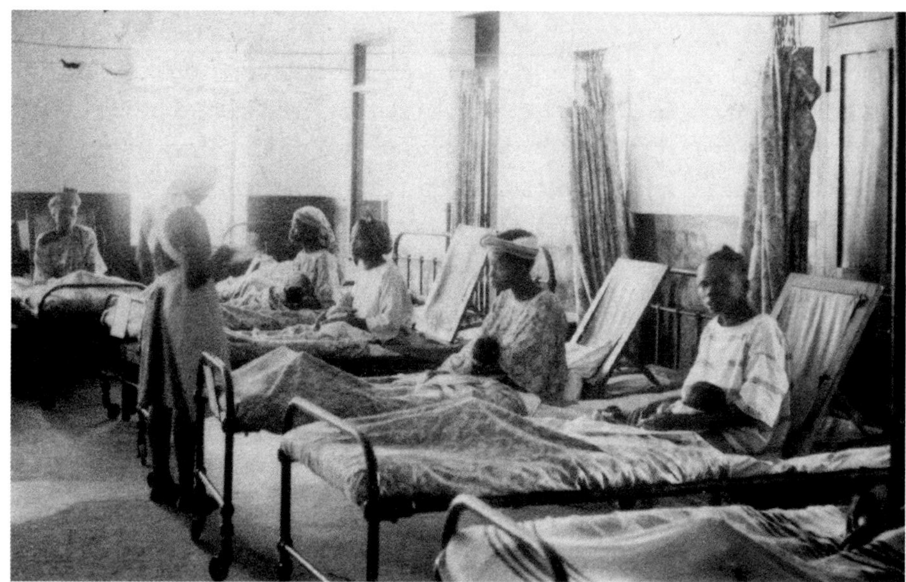

Happy mothers, busy ward – WGH, Ilesha

Build for the Future

Outpatients was busy as usual, increasing week by week. Another chap with a large hernia, inguinal and direct and sounding as if the bladder was involved. It would not strangulate, but was irreducible. Could we find him a bed next week? That would be the third one with a hernia this morning and beds were full.

An elderly woman, perhaps 60 years of age, presented herself, led by the hand by her daughter. She had no sight at all. It only needed one look at her eyes to find that two very advanced cataracts were present. We found her a chair in the examination room and asked her to wait for a while. We carried on with Outpatients till 11 a.m. when all were finished and morning coffee in Sister's office would be on the menu.

"Hello Sister, how's tricks?"

"Very busy, very full. Beds down the centre of Male Ward and on both eight-foot verandas. Maternity overflowing. Female choc-a-bloc. Children are quite full but two of the kwashiorkor kiddies have died."

"Oh dear! I'm sorry about that." It happened so often that our minds accepted the tragedy but pressed on with the immediate emergencies of the hospital.

I told her of the Outpatients and asked if any hope of beds next week was possible. "Well, in the Female Ward the laparotomy for fibroid removal, the chief's wife, is healing well and could be discharged on Monday. The vesico-vaginal fistula with ureteric transplantation has settled down nicely; she is very happy and the wound is healed, so she could go too."

That would enable our cataract patient to be admitted on Monday. That helped.

"What about male beds, Sister? I've got three hernias to keep us out of mischief."

"Oh well, let's see. That huge thigh abscess has drained well and is healing. He could go home and come for daily dressings. Then the fractured tibia is getting about with two sticks, so he could go home. There are four hernias, one of which is ready, and maybe a lacerated arm could be discharged to attend Outpatients. How would that suit? Provided no weekend troubles or emergency ops."

"Thank you Sister, that could solve my problems." And I returned to tell Hezekiah that we could admit the old lady and the three hernias on Monday. All seemed well.

Monday came, and three hernias, but no old lady. We sent a messenger to enquire about her. He returned and spoke at length to Hezekiah, who translated "The old lady told her people that the Doctor had sent her away because he could not help her. She went to her bed, turned her face to the wall, and next morning she was dead."

Sadly she had understood that, as was the common custom, she had been politely 'put off' because we could do nothing for her. What a pity! Those cataracts could have been popped out on the slightest encouragement, and our dispenser had quite a good collection of lenses and frames which would have given her a degree of vision in her advancing years. We felt so sorry for the old dear, but understood that the practice of 'putting them off' was well known by the local populace, and indeed not only in that country...

The morning stint finished at last. As I turned my steps homeward Sister called, "Don't forget the staff meeting after chop at 7 p.m." This was a get together of doctors and Sisters to discuss hospital affairs such as pay for the nurses and employees, work as affected all of us, the state of buildings and compound, transport, lighting and heating. These matters were our responsibility primarily. To Sister's nice big double storey house at 7 p.m. we all repaired, and to all the questions involved we succeeded in finding answers that would fit the bill.

Then came the all important question, "How are we to extend?" How indeed! We were very well aware that the work was increasing, the demand was heavier as people of town and district came to appreciate the hospital's services. The Maternity and Child Welfare Wards overflowed, the Men's Ward always bulged with beds and occupants, and the Women's Ward too was now full, as the men undertook more financial responsibility towards their women. The Francis Ream Theatre saw a huge increase of operations, and let us not forget maternity, vastly increased to the intense satisfaction of all concerned. As for Outpatients' Departments - well…!

Building materials for the new Hospital

The compound was a triangular area of land occupying the apex quite fully, roads on either side, and our leprosy compound nearby was across the road. No chance there. Below were staff houses and nurses quarters, and further down at the base of the isosceles triangle the land was swampy, growing mosquitoes! We thought, talked, mulled over the problems for an hour or more. The matter seemed insoluble, so giving up once again we retired to rest our brains in refreshing slumber.

Not long afterwards a youngish Englishman came to visit. He was a very pleasant chap and described himself as a Development

Officer. He was interested in matters that affected improvement and development of facilities in the country, and to him we unburdened our souls regarding the expansion difficulties. After listening to our version of the problem he said simply, "Well why don't you build a new hospital?"

"Money!" we responded with emphasis! Where would that come from?

New Hospital site, December 1951

He didn't seem unduly concerned and suggested a visit to the D.O.'s office where, on the wall was pinned a large-scale map of Ilesha and its environs, and there we found a large stretch of land on the other side of town on top of a hill. A flat ridge comprising some thirty odd acres and only gradually declining towards the further 'bush' area. We discovered that it belonged to Chief Lejofi. Excitement began to bubble up within us. Was it really possible? Could this be the right answer?

It was 1947, and shortly I was due for furlough in the U.K. From holiday with my family in Brean Down I wrote a long letter to Dr Bolton, the medical secretary of the Methodist Missionary Society, putting forward the desirability of rebuilding the Wesley Guild Hospital. Letters began to flow to and fro, to and from the Mission House, our Lagos headquarters, Government authorities and local important people. Dr Bolton came to visit after my return to the field in 1948 and inspected the site, partly cleared after agreement with Chief Lejofi. A great palaver was held in the Council Hall when the chiefs, apprised of our new hospital idea and full of enthusiasm, were at great pains to persuade Chief Lejofi to allow us to use the land. At length he agreed, at £1 per acre per annum (33 acres), but would like 30 years rent in advance! No can do!

At long last all was finally approved, – see my successor's book, *Front Line Hospital.*

The news spread quickly in the town and district. Excitement! Boost for Ilesha!!

On a number of occasions there came early in the morning a succession of traders, experts in supplying building sand and stone of varying dimensions, and of course each one said to us:

"Don't tell anybody else, but I can sell you stone and sand at very special price, (whispering) very special price indeed."

Each offer was lower than the last – a Methodist trader put in the highest bid! But a Mohammedan merchant sent a message asking the doctors to meet him at his quarry, and thither Jack and I proceeded one day.

Morning Outpatients was finished, minor ops too, and we had time to go the few miles to the gentleman's gravel pits before lunch. What a very good thing that was. He told us that he had long admired the work at the Wesley Guild Hospital, the dedication of all the staff, by day and by night, and wished to offer help in the only way he could, namely by supplying the building stone and river sand at rock bottom prices. They were remarkably low.

This offer opened the way to bring real life to our proposed rebuilding project. We thankfully accepted the excellent offer, and informed Mr Jobling of the Blaize Memorial Institute of Abeokuta who would undertake the building work. The job could begin!

We bought a 5-ton diesel lorry; sent down loads of cocoa for local farmers and brought back from Lagos cement, timber and building supplies, as has already been mentioned. Stacks of roofing sheets arrived in huge lorries, off-loaded beside my bungalow for security, in our old compound. The Liaison Committee assembled on the new site, now partly cleared, where Dr Bolton had barked his shins trying to climb a palm tree. I showed them the new hospital plans. The news sped round the town - great joy and a really great triumph for Ilesha! This would be fun indeed!

A first trench was dug on the new site, which we visited daily. A service was held there conducted by our church minister, Rev. N. Salako, and Owa and Chiefs attended with a big crowd. The 'Cutting of the First Sod' was an important ceremony, and duly performed by the Owa who ceremonially tipped a little soil into the trench. The chiefs followed suit one by one. My daughter, Carol, was tickled pink and hopped into the trench too! What fun at five years old! Her sister, Gillian at six and three quarters was more sedate!

"Cutting of the First Sod"

The assembled company made lavish contributions and the first £1,000 was collected for their new hospital by the people of Ilesha in the month of December 1951, a grand effort indeed. The Wesley Guild at home should remember the tremendous enthusiasm, effort and sacrifices made by the people of Ilesha town on the occasion of the founding of their new Hospital. It is noteworthy that the Rev. Salako gave up the purchase of new Easter clothes for himself and family in order to make a contribution to the Building Fund.

A vast stack of building blocks, composed of laterite and a little cement and dampened with water slightly, went up ready for use. The blocks had been compressed by a special machine and stood out to dry, some 10,000 of them. Concrete filled the trenches; foundations were to be such as to withstand a second storey if needed, and stone block footings followed. A first block of buildings for storage purposes was ready by March 1952.

The New Hospital gets going

The time came when my departure from the scene became necessary, to escape rather frequent malarial attacks and provide education for my family. The Wesley Guild Hospital had proved its value as a place where medical expertise and Christian Witness together gave light and hope to the community. Its further development was solidly planned and its future was assured. It was time to go, and time for others to build on the foundations laid.

Farewells were being said by Church and people. The Owa gave a party at the Council Hall, and there were gathered many invitees, chiefs and businessmen of African and European origin. This was a happy occasion and left a warm glow in our hearts, as indeed did the similar parting ceremony where our own Church said an effusive "Thank you" and a sad "Goodbye". For our family to be photographed with the Owa, now restored to health and strength, was a great honour. To receive from the hands of our Church officers a neatly framed, illuminated address was a touching tribute of which I have been very proud.

Procession from old Hospital to new

There was more sadness at the hospital gate where a crowd surrounded our car and waved vigorously as we shook many hands in farewell. But where was Hezekiah? I discovered him within the gate office. He was too overcome to emerge for a final emotional parting...

We retraced our journey to Lagos for the last time. A day or two afterwards we embarked on our ship for another home. On this occasion we gathered in the stern of the ship and gazed at the receding harbour and shore. An hour passed and the mole, the buildings, the waving palm leaves and the white waters of the bar sank below the horizon.

So was that the last of Africa? Oh no! Two years later in September 1954 I made my first plane flight with a donated airline ticket from the Hospital, crossed France, the Mediterranean, Tripoli and the Sahara and entered Nigeria by the back door so to speak. At Ilesha things were about to move. Welcomed by my successor, Dr. Pearson, I had the great joy of leading, with Dr. Cannon, the procession of nursing staff from the old Hospital to the new. Arriving there I found a vast crowd of some three thousand African folk with Europeans peppered among them outside the new gates. The Owa and the Minister of Health were there. After a short service and speeches the Minister unlocked the gates and the crowd streamed in to inspect the New Hospital.

Dr. Pearson places the Wesley Guild Badge

May the Christian Witness of this Hospital long continue in the life of Nigeria, and may its healing efforts bring comfort and health to the people of Ilesha for many future years.

GLOSSARY

aneurysm	swollen area in an artery
antenatal	prior to birth
arthrodesis	surgical union of bones in arthritic joint
auscultation	listening with a stethoscope
cancrum oris	cancroid condition of the cheek
clavicle	collar bone
D & C	surgical scraping of the womb lining under anaesthetic
dorsal	of or on the back
elephantiasis	gross limb swelling due to blockage of lymph vessels
Fallopian tube	tube from ovary to womb
filarial	tiny worm in body tissues / lymph vessels.
hernia	protrusion of part of an organ via an enclosing membrane: sites of potential weakness
inguinal	of the groin
laparotomy	surgical opening of the abdomen
lipoma	a benign growth of fatty tissue
kerosene	paraffin
mastoid	the bone behind the ear.
mastoid muscle	muscle of neck from breast bone to mastoid
M&B 693	germ killing product made by May and Baker, originally in the 1930's
mosquitoes	tiny insects carrying malaria parasites, dengue and other diseases
oedematous	of a limb swollen with fluid

GLOSSARY (continued)

omentum	a sheet of tissue hanging down from the stomach
peritoneum	the thin tissue that lines the whole of the abdomen
salpingitis	inflammation of the Fallopian tubes
strangulation	severe squeezing of blood vessels, windpipe or intestines cutting off vital supplies
stridor	noisy rasping sound when air is inhaled
subcutaneous	underneath the skin
thyroid	the gland in the front of the neck which makes hormones to regulate metabolism
trachea	the main breathing tube in the neck
trocar and cannula	sharp bulky needle within a metal tube for draining body fluids
trypanosome	a very minute organism that causes sleeping sickness
tsetse fly	tropical fly whose bite can cause sleeping sickness in Africa
umbilical	at the navel
urethra	tube that carries urine away from the bladder
wen	swelling, often of the scalp, containing sebaceous material